the art of SLIP-STITCH KNITTING

TECHNIQUES, STITCHES, PROJECTS

FAINA GOBERSTEIN &
SIMONA MERCHANT-DEST

INTERWEAVE
interweave.com

EDITOR Michelle Bredeson

TECHNICAL EDITOR
Kristen TenDyke

ASSOCIATE ART DIRECTOR
Charlene Tiedemann

DESIGNER Pamela Norman

BEAUTY PHOTOGRAPHER
Joe Hancock

SWATCH PHOTOGRAPHER
Ann Swanson

ILLUSTRATOR Kathie Kelleher

PHOTO STYLIST Tina Gill

HAIR AND MAKEUP
Kathy MacKay

PRODUCTION Kerry Jackson

Interweave
A division of F+W Media, Inc.

4868 Innovation Drive
Fort Collins, CO 80525
interweave.com

Manufactured in China by
RR Donnelley Shenzhen.

Library of Congress Cataloging-in-Publication Data

Merchant-Dest, Simona.

The art of slip-stitch knitting : techniques, stitches, projects / Simona Merchant-Dest and Faina Goberstein.

pages cm

Includes bibliographical references and index.

ISBN 978-1-62033-756-1 (pbk.)

ISBN 978-1-62033-757-8 (PDF)

1. Knitting--Patterns. 2. Stitches (Sewing) I. Goberstein, Faina, 1950- II. Title.

TT820.M4756 2015

746.43'2--DC23

2014047041

10 9 8 7 6 5 4 3 2 1

dedication

FAINA: To Simon, Eli, Rebecca, and Geoff with much love.

SIMONA: To my daughters, Eliška, Marina, and Sofia, you are the force and bottomless pit of inspiration behind everything I do; and to my grandmother who introduced me to the love of knitting.

Contents

introduction

WORKING ON THIS book was an interesting and rewarding experience. We both grew up in Europe and saw the use of slip stitch in many folk-knitting projects from different countries, including Estonia, Russia, Czech Republic, Bulgaria, and others. Slip-stitch patterns are often combined with other more popular techniques such as Fair Isle (also known as Jacquard) and textured stitches. As a matter of fact, in Russia, slip stitch is referred to as a "Lazy Jacquard," referring to the visual resemblance between multicolored slip stitch and Fair Isle.

As knitters and designers, we are always on the lookout for unique or unusual stitch patterns that produce interesting textures and appearances. Going through stitch dictionaries in search of slip-stitch patterns that are different is often difficult and a disappointment.

The unsuccessful search for distinctly different slip-stitch patterns and our desire to research these types of patterns in depth to give them the attention they deserve developed into more than enough material for this book.

The slip-stitch patterns in this collection are divided into four groups: traditional, woven, fancy, and reversible. Some of these are classic and well known, and some we engineered and developed in the process of doing research for this book.

We begin each chapter with a dictionary of stitches representing that group of slip-stitch patterns. You can choose between written instructions or a chart to knit each stitch pattern.

We've found that slip-stitch patterns are unpredictable and absolutely fascinating. The more we work, rework, and "play" with them, the more we find that even with a small change you can make a completely new stitch that has no resemblance to a previous one.

In addition to the forty slip-stitch patterns, there are sixteen stunning, yet easy-to-make projects. Among them are six full garments, two vests, and eight accessories. Each features one or more slip-stitch patterns and demonstrates the possibilities for using these stitches. The stylish and well-fitting projects are made from soft and beautiful yarns that we hope will help change the notion some knitters have that slip stitch creates a bulky fabric. Not anymore! When worked with thoughtfully chosen modern yarns paired with correct needle sizes, slip-stitch fabric can be lacy, as you can see in the Bordo Shawl (page 48) or the breezy, light, and reversible Zlatý déšť Cowl (page 124). Use slip stitch as an overall pattern to "fake" Fair Isle as in the Čekanka Jacket (page 54) or play with color sequences as in the Svítání Pullover (page 42). Add just an accent on the sophisticated background of stockinette as in the Kromka Hoodie (page 64), Nebo Pullover (page 112), or Koketka Sweater (page 128). Experiment with woven slip-stitch patterns to make head-turning projects such as the Gobelen Bag (page 82) or the Volna Scarf (page 98).

PROJECT NAMES

For the projects in this book, we chose Czech and Russian (our native languages) names that describe our inspiration for the design, color, construction elements, or other aspects of the designs. See page 174 for the translations and pronunciations.

It is our hope that you will catch on to our excitement over this fresh look at this family of stitches. Follow our lead and experiment with fibers, colors, textures, and needle sizes while working the same patterns we present to you. If you are like us and love adventure, you will come up with almost countless variations of these stitches.

We are very excited to share with you our findings of what slip stitch can do: its beauty, its endless possibilities, and the great versatility it offers. We're looking forward to seeing your variations of the slip-stitch patterns in your projects.

EAT
drink
knit

CHAPTER 1

all about SLIP-STITCH KNITTING

SOMETIMES AFTER KNITTING a row we notice that we've made a mistake; one or more stitches do not have a yarn pulled through them. Rather, the yarn is floating between the flanking stitches on the back of the work, and the skipped stitches are taller than the others. It's probably safe to say that in the early days of knitting, this mistake drew the attention of some curious knitters. They began experimenting with this effect to obtain interesting patterns just by skipping some stitches in an orderly fashion.

The evidence of slip-stitch patterns can be traced to the early days of knitting in various parts of the world, but most of the time it was not isolated as a separate and distinct technique. Because the earliest written knitting instructions known to us date to the nineteenth century, and not all techniques were popular and developed at the same time, it's hard to say when and where the slip-stitch technique, as we now know it, originated. There is evidence of slipped stitches used in decreases as early as the nineteenth century.

Although the focus of this book is on exploring slip-stitch technique and its usage, let's first take a closer look at the slipped stitch itself and how it's used.

A stitch can be slipped with the yarn held in front or back. We choose one or the other depending on the effect we want to achieve. We can then work slipped elongated stitches into a pattern as knit, purl, or tuck stitches. They can also be used to form cables or traveling stitches, horizontal chains, herringbone patterns, and much more.

the formation of slip stitch

In certain patterns and techniques, a stitch is intentionally slipped with no yarn looped through it. In order for us to work the next stitch, we strand the yarn either in the back or front of the stitch, or sometimes over the needle.

Let's call a stitch that is transferred from the left-hand needle to the right-hand needle as if to knit or purl without being worked a standard slipped stitch and the strand of yarn a float.

It's very important to pay attention to the length of the float. If it's too short, the flanking stitches will come much closer together than the pattern requires. In this case, the gauge and the look of the fabric will change. If the float is too long, it will make the flanking stitches looser, while the rest of the float will sag, making the fabric look untidy.

We suggest checking the float after working the next stitch. At this point you can pull the yarn to shorten the float or give it a little more length.

Note: A standard slipped stitch is always slipped as if to purl. If the instructions call for slipping a stitch as if to knit, there will be specific instructions to do so.

TERMINOLOGY

The abbreviations and terminology of carrying yarn to form a float varies from publication to publication and can become a bit confusing. There's a difference between stating to "carry yarn on (or along) the back of work" versus "with yarn in back."

The first statement means that no matter if we are working the right side or a wrong side of the work, we carry the yarn on the wrong side of the project. In other words, if we are working a RS row, then we carry the yarn behind the slipped stitch. If we are on the WS row, we carry the yarn in front of the slipped stitch.

The statement "with yarn in back" describes the yarn always being carried behind the slipped stitch no matter which side we're working on. So if we're working the RS row and we're slipping a stitch "with yarn in back," the float will be carried on the WS of the project. Consequently, if we're working a WS row, the float will be carried on the RS of the project.

In this book, we use the following descriptions and abbreviations.

SLIP STITCH PURLWISE WITH YARN IN BACK (WYB)

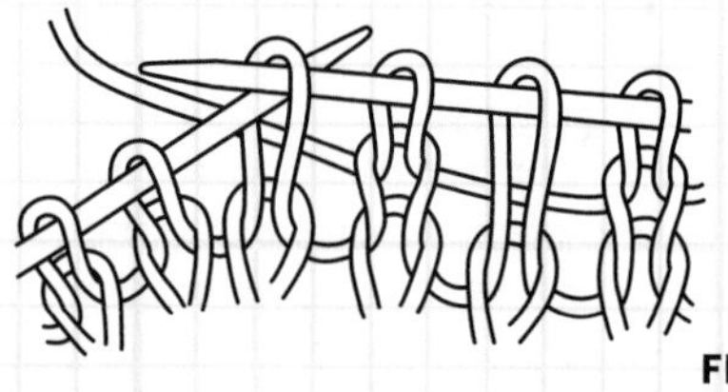

FIG. 1

1 Hold the working yarn in back of the stitch.

2 Slip the next stitch to the right needle as if to purl **(FIG. 1)**.

3 Work the next stitch in the pattern.

4 If you're working a RS row, the float will be carried and visible on the WS of the work. If you're working a WS row, the float will be carried and visible on the RS of the work.

SLIP STITCH PURLWISE WITH YARN IN FRONT (WYF)

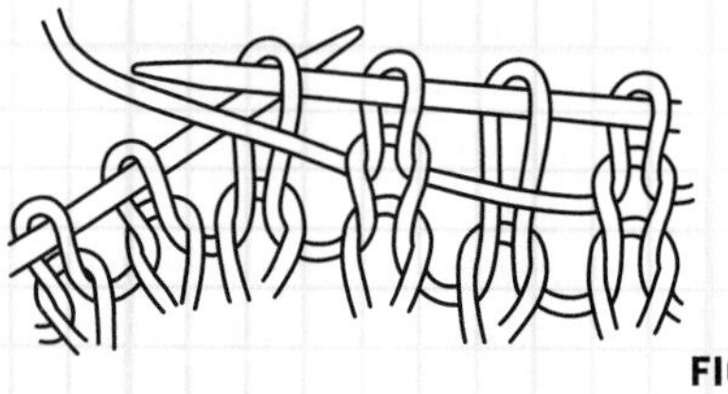

FIG. 2

1 Hold the working yarn in front of the stitch.

2 Slip the next stitch to the right needle as if to purl **(FIG. 2)**.

3 Work the next stitch in the pattern.

4 If you're working a RS row, the float will be carried and visible on the RS of the work. If you're working a WS row, the float will be carried and visible on the WS of the work.

SLIP STITCH KNITWISE WITH YARN IN BACK (WYB)

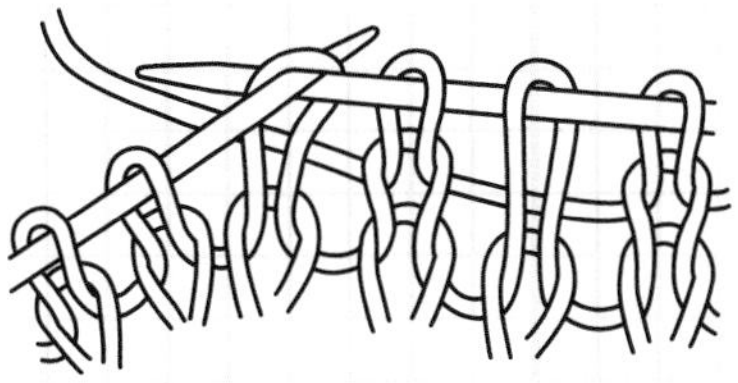

FIG. 3

1. Hold the working yarn in back of the stitch.
2. Slip the next stitch to the right needle as if to knit **(FIG. 3)**.
3. Work the next stitch in the pattern.
4. If you're working a RS row, the float will be carried and visible on the WS of the work. If you're working a WS row, the float will be carried and visible on the RS of the work.

SLIP STITCH KNITWISE WITH YARN IN FRONT (WYF)

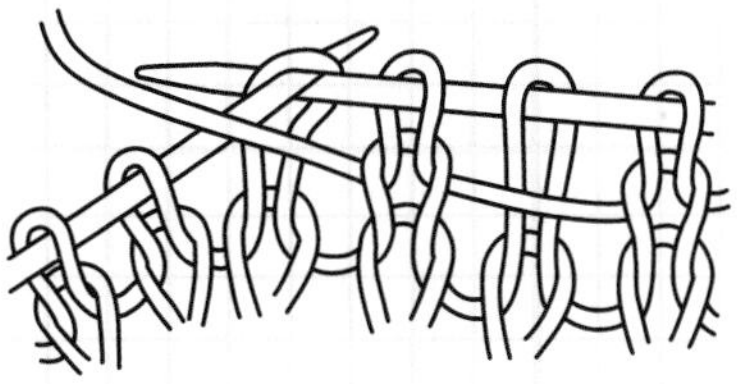

FIG. 4

1. Hold the working yarn in front of the stitch.
2. Slip the next stitch to the right needle as if to knit **(FIG. 4)**.
3. Work the next stitch in the pattern.
4. If you're working a RS row, the float will be carried and visible on the RS of the work. If you're working a WS row, the float will be carried and visible on the WS of the work.

SLIP STITCH AS A HELPING TOOL

There are many reasons why we may need to slip a stitch. Some are obvious and some are not. Although there are only a few ways of slipping a stitch, there are many ways of manipulating and using slipped stitches. Without slipped stitches, our knitting repertoire would be very limited, and we would not have the many techniques and stitch patterns that we see and use today. In other words, the slipped stitch is essential to knitting! We use slip stitch:

TO CREATE TEXTURE

- to build slip-stitch patterns in solid or semisolid yarns
- to form clusters, knots, and bobbles
- to produce three-dimensional knitted fabrics
- to work brioche stitches
- to work many interesting stitches that are formed with the use of a slipped stitch, but not classified as a slip-stitch technique
- to produce horizontal chains and cables
- to help cross stitches in cables

TO CREATE COLOR

- to imitate Fair Isle patterns using different color yarns while working both flat and in the round
- to produce decorative accents such as embossed stripes

TO SHAPE

- to produce nice-looking decreases: ssk, skp, sl2tog-k1-p2sso
- to decrease a large number of stitches simultaneously
- to make multiple-stitch increases
- to cinch fabric horizontally or vertically
- to gather fabric

FOR FINISHING

- to make a crisp edge at the fold of pleats, hems, and buttonbands
- to make a nice selvedge edging
- to bind off stitches
- to correct jogs in circular knitting

SLIP STITCH WITH YARN ON (OR OVER) THE NEEDLE (WYON)

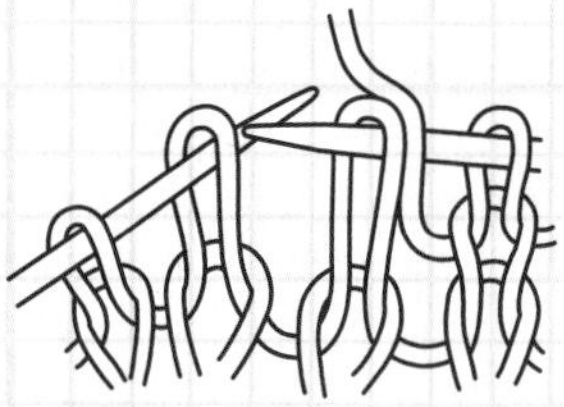

FIG. 5

The yarn carried on (or over) the needle is worked on both WS and RS the same way.

1 Hold the working yarn in front of the stitch.

2 Insert the right needle into the next stitch from back to front as if to purl.

3 Slip the stitch from the left needle onto the right needle.

4 Bring the yarn over the needle from front to back, placing it next to the slipped stitch **(FIG. 5)**.

5 Work next stitch in the pattern.

A pattern can call for a certain stitch to be slipped on a few consecutive rows. For example, in the waffle stitch (see page 40 for the pattern and chart), stitch number 3 is slipped in 4 consecutive rows. On Row 5, we see 4 floats on the back of that stitch. When we work this row, we knit stitch number 3. Thus, the floats just stay as part of the pattern on the WS of the fabric.

The stitch itself is drawn up from row to row and becomes elongated.

Even if this stitch pattern is done in a solid-color yarn, we will see a difference in texture. Because the elongated stitch does not have as much yarn to stretch over 4 rows with ease, it gathers the fabric around it and gives it a textured and interesting structure.

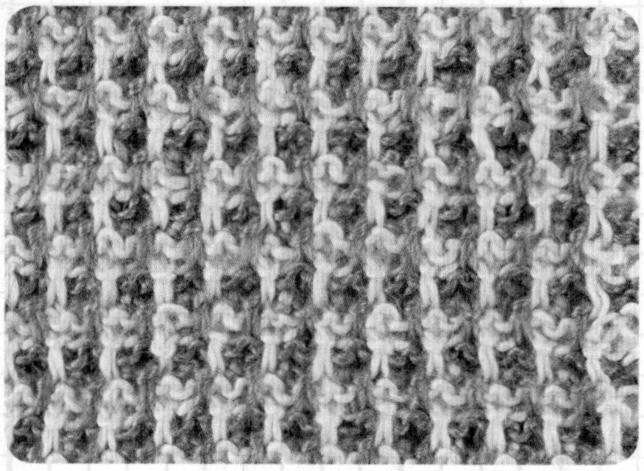

Waffle Stitch

TUCK STITCH

In some patterns, the floats from previous rows are picked up and incorporated into a stitch on the next row. This stitch is called a tuck stitch. A tuck stitch can be done knitwise or purlwise. It makes no difference whether the floats are carried in front or in back of the work. It can make a slight difference in the appearance of the fabric when the float is formed by carrying the yarn over the needle (see Reengineering with Floats and Tucks, page 20).

Knit tuck stitch

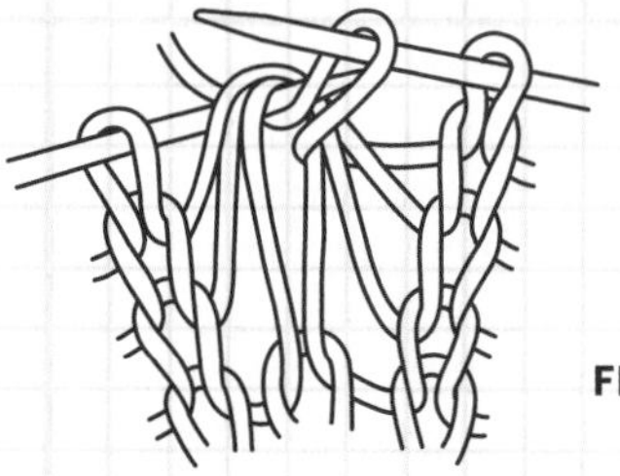

FIG. 6

1 Hold the working yarn in back of the stitch.

2 With the left needle, catch the floats on the back or front of the next elongated stitch, so the floats are on top of the needle in front of the next stitch.

3 Knit the floats together with the next stitch **(FIG. 6)**.

4 Work the next stitch in pattern.

Purl tuck stitch

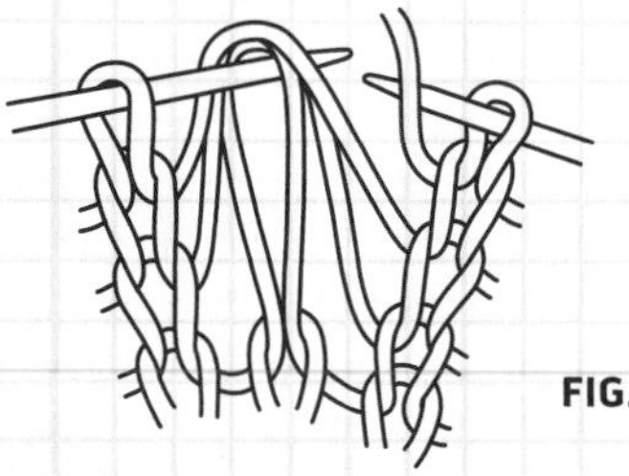

FIG. 7

1 Hold the working yarn in front of the stitch.

2 With the left needle, catch the floats on the back or front of the next elongated stitch, so the floats are on top of the needle in front of the next stitch.

3 Purl the floats together with the next stitch **(FIG. 7)**.

4 Work the next stitch in pattern.

Tuck stitches take some practice, but after working through them a few times, you'll see how easy and effective these stitches are. Working tuck stitches adds so much to the texture of a stitch pattern. Most of the time these stitches also make the other side of fabric look attractive enough that the stitch pattern becomes reversible. This is a valuable feature of any stitch pattern.

To understand how a tuck stitch is used in a pattern, let's look at tuck rib (see page 140 for pattern and chart). Stitch number 5 was slipped over 4 rows. On Row 5, we perform knit tuck stitch picking up all 4 floats and knitting them together with the elongated stitch. Because it is a knit tuck, all floats fall to the wrong side of the work and, as with any knit stitch, a knit tuck looks like a purl tuck on the wrong side. Because of that, the wrong side looks dramatically different from the right side and has a nice pattern in its own right.

Tuck Rib (right side)

Tuck Rib (wrong side)

THE ORIENTATION OF STANDARD SLIPPED STITCHES

When working with standard slipped stitches for different purposes, we notice that there are three obvious types of orientation: horizontal, vertical, and diagonal. Let's take a look at each separately.

HORIZONTAL

Slipping a few stitches in one row for a certain appearance or pattern creates a distinct visual or physical horizontal line. This is a very effective tool. Some of the simplest yet most sophisticated-looking patterns have a horizontal line of slipped stitches once every few rows.

Within one row, stitches can be slipped one at a time as in a simple slipped rib that is used as an edging or two at a time as in the slipped checks used for the sleeves in the Nebo Pullover (page 112). The number of slipped stitches can vary from pattern to pattern. In Chapter 3, where we talk about woven stitches, which use the floats to create their woven appearance, there are stitch patterns that periodically use groups of 3 or 4 slipped stitches in one row. Examples are the Gobelen Bag (page 82) and the Volna Scarf (page 98) patterns.

The outcome of slipping stitches horizontally is very apparent, and practically all slip-stitch patterns use it in many variations and combinations with other techniques.

It's also a very easy way to inject an old color into the background of a new one. For example, working a row with a new color and a repeat of one or more slipped stitches followed by a few knit stitches allows bleeding of an old color into a new color stripe (see tricolor waves; pattern and chart on page 38). It can look almost like a watercolor and makes a good accent pattern for many projects.

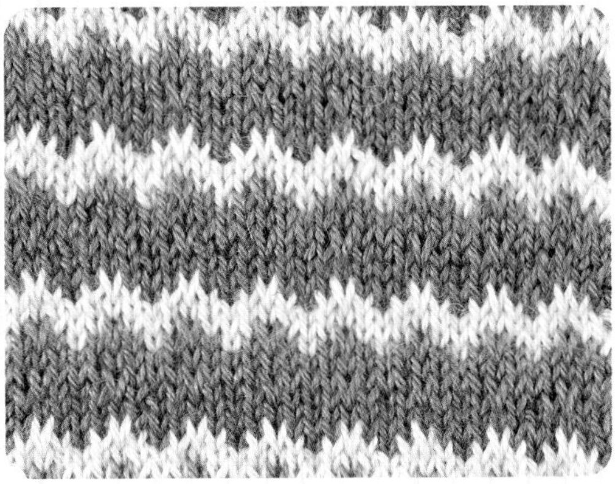

Tricolor Waves

Although it seems like there is an endless supply of stitch patterns with this orientation, we have to realize that there are limitations to how many adjacent stitches can be slipped at the same time. If the float is too long, it sags, and the fabric appears untidy. The long float is also not practical for garments or projects such as afghans because they will snag. On the other hand, if these floats will be picked up by a tuck stitch later in the pattern, you can allow a little longer float.

VERTICAL

When we are talking about vertical orientation of slipped stitches, we mean that we obtain a vertical stripe by slipping the same stitch on alternating rows.

As a variation, the stitch can be slipped with a number of rows in between. One example of this is the main stitch used in the Svítání Pullover (page 42). There is yet another variation in which we slip a stitch for a few rows to make it elongated, then work a few rows. Repeating this sequence will produce a dashed vertical line as in the icicles stitch pattern (see page 36). As long as elongated stitches are not far from each other vertically, you will see the stripe.

Stripes can be narrow or wide depending on the number of stitches involved. The closer the stripes are to each other, the less visible they are. To show off stripes, it helps to spread them horizontally.

As we see in tuck rib (page 140), tuck stitches can be stacked vertically as well.

The use of color also adds many variations. An example of a simple pattern of stripes in color is two-color stripes (see page 37 for pattern and chart).

Two-Color Stripes

Limitations of vertical orientation lie in drawing a stitch over a number of rows to elongate a stitch. The fabric around this stitch is gathered while the stitch is pulled up. The more rows are involved, the more this fabric gathers and eventually makes a bobble or cluster that is raised so high the stripe is not visible. Thus, the distinctive vertical stripe vanishes. On the other hand, if the vertical orientation is used to create such fabric, it is a perfect use of it.

DIAGONAL

This orientation is a combination of horizontal and vertical ones. You can slip every other stitch in the first row and on the next row change the positions of the stitches in checker order (i.e., a knit stitch is now a slipped stitch and a slipped stitch is a knit). By doing this, you visually move the slipped stitch one stitch horizontally and one row vertically, thus along the diagonal.

Spiral Hat

More than one stitch can be successfully moved in a diagonal fashion. The Spiral Hat (page 94) illustrates the use of diagonal orientation. As you see in the diagonal weave chart (page 97), there are 3 stitches that move on a diagonal over a stockinette-stitch background.

Multiple variations include moving stitches on a diagonal, but every other row. We see very striking results in changing directions of diagonals, including zigzag patterns like you see in the Gobelen Bag (page 82), and staggering diagonals of different directions as in the multidirectional weave pattern (page 76), among others. Limitations of both horizontal and vertical orientations apply here.

It's safe to say that some of the patterns show more obvious orientation than others. When you work through any stitch pattern offered in this book, pay attention to the orientation we discussed. It will help you to visualize the stitch pattern.

Horizontal

Vertical

Diagonal

ORIENTATION OF FLOATS

Every slipped stitch comes with a float. The length of a float in a stitch pattern depends on how many consecutive stitches were slipped. The more stitches are slipped, the longer the float. Orientation of floats can also be classified as horizontal, vertical, and diagonal.

For convenience of our discussion, let's take a simple stitch pattern.

Cast on a multiple of 9 stitches + 3.

ROW 1: (RS) Knit.

ROW 2: Purl.

ROW 3: Rep Row 1.

ROW 4: Rep Row 2.

ROW 5: (RS) Sl 3 wyf, *k6, sl 3 wyf; repeat from *.

ROWS 6 AND 8: Rep Row 2.

ROWS 7 AND 9: Rep Row 1.

HORIZONTAL

Floats can be placed in one row with a certain interval between them. For example, in our stitch pattern above, on the RS of our knitting we have 3 stitches—long floats repeated with 6 knit stitches between them. These floats are placed horizontally.

VERTICAL

Following the same instructions, we repeat Rows 5 and 6 three more times. Now we see that floats are placed vertically over the same 3 stitches. Repeating these 2 rows will continue to produce a simple but nice-looking pattern focused on floats.

DIAGONAL

Now, let's use the same pattern and make a little change. Every time we repeat Row 5, we will begin our first float one stitch earlier than the previous one. Here is how the first repeat of Row 5 will be written:

NEXT ROW: (RS) Sl 2 wyf, *k6, sl 3 wyf; repeat from * to last st, k1.

We have moved our float one stitch to the right. Continuing to move floats every time we work a RS row will result in floats placed diagonally.

There are many variations on diagonal floats. We will discuss them in more detail later.

about slip-stitch patterns

Now that we know all about slipped stitches and floats, we can take a closer look at slip-stitch patterns themselves. The more familiar you get with these stitches, the more you realize they're part of a huge family.

Slip-stitch patterns are extremely interesting in their appearances and in their formations. They can be very colorful or worked in one color. Unlike any other stitch patterns, the texture of these stitches stands out as a result of the use of slipped stitches and floats. Therefore, they are commonly portrayed as being dense and not very suitable for light garments. In this book, we're offering not just a classification of all possible slip-stitch pattern types, but also an update on their general image. This is long overdue. With the yarns and tools available to us today, these stitches can have a big range of density and variations from very thick to lace.

One true characteristic of these stitches that is never going to change is the fact that they look more intricate than they are. It's probably the easiest knitting technique after plain stockinette stitch. If you know how to knit, purl, and slip a stitch, you are ready for this adventure.

It does not take much to completely change the texture and appearance of a certain stitch pattern. For example, the same slip-stitch pattern can be worked in one color or a number of colors for an almost completely different look.

In this book, we divide all slip-stitch patterns into four groups: traditional (see Chapter 2), woven (see Chapter 3), fancy (see Chapter 4), and reversible (see Chapter 5). The definition of each group can be found in its corresponding chapter. Here, we will concentrate on how slip-stitch patterns are designed and, in the next section, how we can reengineer them.

EXAMPLES OF SLIP-STITCH PATTERNS

Here are a few basic slip-stitch patterns.

EXAMPLE #1

A very simple slip-stitch pattern that makes a horizontal chain is worked in super-bulky yarn.

CO an odd number of stitches. Work 4 rows of stockinette stitch.

ROW 1: *P1, sl 1 wyf; rep from * to last st, p1.

ROW 2: *Sl 1 wyb, k1; rep from * to last st, k1.

Work 4 rows of stockinette stitch.

Rows 1 and 2 make the chain you see on the background of stockinette stitch.

This is one of many patterns that are worked in a solid color and have a beautiful texture.

EXAMPLE #2

This next stitch pattern is a traditional slip-stitch pattern with a background of stockinette stitch. It is reminiscent of a Fair Isle technique, but in fact, it's a two-color slip-stitch pattern. All floats are on the back of fabric, and it's a very easy play of colors.

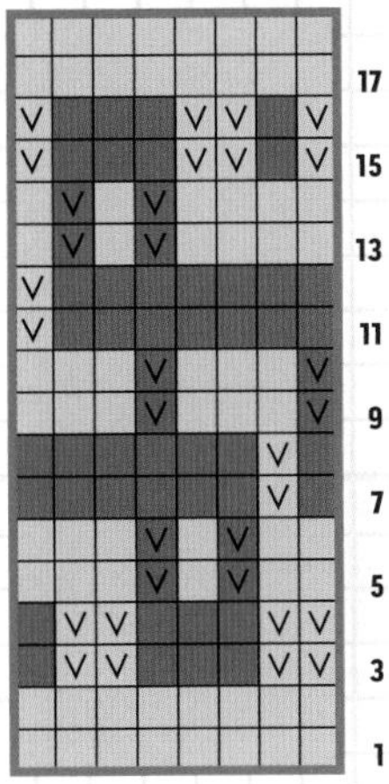

- with A, knit on RS, purl on WS
- with B, knit on RS, purl on WS
- V V sl pwise wyb on RS, wyf on WS
- pattern repeat

EXAMPLE #3

This example of a traditional stitch pattern is a little more obvious. The slipped stitches are stacked vertically and appear more frequently.

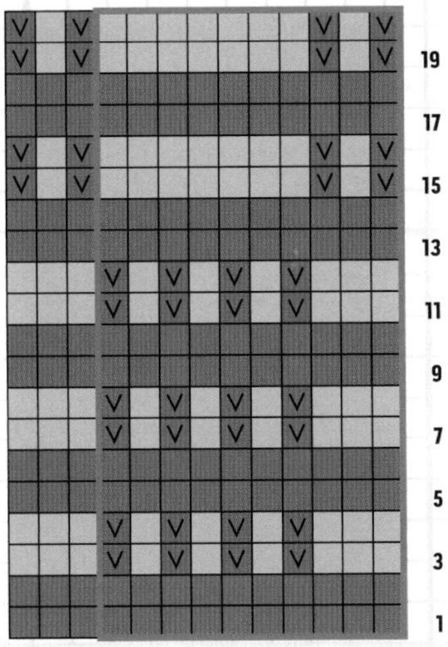

- with A, knit on RS, purl on WS
- with B, knit on RS, purl on WS
- V V sl pwise wyb on RS, wyf on WS
- pattern repeat

EXAMPLE #4

Here is one more traditional swatch. This slip-stitch pattern was first done on a garter-stitch background for the bottom portion and then redone on a background of stockinette stitch.

As you'll notice, the top is showing more of a pattern than the bottom. This is also an example of a less-than-winning combination of colors. Although each color is nice on its own, together they don't work well for this stitch. Neither color pops.

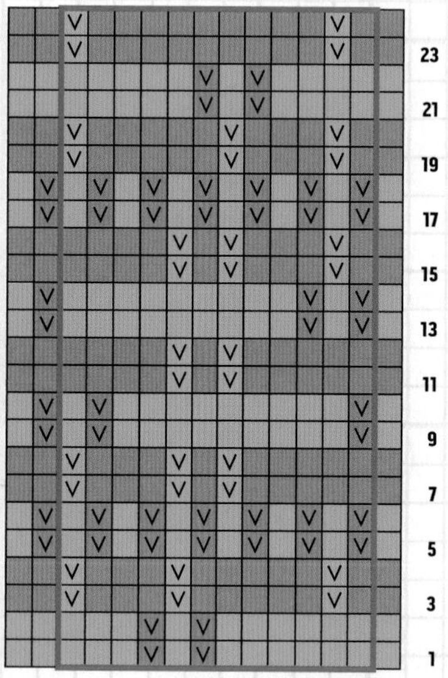

St st background: with A, knit on RS, purl on WS; garter st background: with A, knit

St st background: with B, knit on RS, purl on WS; garter st background: with B, knit

V V sl pwise wyb on RS, wyf on WS

pattern repeat

reading charts in slip-stitch patterns

Working with charts is a good habit even when knitting simple patterns. For patterns such as lace or cables, it helps to visualize the knitted fabric from the beginning and as you work through it.

Basic patterns with small stitch repeats are not a problem. We can't say the same for all slip-stitch patterns. Some of them will stay visually true to the chart after you're done, but some are hard to comprehend by looking at the chart. If this is the case, you might say, what is the reason for having a chart? Well, because most fabrics created with these stitches cinch vertically and some also horizontally, we have a hard time following where we are in the pattern by just looking at our work. Although it's very important to look at stitches on your needles and keep track of where you are, you might find great value in following the chart. In case you're not keen on using charts, we provide written instructions throughout the book. It's your choice.

WHAT IS A CHART?

A chart is a grid that contains columns and rows. Each square represents one stitch. The number of columns equals the number of stitches; and the number of rows equals the number of rows or rounds in the pattern. A symbol (described in chart key) tells you how to work the stitch. There are different symbols, and every publisher chooses their own if they are not a standard symbol such as knit or purl. It's a good practice to read the stitch key and get familiar with symbols before you read the chart. A symbol, when placed in a square, explains that this particular stitch needs to be worked according to the symbol's meaning.

ROW AND COLUMN NUMBERING

In the charts in this book, the numbers on the right-hand side of the chart represent RS rows for knitting flat. The RS rows are read from right to left, and the WS rows are read from left to right. Pay attention to these numbers; some charts begin on the WS row. For patterns that are knit in the round, every other round is numbered on the right-hand side of the chart. All rounds are read from right to left.

READING SYMBOLS

American and European knitting publications treat WS rows differently in charts. European charts show WS symbols as they will be worked on that row. The American way of charting (and the one used in this book) is to show the RS of the pattern throughout the chart, so you can see the fabric you're creating. Thus, the WS row symbols are shown as inverted symbols. For example, when you knit a stitch on the RS of the work and look at the back of it, you will see that it is a purl stitch on the WS. If you are working the WS row and want to create a knit stitch on the RS, you will intentionally make a purl stitch whose inverse is a knit stitch that you want. This applies to all symbols, and it also means that every time you're working the WS row and you're reading a chart from left to right, you invert the symbols you see.

The diagonal weave chart (shown at right and used in the Spiral Hat project on page 94) is a chart for diagonal weave pattern that is worked flat. Read the first row from right to left: Knit first 6 stitches, slip next 3 stitches wyf. Now, read the WS Row 2: Purl 1 stitch, slip next 3 stitches wyb, purl next 5 stitches.

Do you see how we read the stitches? In the key for the chart the meaning of the symbol is stated for RS and WS rows.

STITCH PATTERN REPEATS

In the waffles chart (at right and on page 40) the grid has 5 stitches and 8 rows. There is also a red rectangle inside the chart denoting what is called stitch and row repeat. There is one stitch before and one stitch after the repeat.

Here is how we work through this chart in terms of repeats:

ROW 1: K1, *k1, sl 1 wyb, k1; repeat from * to last st, k1.

The portion of instructions that says "*k1, sl 1 wyb, k1" is the portion inside the red rectangle. This is the repeat for this pattern, and that's why we see "repeat from * to last st" and "k1" after that. How many times you repeat depends on the number of stitches you cast on. When you cast on, multiply the number of stitches in the repeat (3 this time) by some number (let's say 5). This will give you 3 × 5 = 15 stitches. To finish your cast-on calculations, add 2 sts from the chart that you see as extras. Therefore, your calculation will be 15 sts + 2 sts = 17 sts.

If you'd like to have a selvedge, add 2 more stitches that you do not see in the chart and work them separately from the chart. In this case, your cast-on number will be 17 sts + 2 sts = 19 sts.

The row repeat in this case is 8 rows, so when you are done working them, go back to Row 1 and start a new repeat.

It is not as difficult as it might sound to learn to use charts. After you understand the basics, take another chart and read it looking at symbols in the key.

Choose one of the forty stitch patterns offered in the dictionary sections of this book and swatch it working with a chart. You will see how easy these patterns are.

DIAGONAL WEAVE

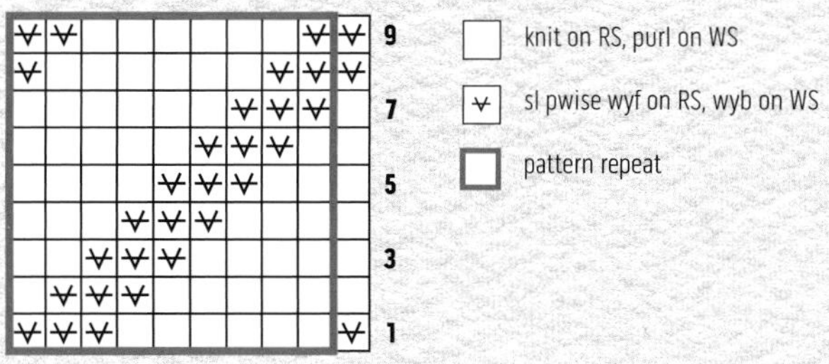

WAFFLES

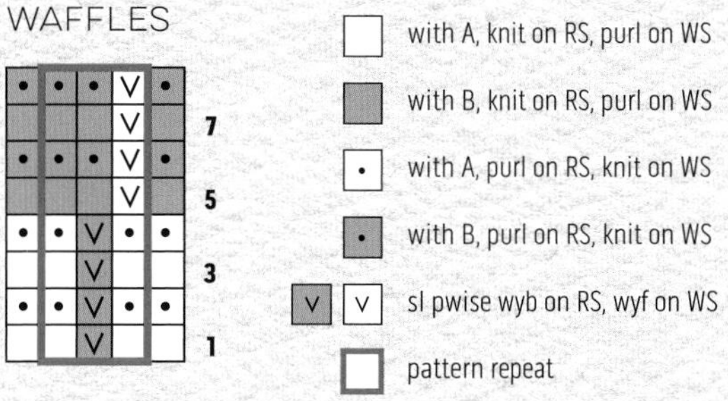

reengineering slip-stitch patterns

What are we talking about when we say we're changing a stitch pattern? What can be changed and how? To answer that, let's look at some examples.

REENGINEERING WITH COLOR

In the Svítání Pullover at right and on page 42, only one simple slip-stitch pattern was used with the 2-stitch over 4 rows repeat.

PATTERN (multiple of 2 sts + 3)

ROW 1: (RS) Knit.

ROW 2: Purl.

ROW 3: K1, *k1, sl 1 wyb; rep from * to last 2 sts, k2.

ROW 4: P1, k1, *sl 1 wyf, p1; rep from * to last st, p1.

Rep Rows 1–4 for patt.

This top would look good in only one color, but we decided to use three different colors. The colors are similar but in different values (light to dark), so the visual effect is subtle. The darkest color makes a horizontal line, while in the yoke the light color makes vertical lines. By changing colors every few rows, we create an ombré effect.

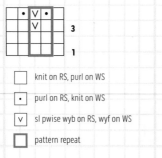

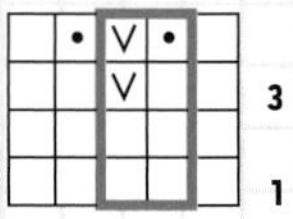

knit on RS, purl on WS

purl on RS, knit on WS

sl pwise wyb on RS, wyf on WS

pattern repeat

Svítání Pullover

REENGINEERING WITH COLOR AND YARN WEIGHT

Changing yarn weights can also affect the look of the same pattern in very unexpected ways.

PATTERN 1 (multiple of 4 sts + 3)

First, we knit a swatch with a single strand of yarn.

ROW 1: (RS) K1, *sl 1 wyf, k3; rep from * to last 2 sts, sl 1 wyf, k1.

ROW 2: P1, sl 1 wyf, * p3, sl 1 wyf; rep from * to last st, p1.

ROW 3: K1, *k2, sl 1 wyf, k1; rep from * to last 2 sts, k2.

ROW 4: P2, *p1, sl 1 wyf, p2; rep from * to last st, p1.

Rep Rows 1–4 for patt.

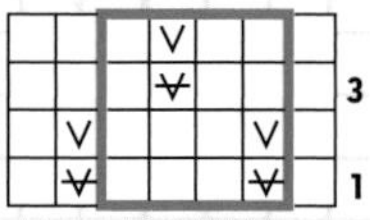

knit on RS, purl on WS

sl pwise wyb on RS, wyf on WS

sl pwise wyf on RS, wyb on WS

pattern repeat

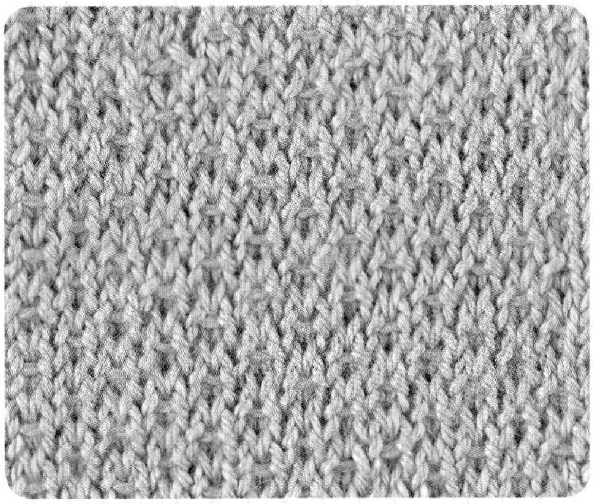

PATTERN 2 (multiple of 4 sts + 3)

Using two colors (single strand of each) creates a completely different-looking swatch.

ROW 1: (RS) With color A, k1, *sl 1 wyf, k3; rep from * to last 2 sts, sl 1 wyf, k1.

ROW 2: With color A, p1, sl 1 wyf, *p3, sl 1 wyf; rep from * to last st, p1.

ROW 3: With color B, k1, *k2, sl 1 wyf, k1; rep from * to last 2 sts, k2.

ROW 4: With color B, p2, *p1, sl 1 wyf, p2; rep from * to last st, p1.

Rep Rows 1–4 for patt.

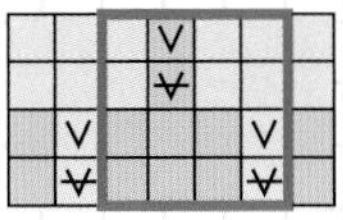

- with color A, knit on RS, purl on WS
- with color B, knit on RS, purl on WS
- sl pwise wyb on RS, wyf on WS
- sl pwise wyf on RS, wyb on WS
- pattern repeat

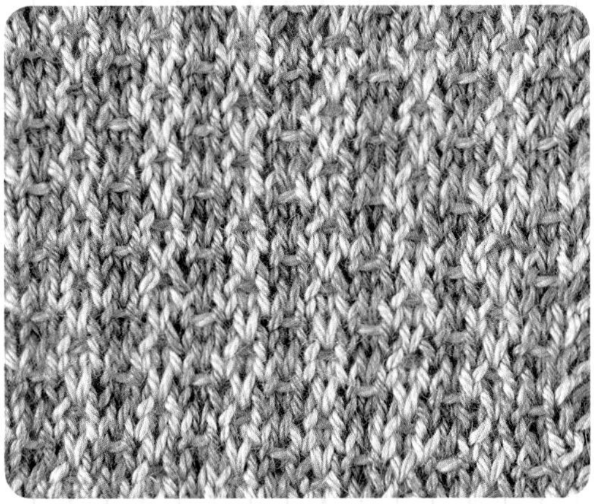

PATTERN 3 (multiple of 4 sts + 3)

Here is an example of using two different yarn weights together and slightly changing the pattern while always carrying floats on the WS. We used a double strand of yarn A and a single strand of yarn B.

ROW 1: (RS) With color A, k1, *sl 1 wyb, k3; rep from * to last 2 sts, sl 1 wyb, k1.

ROW 2: With color A, p1, sl 1 wyf, *p3, sl 1 wyf; rep from * to last st, p1.

ROW 3: With color B, k1, *k2, sl 1 wyb, k1; rep from * to last 2 sts, k2.

ROW 4: With color B, p2, *p1, sl 1 wyf, p2; rep from * to last st, p1.

Rep Rows 1–4 for patt.

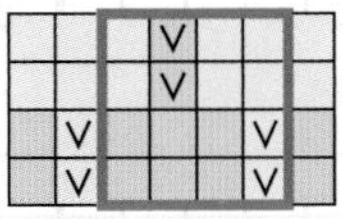

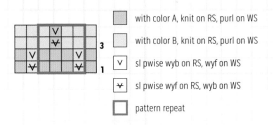

- with color A, knit on RS, purl on WS
- with color B, knit on RS, purl on WS
- sl pwise wyb on RS, wyf on WS
- pattern repeat

PATTERN 4 (multiple of 4 sts + 3)

This swatch, as in Pattern 3, also uses both lighter and heavier yarn weights. The stitch pattern remains the same as in Pattern 3, with a change in color sequence.

ROW 1: (RS) With color A, k1, *sl 1 wyb, k3; rep from * to last 2 sts, sl 1 wyb, k1.

ROW 2: With color A, p1, sl 1 wyf, *p3, sl 1 wyf; rep from * to last st, p1.

ROW 3: With color B, k1, *k2, sl 1 wyb, k1; rep from * to last 2 sts, k2.

ROW 4: With color B, p2, *p1, sl 1 wyf, p2; rep from * to last st, p1.

ROW 5: With color A, k1, *sl 1 wyb, k3; rep from * to last 2 sts, sl 1 wyb, k1.

ROW 6: With color A, p1, sl 1 wyf, *p3, sl 1 wyf; rep from * to last st, p1.

ROW 7: With color A, k1, *k2, sl 1 wyb, k1; rep from * to last 2 sts, k2.

ROW 8: With color A, p2, *p1, sl 1 wyf, p2; rep from * to last st, p1.

ROW 9: With color B, k1, *sl 1 wyb, k3; rep from * to last 2 sts, sl 1 wyb, k1.

ROW 10: With color B, p1, sl 1 wyf, *p3, sl 1 wyf; rep from * to last st, p1.

ROW 11: With color A, k1, *k2, sl 1 wyb, k1; rep from * to last 2 sts, k2.

ROW 12: With color A, p2, *p1, sl 1 wyf, p2; rep from * to last st, p1.

Rep Rows 1–12 for patt.

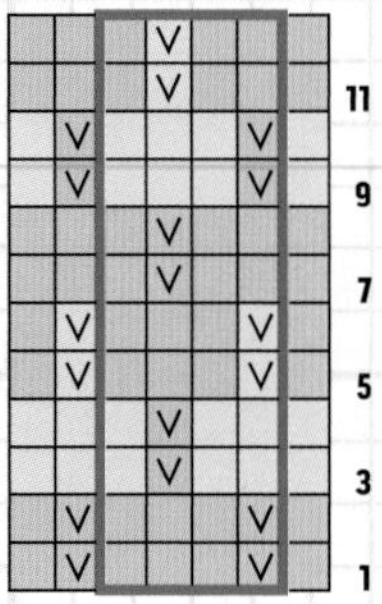

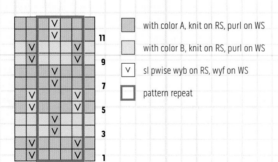

with color A, knit on RS, purl on WS

with color B, knit on RS, purl on WS

sl pwise wyb on RS, wyf on WS

pattern repeat

REENGINEERING WITH FLOATS AND TUCKS

Adding or omitting a tuck stitch as well as changing a front float to back or to carrying the yarn over the needle alters the stitch pattern. Sometimes the change is subtle; other times the pattern is hard to recognize.

PATTERN 1: THREE YON
(multiple of 6 sts + 3)

Here we are working all three slipped stitches and yons together .

STITCH GUIDE

T3-yon: K1tog with all 3 yon (yarn-over-needle loops) on RS.

pT3-yon: P1tog with all 3 yon on WS.

ROWS 1 AND 3: (RS) *K3, p1, sl 1 wyon, p1; rep from * to last 3 sts, k3.

ROW 2: P3, *k1, sl 1 wyon, k1, p3; rep from *.

ROW 4: K1, sl 1 wyon, k1, *p1, pT3-yon, p1, k1, sl 1 wyon, k1; rep from *.

ROW 5: *P1, sl 1 wyon, p1, k3; rep from * to last 3 sts, p1, sl 1 wyon, p1.

ROW 6: K1, sl 1 wyon, k1, *p3, k1, sl 1 wyon, k1; rep from *.

ROW 7: *K1, T3-yon, k1, p1, sl 1 wyon, p1; rep from * to last 3 sts, k1, T3-yon, k1.

ROW 8: Rep Row 2.

ROW 9: Rep Row 1.

Rep Rows 4–9 for patt.

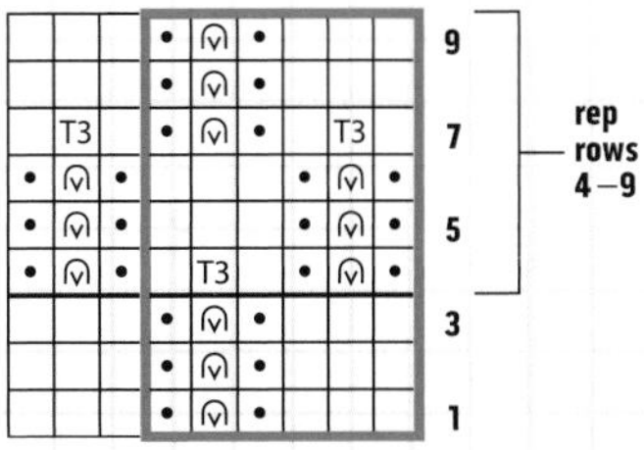

- knit on RS, purl on WS
- • purl on RS, knit on WS
- sl1 wyon
- T3 T3-yon on RS, pT3-yon on WS
- pattern repeat

PATTERN 2: ONE YON

(multiple of 6 sts + 3)

Here we are working only the slipped stitch and one yon (from 3rd row below) together. The floats on the WS of work are left unworked.

STITCH GUIDE

T1-yon: (RS) Knit next stitch together with yon from third row below.

pT1-yon: (WS) Purl next stitch together with yon from third row below.

ROW 1: (RS) *K3, p1, sl 1 wyon, p1; rep from * to last 3 sts, k3.

ROW 2: P3, *k1, sl 1 wyf, k1, p3; rep from *.

ROW 3: *K3, p1, sl 1 wyb, p1; rep from * to last 3 sts, k3.

ROW 4: K1, sl 1 wyon, k1, *p1, pT1-yon, p1, k1, sl 1 wyon, k1; rep from *.

ROW 5: *P1, sl 1 wyb, p1, k3; rep from * to last 3 sts, p1, sl 1 wyb, p1.

ROW 6: K1, sl 1 wyf, k1, *p3, k1, sl 1 wyf, k1; rep from *.

ROW 7: *K1, T1-yon, k1, p1, sl 1 wyon, p1; rep from * to last 3 sts, k1, T1-yon, k1.

ROW 8: Rep Row 2.

ROW 9: Rep Row 3.

Rep Rows 4–9 for patt.

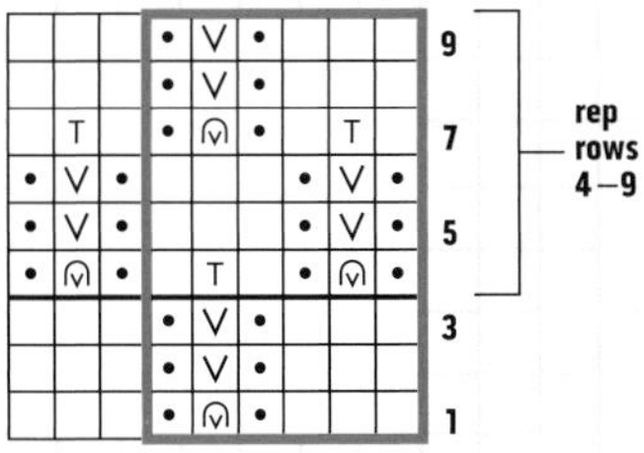

- knit on RS, purl on WS
- • purl on RS, knit on WS
- V sl pwise wyb on RS, wyf on WS
- sl1 wyon
- T T1-yon on RS, pT1-yon on WS
- pattern repeat

PATTERN 3: THREE FLOATS IN THE BACK (multiple of 6 sts + 3)

Here we are working together the slipped stitch and all the floats on the WS of the work.

STITCH GUIDE

T3: (RS) Insert needle into next st from front to back as if to knit, on the WS of the work lift and place back floats from 3 previous rows onto the needle (4 loops on needle; 1 live and 3 floats).

Knit all 4 loops together.

pT3: (WS) Insert needle into next st from back to front as if to purl, on WS of the work lift and place back floats from 3 previous rows onto the needle (4 loops on needle; 1 live and 3 floats). Purl all 4 loops together.

ROWS 1 AND 3: (RS) *K3, p1, sl 1 wyb, p1; rep from * to last 3 sts, k3.

ROW 2: P3, *k1, sl 1 wyf, k1, p3; rep from *.

ROW 4: K1, sl 1 wyf, k1, *p1, pT3, p1, k1, sl 1 wyf, k1; rep from *.

ROW 5: *P1, sl 1 wyb, p1, k3; rep from * to last 3 sts, p1, sl 1 wyb, p1.

ROW 6: K1, sl 1 wyf, k1, *p3, k1, sl 1 wyf, k1; rep from *.

ROW 7: *K1, T3, k1, p1, sl 1 wyb, p1; rep from * to last 3 sts, k1, T3, k1.

ROW 8: Rep Row 2.

ROW 9: Rep Row 1.

Rep Rows 4–9 for patt.

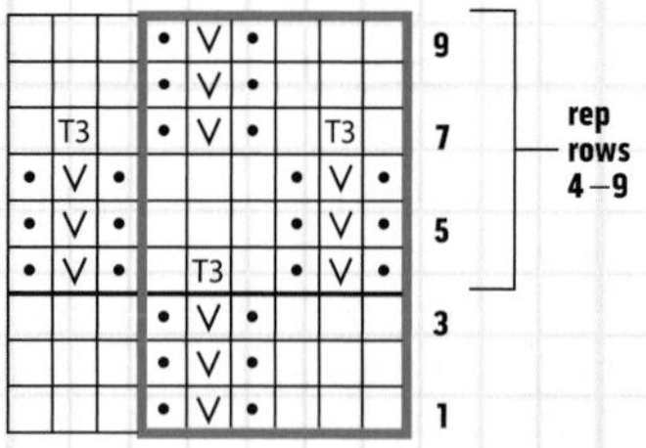

knit on RS, purl on WS

T3 T3-yon on RS, pT3-yon on WS

purl on RS, knit on WS

pattern repeat

sl pwise wyb on RS, wyf on WS

PATTERN 4: TWO FLOATS IN FRONT, ONE IN BACK
(multiple of 6 sts + 3)

Here we are working slipped stitches with floats in front and back with no tuck stitch.

ROWS 1 AND 3: (RS) *K3, p1, sl 1 wyf, p1; rep from * to last 3 sts, k3.

ROW 2: P3, *k1, sl 1 wyf, k1, p3; rep from *.

ROW 4: K1, sl 1 wyb, k1, *p3, k1, sl 1 wyb, k1; rep from *.

ROW 5: *P1, sl 1 wyb, p1, k3; rep from * to last 3 sts, p1, sl 1 wyb, p1.

ROW 6: K1, sl 1 wyb, k1, *p3, k1, sl 1 wyb, k1; rep from *.

ROW 7: *K3, p1, sl 1 wyf, p1; rep from * to last 3 sts, k3.

ROW 8: Rep Row 2.

ROW 9: Rep Row 1.

Rep Rows 4–9 for patt.

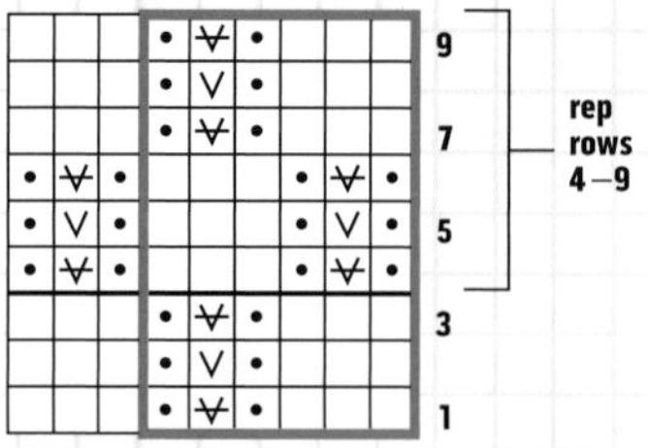

knit on RS, purl on WS

sl pwise wyf on RS, wyb on WS

purl on RS, knit on WS

pattern repeat

sl pwise wyb on RS, wyf on WS

REENGINEERING WITH COLOR AND FLOATS

By manipulating color and floats, you can create an infinite number of patterns. This pattern is a multiple of 4 sts and uses two colors: cream and blue. First, we used the blue color as a background (color A) and cream (color B). The blue color is slipped and drawn over the cream color. It is nice and crisp.

ORIGINAL STITCH

(multiple of 4 sts)

ROW 1: (RS) With A, knit.

ROW 2: Purl.

ROW 3: With B, *k2, sl 1 wyb, k1; rep from *.

ROW 4: *P1, sl 1 wyf, p2; rep from *.

ROW 5: Rep Row 3.

ROW 6: Rep Row 4.

ROW 7: With A, knit.

ROW 8: Purl.

ROW 9: With B, *k1, sl 1 wyb; rep from *.

ROW 10: *Sl 1 wyf, p1; rep from *.

Rep Rows 1–10 for patt.

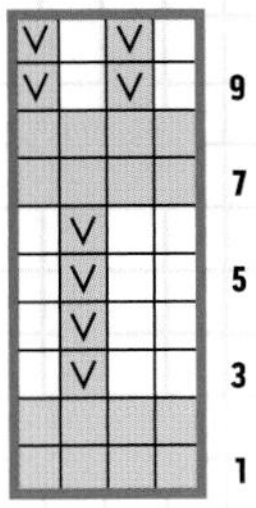

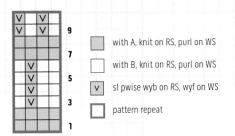

- with A, knit on RS, purl on WS
- with B, knit on RS, purl on WS
- sl pwise wyb on RS, wyf on WS
- pattern repeat

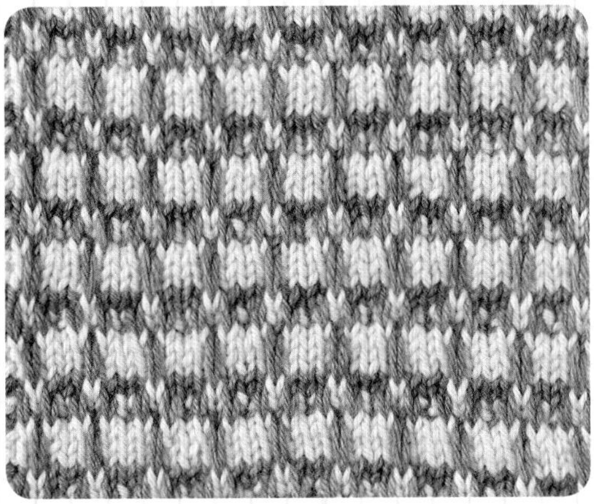

Then, we used the cream color as a background (color A) and blue (color B). This time the cream was carried over the blue, and the pattern does not look as crisp anymore.

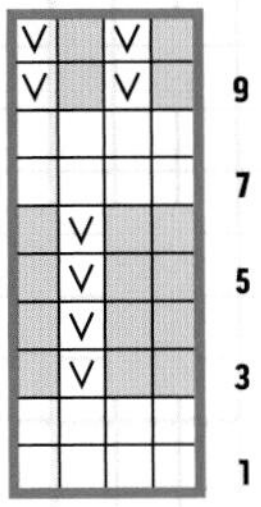

- with A, knit on RS, purl on WS
- with B, knit on RS, purl on WS
- sl pwise wyb on RS, wyf on WS
- pattern repeat

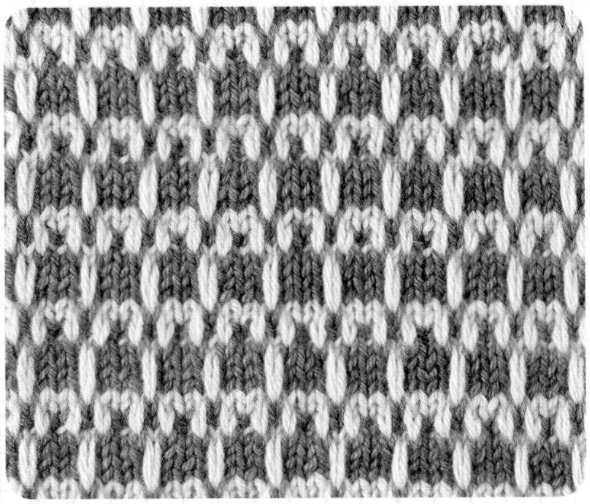

MODIFIED PATTERN 1

(multiple of 4 sts)

Next, we wanted to change the way the floats are oriented, slanting them in one direction and then changing to the other. The chart and pattern needed some changes to adapt to slanting floats. This creates a very attractive new pattern with minimal change from the original pattern.

STITCH GUIDE

1/3RC: Sl 3 sts to cn and hold in back, k1, k3 from cn.

1/3LC: Sl 1 st to cn and hold in front, k3, k1 from cn.

ROW 1: (RS) With A, knit.

ROW 2: Purl.

ROW 3: With B, *k3, sl 1 wyb; rep from *.

ROW 4: *Sl 1 wyf, p3; rep from *.

ROW 5: Rep Row 3.

ROW 6: Rep Row 4.

ROW 7: With A, *1/3RC; rep from *.

ROW 8: Purl.

ROW 9: With B, *sl 1 wyb, k1; rep from *.

ROW 10: *P1, sl 1 wyf; rep from *.

ROW 11: With A, knit.

ROW 12: Purl.

ROW 13: With B, *sl 1 wyb, k3; rep from *.

ROW 14: *P3, sl 1 wyf; rep from *.

ROW 15: Rep Row 13.

ROW 16: Rep Row 14.

ROW 17: With A, *1/3LC; rep from *.

ROW 18: Purl.

ROW 19: Rep Row 9.

ROW 20: Rep Row 10.

Rep Rows 1–20 for patt.

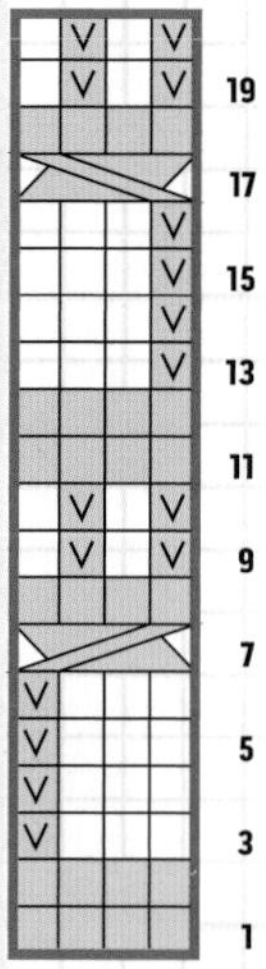

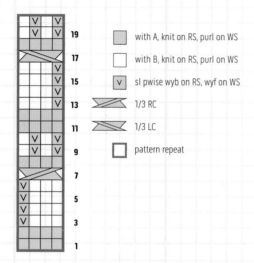

■	with A, knit on RS, purl on WS
□	with B, knit on RS, purl on WS
v	sl pwise wyb on RS, wyf on WS
⤬	1/3 RC
⤬	1/3 LC
▫	pattern repeat

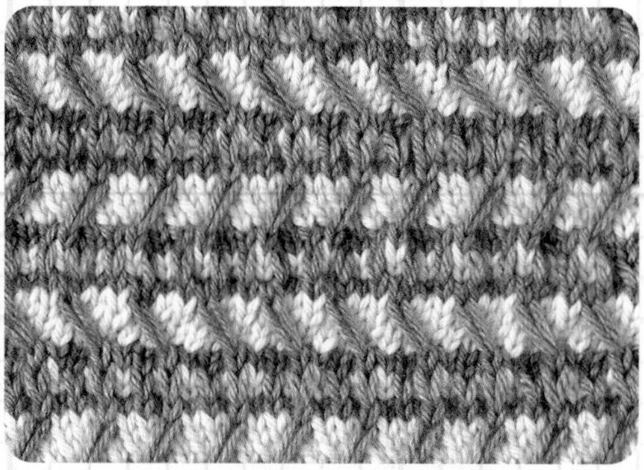

MODIFIED PATTERN 2
(multiple of 8 sts)

Finally, we thought it would be interesting to cross the floats. Here is the result. This variation involved more manipulation and is not that simple anymore. It looks nice, but we think that the slanted floats looked better.

STITCH GUIDE

5-st Cross: Sl 1 st to cn and hold in front, k1, sl 2 sts to 2nd cn and hold in back, k1, k2 from back cn, k1 from front cn.

Variation on 5-st Cross: (uses only 1 cn) Sl 1 st to cn and hold in front, k1, skip 2 sts on the left needle, k1 (slipped st), and do not slip it off the needle, go back to skipped sts, k2, k1 from cn.

ROW 1: (RS) With A, knit.

ROW 2: Purl.

ROW 3: With B, *sl 1 wyb, k3; rep from *.

ROW 4: *P3, sl 1 wyf; rep from *.

ROW 5: Rep Row 3.

ROW 6: Rep Row 4.

ROW 7: With A, *5-st cross, k3; rep from *.

ROW 8: Purl.

ROW 9: With B, *k1, sl 1 wyb; rep from *.

ROW 10: *Sl 1 wyf, p1; rep from *.

Rep Rows 1–10 for patt.

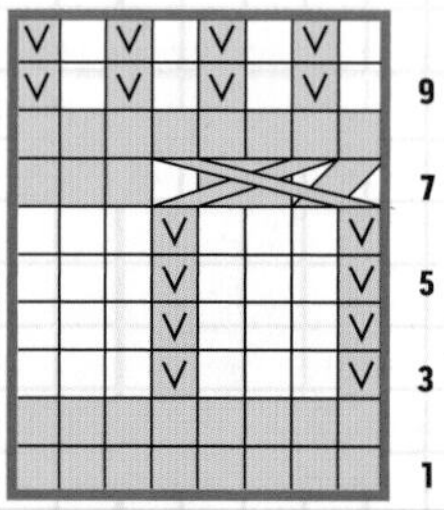

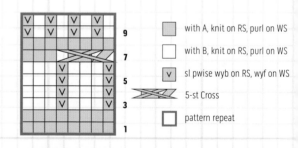

■	with A, knit on RS, purl on WS
□	with B, knit on RS, purl on WS
v	sl pwise wyb on RS, wyf on WS
⤬	5-st Cross
▫	pattern repeat

All of these examples illustrate the work you can do by reengineering the pattern you see in the stitch dictionaries. Use your creativity and come up with more ways to change these patterns. You might end up with much nicer patterns than you see here.

designing with slip-stitch patterns

After you make some of the projects from this book, you will see how we used the stitches for designing purposes. Many stitch patterns were changed to fit the aesthetics of the design or to support the shape and the fit of the garment. For some projects, we combined a few slip-stitch patterns or mixed them with other techniques.

Sometimes it's enough to place colorwork at the edges and leave the rest of the garment in stockinette stitch as in the Kromka Hoodie (page 64) or the Koketka Sweater (page 128).

When a color pattern is introduced in small amounts, it doesn't overwhelm the overall look of a garment. Although, when it's done elegantly such as in the Čekanka Jacket on page 54, it's a head-turning piece. Accessories are the easy application of strong color patterns. For example, the Gobelen Bag (page 82) and the Volna Scarf (page 98) really benefit from the use of bold colors.

FLAT VERSUS IN THE ROUND

Most slip-stitch patterns can be worked either flat or in the round with minimal or no adjustment of the chart. Depending on your project, choose one way or the other. There is a definite advantage to working a woven stitch pattern with a diagonal float orientation in the round; it's simply easier to see where you are in the pattern when you are looking at the RS of the work.

For some stitch patterns, the chart is exactly the same for working in rows or circular knitting. When working in the round from such a chart, just read it from right to left on all rounds to produce the same pattern. For example, the raindrops chart (page 38) can be worked flat or in the round without any adjustments.

Seren' Vest

Other patterns have so-called *balance* stitches included in their charts. These are the stitches that are shown on the outside of the repeat rectangle as in the chart for the waffles stitch (page 40).

Balance stitches are needed here when this pattern is worked flat and must look like the stitch repeat is complete on each side of a finished piece. These stitches are not part of the repeat itself, but rather are extra stitches before and after all repeats are done.

If the waffles stitch pattern is worked in the round, these stitches will be not needed at all. In fact, they will create wider purl column at the beginning of round and throw off the balance. To prevent this from happening, consider using stitch repeats only for continuity of the pattern.

Gobelen Bag

With some patterns there is an issue of a jog at the beginning of round. Since slip-stitch patterns vary in their structure, you will need to deal with that on case-by-case basis.

STITCH PLACEMENT IN A GARMENT

Placement of stitch patterns in a garment is very important for gauge and aesthetic reasons. Many slip-stitch patterns have horizontal orientation. If you overdo it and place a big stripe around the bust or hip area, the garment will not be flattering. Instead, if you choose to use this pattern for an accent here and there as on the edges of the Kromka Hoodie (page 64) or on the sleeves and next to the hem of the Mák Cardigan (page 88), it could be very nice.

Because many slip-stitch patterns are reversible, it makes sense to use both sides of the pattern in one garment. In Seren' Vest (page 158), the attached scarf is reversible and worked in two colors. As an allover pattern it would be too much, but for an accent as a scarf that wraps around the neck showing both sides of the stitch pattern, it becomes an attractive feature of the design.

Making many swatches and trying different colors and yarn weights is very helpful for choosing where to place the stitch pattern in the project.

MAKE IT YOURS

Our hope is that with all the discussions on how to reengineer patterns, how to use yarns to your advantage, and how to work slip-stitch patterns, you will be brave enough to change patterns for the designs in this book, whether you're changing the stitch pattern or design elements. For example, in the Nebo Pullover (page 112), it's so easy to change the front panel or the pattern for a sleeve. Make sure you have the right gauge when you're replacing stitch patterns. Another change can be done in the length of a sleeve or the sweater itself. In other words, we encourage you to try new stitches and play with designing along the way.

Kromka Hoodie

gauge in slip-stitch patterns

Gauge is a measurement of the number of stitches and rows/rounds per inch of knitted fabric. Finding a precise gauge is imperative to achieving a successful, well-fitting knitted project. Another reason for correct gauge reading is when planning to substitute stitch patterns in a project. One, you need to ensure that the stitch patterns that are worked simultaneously have similar, ideally equal, row gauges. Otherwise, you would experience puckering of the fabric that has looser gauge and pulling of the pattern that has tighter gauge. Two, if planning to substitute a pattern in a project with a slip-stitch pattern, you will need to account for extra yarn. As we have seen, slip-stitch patterns take more rows per inch than, say, stockinette, and thus more yarn will be needed.

MEASURING GAUGE

To determine your gauge, you'll need to knit a generous swatch—at least 6" (15 cm) square—using the yarn, needles, and the stitch pattern that you'll use in the garment. This will allow you to measure 4" (10 cm) both horizontally and vertically without influence from the edge, cast-on, or bind-off stitches, which can distort the fabric. It's a good idea to include at least two pattern repeats both horizontally and vertically in the swatch.

In most cases, the gauge called for in a pattern is based on the finished garment measurements after blocking. Therefore, you need to block your swatch in the same manner you will block the garment after it's finished. We recommend washing the swatch, then placing the damp swatch on a flat surface, patting it lightly to set the stitches. In some cases of slip-stitch patterns, it might be suitable to pull the swatch slightly lengthwise to "open" up the stitch to reveal its true beauty. For example, the Zlatý déšť Cowl (page 124) will not reveal the zigzag and the lacy stars unless it is blocked slightly stretched in both directions. Let the swatch air-dry completely before taking measurements.

ALTERNATIVE METHOD FOR MEASURING GAUGE

For many slip-stitch patterns, it might be really difficult to determine the correct row gauge if we're not careful. Depending on where we place a ruler to count stitches, we may count a completely different number of rows than we had actually worked. This happens because when working slip-stitch patterns, we are slipping some stitches over one or more rows and bringing the rows closer together. If we are not paying attention to it, our row gauge will be drastically different from the actual one. There are a few alternative methods for measuring gauge that ensure an accurate gauge reading. Here's one we like to use.

With this method, you do not have to count the number of stitches and rows; rather, you measure across whole stitch pattern repeats, which are usually much easier to see and identify. Cast on the number of stitches needed to knit enough stitch repeats to obtain a swatch of about 6" (15 cm) wide. Then add 2 selvedge stitches for each side to obtain the total stitch count.

Here's an example: A project's pattern has 5 sts and 6 rows in each pattern repeat; and the yarn's stitch gauge on the yarn label states 24 sts over 4" (10 cm), or in other words 6 sts per 1" (2.5 cm). To achieve a 6" (15 cm) wide swatch, we will need to cast on 6 times 6 sts, or 36 sts. Our pattern has 5 sts in one repeat, so we divide 36 by 5 to determine the number of full repeats. In this case, we have 7 repeats, which equals 35 sts. Adding 2 selvedge stitches at each edge will give us a total of 39 sts (2 sts + 35 sts + 2 sts) to cast on for the swatch.

So after casting on the appropriate number of stitches, work 2 selvedge stitches, the number of predetermined pattern repeats (7 in our example), and then 2 selvedge stitches. Work 3 or 4 rows in garter stitch to secure the edge of the swatch and prevent rolling. Begin swatching the stitch pattern and work until swatch measures about 6" (15 cm) from

Zlatý déšť Cowl

the end of the garter edge, ending with a last row of the stitch pattern repeat. Work an additional 3 or 4 rows of garter stitch for the upper edge and bind off. After your swatch is blocked and completely dry, proceed with measuring your swatch. Unlike with regular gauge reading, measure across all (7 in our example) stitch repeats widthwise for stitch gauge and lengthwise for row gauge. Divide the number of stitches you cast on less selvedge stitches (35 sts in our example) by the measurement you obtained for the width of these repeats. This will be your stitch gauge per inch. Then multiply by 4" (10 cm) to match the pattern's gauge per 4" (10 cm).

Similarly, to obtain row gauge, multiply the number of rows in one repeat by the number of repeats you worked and divide the result by your measurement reading to obtain the number of rows per inch. Multiply that by 4" (10 cm) to obtain row gauge per 4" (10 cm).

yarn choices

The choice of yarn for slip-stitch designs is very important as it will determine the look, the feel, and the style of your project. Today, we have an unimaginable number of yarn choices. We can choose yarn by weight, texture, or color; we can pair yarns with larger or smaller needles than called for on a yarn band to create various effects; and we can combine yarns of different weights, textures, and colors. With all these possibilities, we can achieve dramatic differences in the looks and styles of finished projects even if using the same basic slip-stitch pattern.

For slip-stitch patterns, it's best to avoid strongly multicolored and variegated yarns, especially if the pattern is used as an overall pattern. Because slip stitch creates textures, using visually busy yarns will hide the effects of the slipped stitch. These yarns should be used sparingly and only as accents or complementing yarns in this family of stitches.

Choosing a suitable yarn depends on the project you want to make. If you want to make a shawl or a summer cardigan, you would choose lighter weight yarn for a slip-stitch pattern that is more open or airy. See the swatches for fancy stitches in Chapter 4, the Zlatý déšť Cowl (page 124) or the Bordo Shawl (page 48).

On the other hand, if your project is a bag, such as the Gobelen Bag (page 82), you would choose slightly heavier yarn paired with a denser slip-stitch pattern so the bag will be more durable and keep its shape.

Let's take a closer look at some of the possibilities for how we can "manipulate" (or experiment with) yarn to open the door to endless slip-stitch designs.

WEIGHT

One classification of yarns is done by weight, ranging from fingering to bulky; the choices are ample. Depending on your project, the most suitable weights for slip stitch range from light DK to Aran. Using lighter yarn will produce textured fabric that might be too dainty to see it. Using heavier yarns will produce very dense fabrics. You can increase the needle size to reduce the density, thus the stiffness of the fabric, if you desire.

SAME YARN WEIGHT

Making a project in the same yarn weight will create a uniform look throughout the pattern. Using the same yarn weight is suitable for any slip-stitch pattern.

THIN AND THICK

Using two different yarn weights will create significant changes in a stitch pattern. Depending on the sequence in which you alternate them and use them in a pattern, you will get different results and looks.

One nice combination is thick and thin where the thin yarn is worked on the same needle size as the thicker one, thus producing airy, lacelike fabric against a contrasting sturdier fabric.

TEXTURE

Slip-stitch patterns by their nature create textured fabric. That is one of the most exciting features of the slip-stitch pattern family.

Yarns themselves, though, have their own textures because of how they are spun or the fiber they are made from. For example, one-ply yarns are smooth as are yarns made from alpaca. When knitted in slip-stitch patterns, these smooth yarns will still produce quite textured knitted fabric. If we introduce an additional element of yarn textures, such as a novelty yarn, we add a whole new dimension to a basic slip-stitch pattern. As with multicolored or variegated yarns, novelty yarns should be used sparingly and as an accent in slip-stitch patterns. For example, a novelty yarn would be a nice accent as color B in the bricks stitch pattern (see page 41). The novelty yarn would add a three-dimensional effect against a smooth yarn.

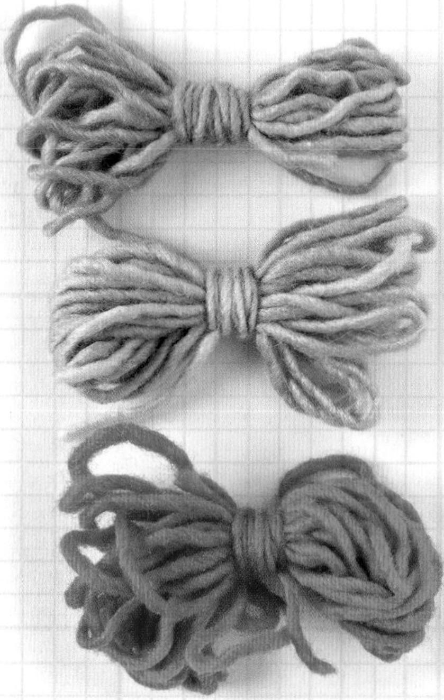

FIG. 1

FIG. 2

Another yarn characteristic to be aware of is yarn's "memory." Yarns with good memory are the ones that produce beautiful stitch definition. Yarns that produce poor stitch definition, such as most 100% cotton yarns, are considered to have bad memory. Yarns with poor memory will produce a non-unified look in a stitch pattern, will not be as bouncy, will not conform to a slip-stitch pattern as well, and will not "pop" as much as yarns with good memory.

COLOR

Choosing yarn colors is another dimension that can completely change a pattern's feel and look. Choosing colors can be very unpredictable.

In today's market, you can choose any color imaginable. Yarn companies create beautiful ranges of colors that you can choose from in any yarn weight you please, and in a way, they make it easier to combine colors that go together well. There is a wide variety of combinations you can use to work a slip-stitch pattern into a knitted fabric that will look fresh, modern, stylish, and fashion-forward.

For example, you can choose muted colors (see fancy stitches in Chapter 4), you can choose highly contrasting colors (see the Čekanka Jacket at right and on page 54), or you can choose colors for an ombré look (see the Svítání Pullover on page 42). You can choose pastel colors or you can choose earthy colors. The possibilities are endless.

CONTRASTING COLORS

What may seem like a contrasting color scheme when yarn skeins are placed next to each other may not work well in the slip-stitch pattern you choose to work with. For example, see the blue and green Manos del Uruguay Silk Blend yarns in **FIG. 1**. When these two colors are placed together, they nicely complement each other; they both "pop" and look like good colors to combine for a slip-stitch pattern. Though when used together in a simple slip-stitch pattern **(FIG. 2)** you can see that they blend together because they're the same value (i.e., they're both light colors). The stitch pattern used at the lower portion of the swatch is the same stitch pattern used in Pattern 3 on page 19, and the upper portion of the swatch is the same pattern as in Pattern 4 on page 20.) In these swatches, the colors we used are Blue Sky Alpaca's Silk Alpaca. The colors are the same color of

Čekanka Jacket

different values. One would think that these colors would not contrast well, but they do.

On the other hand, if we contrast the blue and green Manos del Uruguay Silk Blend with another color such as the hibiscus red shown in **FIG. 1**, the colors pop right out against the background, as in the Čekanka Jacket (above).

BLENDING COLORS

To achieve an ombré look such as the one you see in the Svítání Pullover (page 42), choose colors that are of the same hue but different values. This design uses different shades of gray, but you could use light and dark blues or other colors. The stitch pattern you use should be simple enough, like in this project where 2-st and 4-row stitch repetition is used as an overall pattern. The right color sequence can produce an ombré look. See more in Reengineering Slip-Stitch Patterns (page 18).

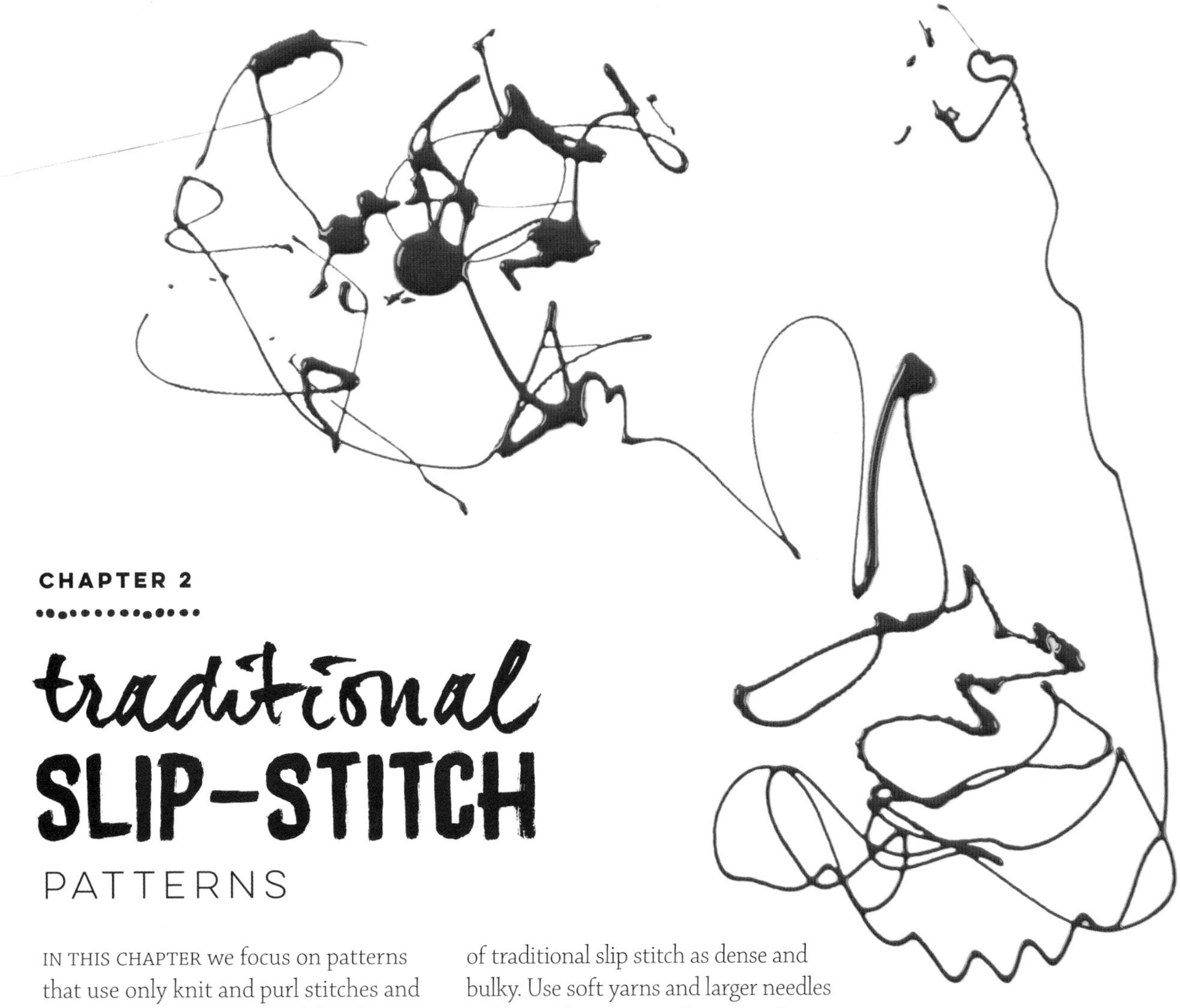

CHAPTER 2

traditional SLIP-STITCH PATTERNS

IN THIS CHAPTER we focus on patterns that use only knit and purl stitches and a standard slipped stitch. It's hard to believe that simple manipulations of these basic stitches can produce such a variety of beautiful stitch patterns. These patterns have a wonderful texture whether knit in a single color or multiple colors.

The ten stitch patterns shown here represent just a few of the many possible ways to combine these basic stitches. You'll find textures, stripes, checked patterns, colorful waves, and more. Some of these stitches are reversible, so we show the wrong side of the swatches for your convenience.

Gentle colors and yarns are used for these swatches with the hope that you will see the beautiful textures and not think of traditional slip stitch as dense and bulky. Use soft yarns and larger needles to loosen the texture when it tends to be tight. Take care of float lengths. Controlling the float tension allows you to have a stitch pattern that pops.

Barbara Walker was instrumental in her research on slip-stitch techniques. Her original mosaic knitting is a variation of traditional stitches. With the way she developed charts, you can choose between working a stitch with stockinette or garter stitches and obtain different results.

Swatch the given stitch patterns, then try reengineering them as we discussed in All About Slip-Stitch Knitting (page 6). You'll increase the number of possible patterns, and the fun you can have with them, exponentially!

ZIGZAG SHADOW

(MULTIPLE OF 8 STS + 2)

– This is a two-color swatch. White is named A, brown is named B. Each color is worked for two rows.

ROW 1: (RS) With A, knit.

ROW 2: Purl.

ROW 3: With B, *sl 2 wyb, k6; rep from * to last 2 sts, sl 2 wyb.

ROW 4: Sl 2 wyf, *k6, sl 2 wyf; rep from *.

ROW 5: With A, rep Row 1.

ROW 6: Rep Row 2.

ROW 7: With B, *sl 3 wyb, k4, sl 1 wyb; rep from * to last 2 sts, sl 2 wyb.

ROW 8: Sl 2 wyf, *sl 1 wyf, k4, sl 3 wyf; rep from *.

ROW 9: With A, rep Row 1.

ROW 10: Rep Row 2.

ROW 11: With B, *k2, sl 2 wyb; rep from * to last 2 sts, k2.

ROW 12: K2, *sl 2 wyf, k2; rep from *.

ROW 13: With A, rep Row 1.

ROW 14: Rep Row 2.

ROW 15: With B, *k3, sl 4 wyb, k1; rep from * to last 2 sts, k2.

ROW 16: K2, *k1, sl 4 wyf, k3; rep from *.

ROW 17: With A, rep Row 1.

ROW 18: Rep Row 2.

ROW 19: With B, *k4, sl 2 wyb, k2; rep from * to last 2 sts, k2.

ROW 20: K2, *k2, sl 2 wyf, k4; rep from *.

Rep Rows 1–20 for pattern.

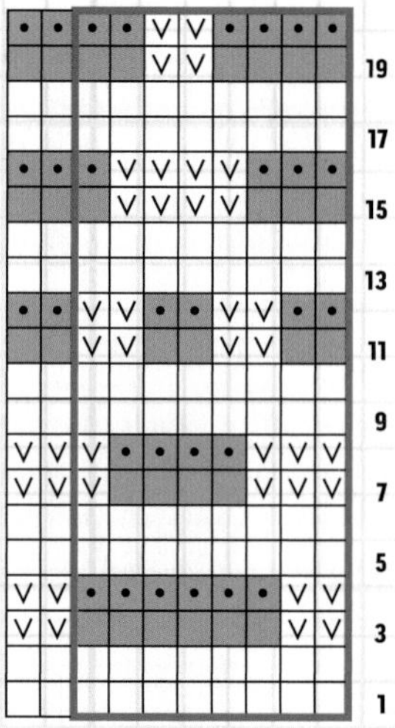

- with A, knit on RS, purl on WS
- with B, knit on RS, purl on WS
- with A, purl on RS, knit on WS
- with B, purl on RS, knit on WS
- sl pwise wyb on RS, wyf on WS
- pattern repeat

MOSAIC SHADOW

(MULTIPLE OF 10 STS + 3)

- This is a two-color swatch. Gray is named A, white is named B. Each color is worked for two rows.
- Worked on a garter-stitch background, but can be worked on a stockinette-stitch background.
- Dark and light colors feature the same patterns that are vertically flipped.

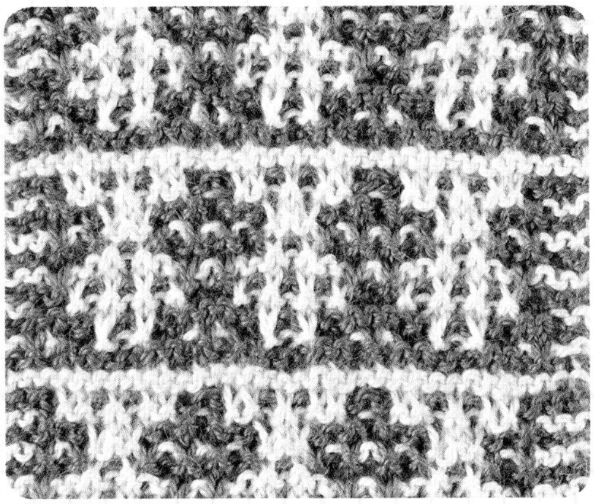

ROW 1: (RS) With A, knit.

ROW 2: Knit.

ROW 3: With B, k1, *sl 1 wyb, k1, sl 2 wyb, k3, sl 2 wyb, k1; rep from * to last 2 sts, sl 1 wyb, k1.

ROW 4: K1, sl 1 wyb, *k1, sl 2 wyb, k3, sl 2 wyb, k1, sl 1 wyb; rep from * to last st, k1.

ROW 5: With A, k1, *k4, sl 1 wyb, k1, sl 1 wyb, k3; rep from * to last 2 sts, k2.

ROW 6: K2, *k3, sl 1 wyb, k1, sl 1 wyb, k4; rep from * to last st, k1.

ROW 7: With B, k1, *sl 2 wyb, k7, sl 1 wyb; rep from * to last 2 sts, sl 1 wyb, k1.

ROW 8: K1, sl 1 wyb, *sl 1 wyb, k7, sl 2 wyb; rep from * to last st, k1.

ROW 9: With A, k1, *k2, (sl 1 wyb, k1) 4 times; rep from * to last 2 sts, k2.

ROW 10: K2, *(k1, sl 1 wyb) 4 times, k2; rep from * to last st, k1.

ROW 11: With B, k1, *k1, sl 1 wyb, k7, sl 1 wyb; rep from * to last 2 sts, k2.

ROW 12: K2, *sl 1 wyb, k7, sl 1 wyb, k1; rep from * to last st, k1.

ROW 13: With A, k1, *k4, sl 1 wyb, k1, sl 1 wyb, k3; rep from * to last 2 sts, k2.

ROW 14: K2, *k3, sl 1 wyb, k1, sl 1 wyb, k4; rep from * to last st, k1.

ROW 15: With B, k1, *(k1, sl 1 wyb) twice, k3, sl 1 wyb, k1, sl 1 wyb; rep from * to last 2 sts, k2.

ROW 16: K2, *sl 1 wyb, k1, sl 1 wyb, k3, (sl 1 wyb, k1) twice; rep from * to last st, k1.

ROW 17: With A, k1, *k4, sl 3 wyb, k3; rep from * to last 2 sts, k2.

ROW 18: K2, *k3, sl 3 wyb, k4; rep from * to last st, k1.

ROW 19: With B, k1, *k1, sl 1 wyb, k7, sl 1 wyb; rep from * to last 2 sts, k2.

ROW 20: K2, *sl 1 wyb, k7, sl 1 wyb, k1; rep from * to last st, k1.

ROW 21: With A, k1, *k2, sl 2 wyb, k1, sl 1 wyb, k1, sl 2 wyb, k1; rep from * to last 2 sts, k2.

ROW 22: K2, *k1, sl 2 wyb, k1, sl 1 wyb, k1, sl 2 wyb, k2; rep from * to last st, k1.

ROW 23: With B, knit.

ROW 24: Knit.

Rep Rows 1–24 for patt.

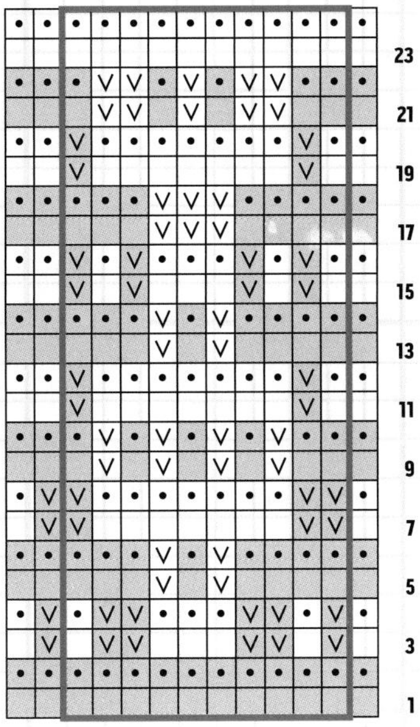

- with A, knit on RS, purl on WS
- with B, knit on RS, purl on WS
- • with A, purl on RS, knit on WS
- • with B, purl on RS, knit on WS
- V V sl pwise wyb on RS, wyf on WS
- pattern repeat

ICICLES

(MULTIPLE OF 6 STS)

- This swatch is reversible and has a very distinct pattern on each side. Works well for projects that show RS and WS, such as scarves.
- Makes soft but sturdy fabric when larger needle is used.

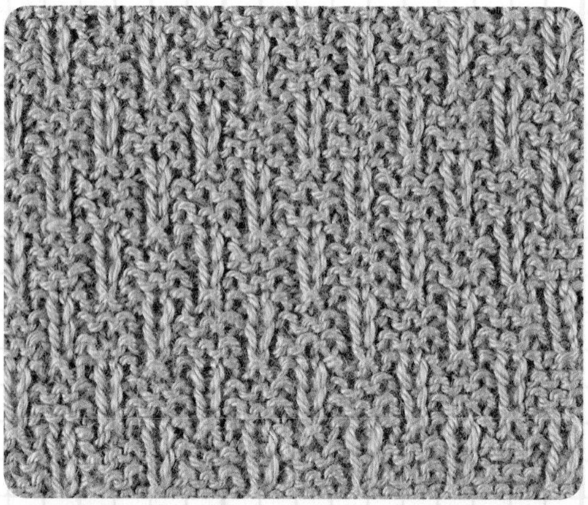

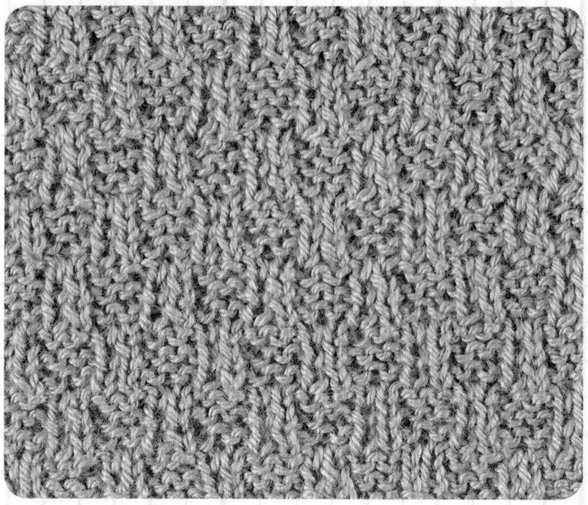

ROW 1: (RS) *K1, sl 1 wyb, k4; rep from *.

ROW 2: *P3, k1, p1, k1; rep from *.

ROW 3: Rep Row 1.

ROW 4: Rep Row 2.

ROW 5: Rep Row 1.

ROW 6: Rep Row 2.

ROW 7: *K4, sl 1 wyb, k1; rep from *.

ROW 8: *K1, p1, k1, p3; rep from *.

ROW 9: Rep Row 7.

ROW 10: Rep Row 8.

ROW 11: Rep Row 7.

ROW 12: Rep Row 8.

Rep Rows 1–12 for patt.

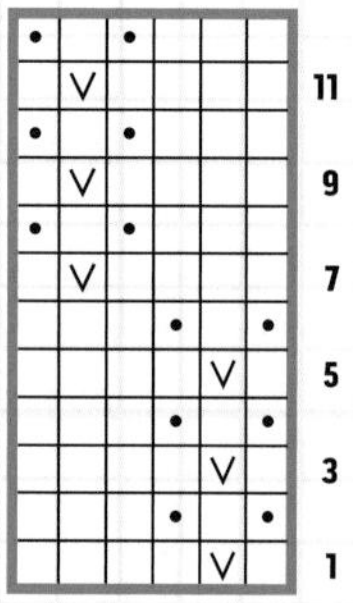

- ☐ knit on RS, purl on WS
- • purl on RS, knit on WS
- V sl pwise wyb on RS, wyf on WS
- ☐ pattern repeat

TWEED

(MULTIPLE OF 4 STS)

– Swatch is reversible.

– Use a large needle for a lacy look.

ROW 1: (WS) *P1, k2, sl 1 wyf; rep from *.

ROW 2: (RS) *K1, sl 1 wyf, k2; rep from *.

ROW 3: *K1, sl 1 wyf, p1, k1; rep from *.

ROW 4: *K3, sl 1 wyf; rep from *.

Rep Rows 1–4 for patt.

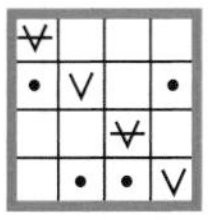

knit on RS, purl on WS

purl on RS, knit on WS

sl pwise wyb on RS, wyf on WS

sl pwise wyf on RS, wyb on WS

pattern repeat

TWO-COLOR STRIPES

(MULTIPLE OF 8 STS + 6)

– This is a two-color swatch. White is named A, brown is named B. Each color is worked for two rows.

– This stitch is not reversible, but it has a subtle patterning on the WS, which is interesting when used for scarves.

– Vertical stripes are slimming and could be used for an overall garment pattern.

– Change order of colors for a different look.

ROW 1: (RS) With A, k2, *sl 2 wyb, k6; rep from * to last 4 sts, sl 2 wyb, k2.

ROW 2: P2, sl 2 wyf, *p6, sl 2 wyf; rep from * to last 2 sts, p2.

ROW 3: With B, k2, *k4, sl 2 wyb, k2; rep from * to last 4 sts, k4.

ROW 4: K4, *k2, sl 2 wyf, k4; rep from * to last 2 sts, k2.

Rep Rows 1–4 for patt.

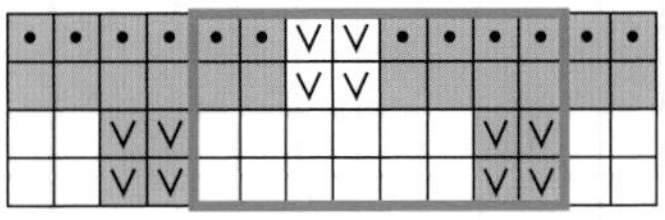

with A, knit on RS, purl on WS

with B, knit on RS, purl on WS

with B, purl on RS, knit on WS

sl pwise wyb on RS, wyf on WS

pattern repeat

TRICOLOR WAVES

(MULTIPLE OF 4 STS + 1)

- This is a three-color swatch. Gray is named A, brown is named B, and white is named C. Each color is worked for four rows.
- Drapey fabric with a subtle pattern on WS.
- Suitable for projects that require drape.

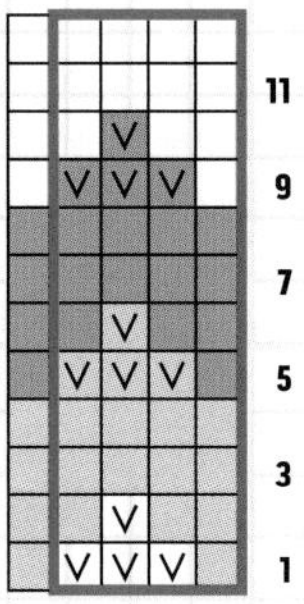

with A, knit on RS, purl on WS

with B, knit on RS, purl on WS

with C, knit on RS, purl on WS

V V V sl pwise wyb on RS, wyf on WS

pattern repeat

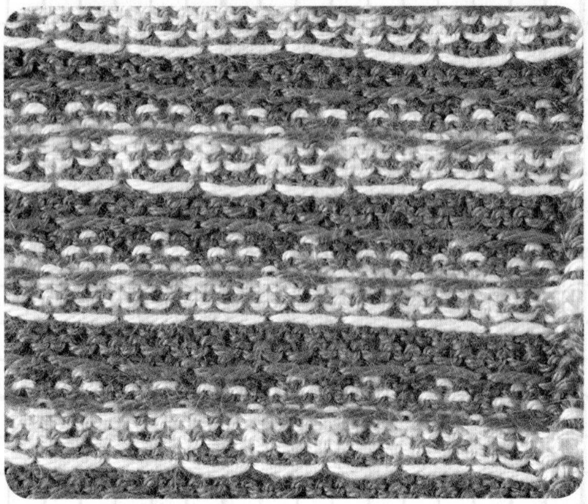

ROW 1: (RS) With A, *K1, sl 3 wyb; rep from * to last st, k1.

ROW 2: P1, *p1, sl 1 wyf, p2; rep from *.

ROW 3: Knit.

ROW 4: Purl.

ROWS 5–8: With B, rep Rows 1–4.

ROWS 9–12: With C, rep Rows 1–4.

Rep Rows 1–12 for patt.

RAINDROPS

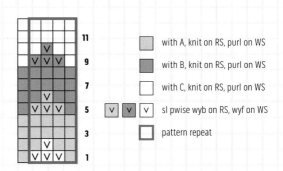

(MULTIPLE OF 4 STS)

- Works best in solid-color yarn with a little sheen.
- Change needle size for a different look.

ROW 1: (RS) *K3, sl 1 wyb; rep from *.

ROW 2: *Sl 1 wyf, p3; rep from *.

ROW 3: *P3, k1; rep from *.

ROW 4: *P1, k3; rep from *.

ROW 5: *K1, sl 1 wyb, k2; rep from *.

ROW 6: *P2, sl 1 wyf, p1; rep from * to end.

ROW 7: *P1, k1, p2; rep from *.

ROW 8: *K2, p1, k1; rep from *.

Rep Rows 1–8 for patt.

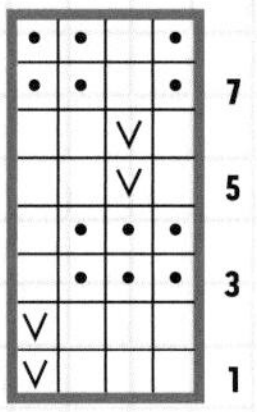

knit on RS, purl on WS

• purl on RS, knit on WS

V sl pwise wyb on RS, wyf on WS

pattern repeat

THREE-COLOR TILES

(MULTIPLE OF 4 STS)

- This is a three-color swatch. White is named A, brown is named B, and green is named C. Each color is worked for three rows.
- Makes a dense fabric with reversible patterns.
- WS pattern displays floats in checks pattern.
- Suitable for accessories.

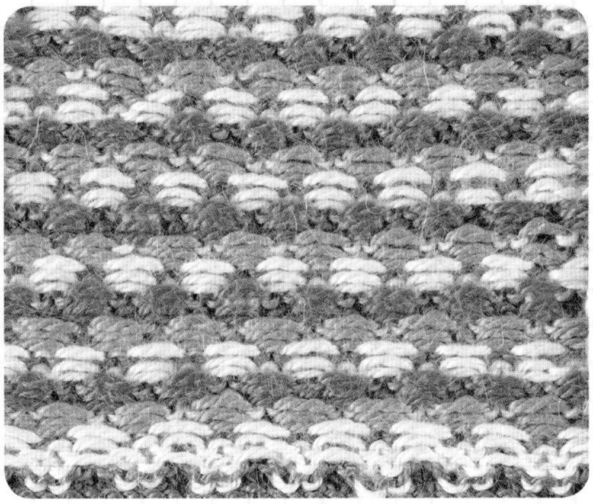

ROW 1: (RS) With A, *k2, sl 2 wyb; rep from *.

ROW 2: *Sl 2, wyf, p2; rep from *.

ROW 3: Rep Row 1.

ROW 4: With B, *p2, sl 2 wyf; rep from *.

ROW 5: *Sl 2, wyb, k2; rep from *.

ROW 6: Rep Row 4.

ROW 7: With C, rep Row 1.

ROW 8: Rep Row 2.

ROW 9: Rep Row 1.

ROW 10: With A, rep Row 4.

ROW 11: Rep Row 5.

ROW 12: Rep Row 4.

ROW 13: With B, rep Row 1.

ROW 14: Rep Row 2.

ROW 15: Rep Row 1.

ROW 16: With C, rep Row 4.

ROW 17: With A, rep Row 5.

ROW 18: Rep Row 4.

Rep Rows 1–18 for patt.

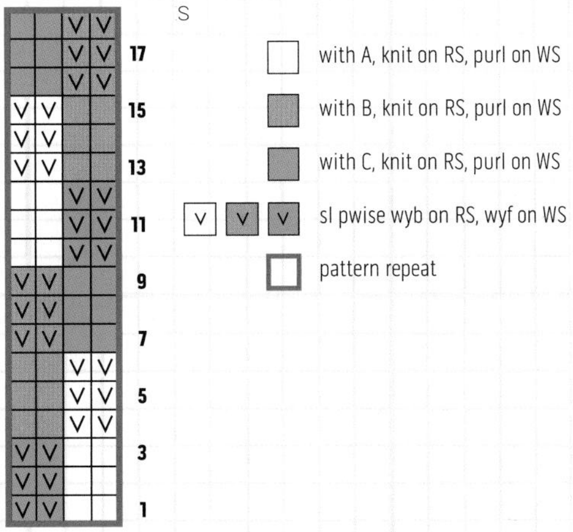

WAFFLES

(MULTIPLE OF 3 STS + 2)

– This is a two-color swatch. White is named A, brown is named B. Each color is worked for four rows.

– This stitch is reversible, making it great for scarves or details such as collars, pockets, and more.

– Change the order of the colors for a different look.

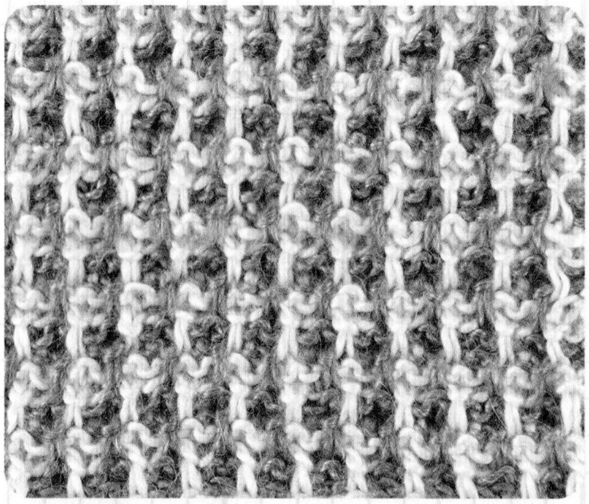

ROW 1: (RS) With A, k1, *k1, sl 1 wyb, k1; rep from * to last st, k1.

ROW 2: K1, *k1, sl 1 wyf, k1; rep from * to last st, k1.

ROW 3: Rep Row 1.

ROW 4: Rep Row 2.

ROW 5: With B, k1, *sl 1 wyb, k2; rep from * to last st, k1.

ROW 6: K1, *k2, sl 1 wyb; rep from * to last st, k1.

ROW 7: Rep Row 5.

ROW 8: Rep Row 6.

Rep Rows 1–8 for patt.

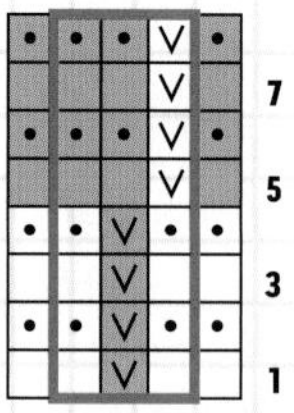

with A, knit on RS, purl on WS

with B, knit on RS, purl on WS

with A, purl on RS, knit on WS

with B, purl on RS, knit on WS

sl pwise wyb on RS, wyf on WS

pattern repeat

BRICKS

(MULTIPLE OF 10 STS + 2)

- This is a two-color swatch. White is named A, dark green is named B. Each color is worked for four rows.
- Three-dimensional reversible fabric.
- Use different thickness of yarns or different fibers to get the most of this pattern.

ROW 1: (RS) With A, purl.

ROW 2: Knit.

ROW 3: Rep Row 1.

ROW 4: Rep Row 2.

ROW 5: With B, *sl 2, wyb, k8; rep from * to last 2 sts, sl 2 wyb.

ROW 6: Sl 2, wyf, *p8, sl 2 wyf; rep from *.

ROW 7: Rep Row 5.

ROW 8: Rep Row 6.

ROW 9: With A, rep Row 1.

ROW 10: Rep Row 2.

ROW 11: Rep Row 1.

ROW 12: Rep Row 2.

ROW 13: With B, *k5, sl 2 wyb, k3; rep from * to last 2 sts, k2.

ROW 14: P2, *p3, sl 2 wyf, p5; rep from *.

ROW 15: Rep Row 13.

ROW 16: Rep Row 14.

Rep Rows 1–16 for patt.

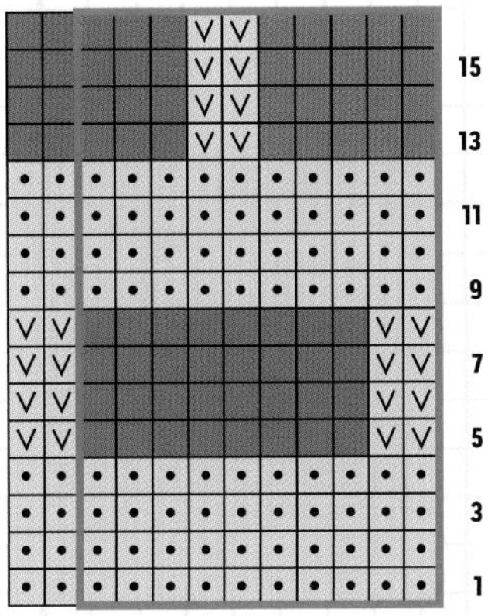

with B, knit on RS, purl on WS

• with A, purl on RS, knit on WS

V sl pwise wyb on RS, wyf on WS

pattern repeat

THIS TOP IS worked in a very simple, though extremely effective slip-stitch pattern. The choice of color sequence over the four-row repetition influences and changes the look and feel of the knitted fabric and style of the project. In this pattern, the colors are chosen to portray soft wide ombré horizontal stripes, and the yoke forms one-color vertical lines with underlying narrow horizontal stripes.

// *designed by* **SIMONA MERCHANT-DEST**

svítání PULLOVER

FINISHED SIZE

About 29½ (33½, 36¾, 40¾, 44¾, 48¾, 52¾)" (75 [85, 93.5, 103.5, 113.5, 124, 134] cm) bust circumference.

Top shown meas 33½" (85 cm).

YARN

Worsted weight (#4 Worsted).

Shown here: The Fibre Company Organik (70% organic merino, 15% baby alpaca, 15% silk; 98 yd [90 m]/1¾ oz [50 g]): loam (color A), 1 (2, 2, 2, 2, 2, 2) skeins; claystone (color B), 3 (4, 4, 4, 5, 5, 5) skeins; crater lake (color C), 2 (3, 3, 3, 3, 4, 4) skeins; cumulus (color D), 3 (3, 3, 4, 4, 4, 5) skeins.

NEEDLES

Hips, Bust, and Yoke: Size U.S. 9 (5.5 mm): 32" (80 cm) and 24" (60 cm) circular (cir) and set of 5 double-pointed (dpn).

Waist: Sizes U.S. 8 (5 mm) and 7 (4.5 mm): 32" (80 cm) cir, and set of 5 double-pointed (dpn).

Adjust needle sizes if necessary to obtain the correct gauge.

NOTIONS

Markers (m); tapestry needle; stitch holders or waste yarn.

GAUGE

20 sts and 34 rnds = 4" (10 cm) in slip-stitch patt (see Stitch Guide or chart) on size 9 (5.5mm) needles.

22 sts and 40 rnds = 4" (10 cm) in slip-stitch patt on size 8 (5 mm) needles.

23 sts and 42 rnds = 4" (10 cm) in slip-stitch patt on size 7 (4.5 mm) needles.

NOTES

All slipped stitches are slipped purlwise with yarn in back (wyb) on RS or with yarn in front (wyf) on WS.

To make top completely reversible, with each color change, break off yarn and attach new ball of yarn. Otherwise, carry unused colors along WS of work at beg of rnd.

STITCH GUIDE

SLIP-STITCH PATT

(multiple of 2 sts)

RND 1: *K1, sl 1; rep from *.

RND 2: *P1, sl 1; rep from *.

RNDS 3 AND 4: Knit.

Rep Rnds 1–4 for patt.

BODY COLOR SEQUENCE

RNDS 1–8: [2 rnds in color B, 2 rnds in color A] twice.

RNDS 9–16: 8 rnds in color B.

RNDS 17 AND 18: 2 rnds in color C.

RNDS 19 AND 20: 2 rnds in color B.

RNDS 21–24: 4 rnds in color C.

RNDS 25–28: 4 rnds in color B.

RNDS 29 AND 30: 2 rnds in color C.

RNDS 31–38: 8 rnds in color B.

RNDS 39 AND 40: 2 rnds in color A.

RNDS 41 AND 42: 2 rnds in color B.

RNDS 43–54: 12 rnds in color A.

RNDS 55 AND 56: 2 rnds in color B.

RNDS 57 AND 58: 2 rnds in color A.

RNDS 59–66: 8 rnds in color B.

RNDS 67 AND 68: 2 rnds in color A.

RNDS 69–76: 8 rnds in color B.

RNDS 77 AND 78: 2 rnds in color C.

RNDS 79 AND 80: 2 rnds in color B.

RNDS 81–84: 4 rnds in color C.

RNDS 85 AND 86: 2 rnds in color B.

RNDS 87–92: 6 rnds in color C.

RNDS 93 AND 94: 2 rnds in color B.

RNDS 95 AND 96: 2 rnds in color C.

RNDS 97–100: 4 rnds in color B.

RNDS 101 AND 102: 2 rnds in color C.

RNDS 103 AND 104: 2 rnds in color B.

RNDS 105 AND 106: 2 rnds in color C.

RNDS 107–112: 6 rnds in color B.

RNDS 113 AND 114: 2 rnds in color C.

RNDS 115 AND 116: 2 rnds in color B.

RNDS 117–120: 4 rnds in color C.

RNDS 121 AND 122: 2 rnds in color B.

RND 123: 1 rnd in color C.

YOKE COLOR SEQUENCE

2 rnds in color B.

2 rnds in color C.

8 (12, 16, 16, 16, 16, 16) rnds in color D.

2 rnds in color C.

2 rnds in color D.

[2 rnds in color B, 2 rnds in color D] 2 (2, 2, 2, 3, 3, 3) times.

2 rnds in color B.

1 rnd in color D.

DEC RND 1: 1 rnd in color D.

[2 rnds in color C, 2 rnds in color D] 1 (1, 1, 1, 2, 2, 2) times.

4 (4, 4, 4, 4, 8, 8) rnds in color C.

2 rnds in color D.

2 rnds in color C.

3 rnds in color D.

DEC RND 2: 1 rnd in color D.

2 rnds in color B.

6 rnds in color D.

[2 rnds in color C, 2 rnds in color D] 2 (2, 2, 2, 2, 2, 3) times.

[2 rnds in color B, 2 rnds in color D] 4 times.

4 rnds in color D.

2 rnds in color C.

2 rnds in color D.

body

With largest cir needle and color A, CO 74 (84, 92, 102, 112, 122, 132) sts, pm for right side "seam," CO 74 (84, 92, 102, 112, 122, 132) sts, pm for left side "seam" and beg of rnd. Join for working in rnds, being careful not to twist sts—148 (168, 184, 204, 224, 244, 264) sts.

Knit 1 rnd.

RNDS 1 AND 3: *K1, sl 1; rep from *.

RND 2: *P1, sl 1; rep from *.

RND 4: Knit.

Work Body Color Sequence (see Stitch Guide) and Rnds 1–4 of Slip-Stitch Patt (see Stitch Guide or chart) until piece meas about 4" (10 cm) from beg, ending after Rnd 34 of Body Color Sequence.

SHAPE WAIST

Change to medium cir, and cont in Slip-Stitch Patt and Body Color Sequence until piece meas about 6" (15 cm) from beg, ending after Rnd 54 of Body Color Sequence.

Change to smallest cir, and cont in Slip-Stitch Patt and Body Color Sequence until piece meas about 7" (18 cm) from beg, ending after Rnd 64 of Body Color Sequence.

SHAPE BUST

Change to medium cir, and cont in Slip-Stitch Patt and Body Color Sequence until piece meas about 9" (23 cm) from beg, ending after Rnd 84 of Body Color Sequence.

Change to largest cir, and cont in Slip-Stitch Patt and Body Color Sequence until piece meas about 14¼" (36 cm) from beg, ending after Rnd 2 of Slip-Stitch Patt and Rnd 122 of Body Color Sequence.

DIVIDE FOR FRONT AND BACK

NEXT RND: Working Rnd 123 of Body Color Sequence and Rnd 3 of Slip-Stitch Patt work 10 (12, 14, 16, 20, 22, 24) sts, place sts just worked onto st holder or waste yarn for underarm; work in patt to 10 (12, 14, 16, 20, 22, 24) sts after the left side m, place 20 (24, 28, 32, 40, 44, 48) sts just worked onto st holder or waste yarn removing m, work in pattern to end of rnd, place last 10 (12, 14, 16, 20, 22, 24) sts just worked onto st holder or waste yarn—54 (60, 64, 70, 72, 78, 84) sts rem for each front and back; and 20 (24, 28, 32, 40, 44, 48) held sts for each underarm. Break yarn.

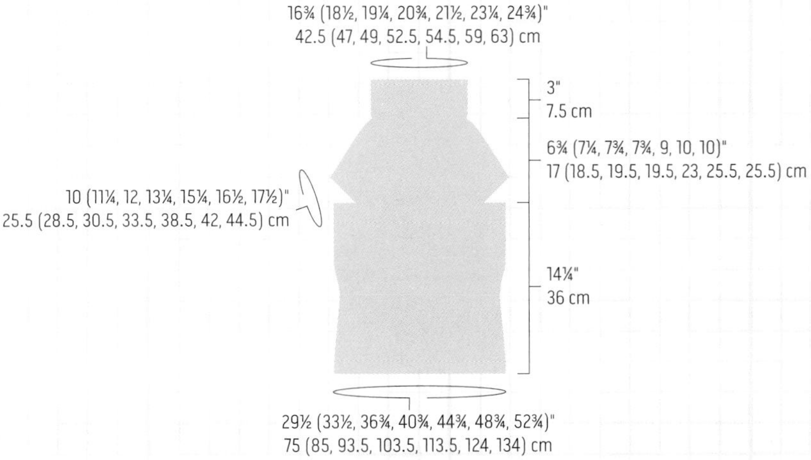

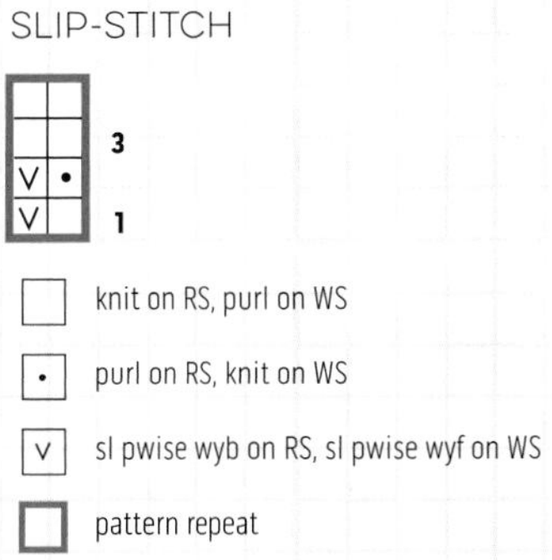

yoke

INC RND: With color C and provisional method (see Glossary), CO 30 (32, 32, 34, 36, 38, 40) sts, work Rnd 4 of Slip-Stitch Patt to end of front, use provisional method to CO 30 (32, 32, 34, 36, 38, 40) sts, work in patt to end of back sts, pm for new beg of rnd—168 (184, 192, 208, 216, 232, 248) sts.

Work 27 (31, 35, 35, 39, 39, 39) rnds in Yoke Color Sequence (see Stitch Guide) while working Rnds 1–4 of Slip-Stitch Patt ending after Rnd 3 of Slip-Stitch Patt.

[Piece meas about 3¼ (3¾, 4, 4, 4½, 4½, 4½)" (8.5 [9.5, 10, 10, 11.5, 11.5, 11.5] cm) from beg of yoke.]

SHAPE YOKE

DEC RND 1: *K5, k3tog; rep from * to end—126 (138, 144, 156, 162, 174, 186) sts rem.

Work 15 (15, 15, 15, 19, 23, 23) rnds in Yoke Color Sequence while working Rnds 1–4 of Slip-Stitch Patt, ending after Rnd 3 of Slip-Stitch Patt.

[Piece meas about 5 (5½, 6, 6, 7, 7½, 7½)" (12.5 [14, 15, 15, 18, 19, 19] cm) from beg of yoke.]

Change to shorter, largest cir.

DEC RND 2: *K3, k3tog; rep from * to end—84 (92, 96, 104, 108, 116, 124) sts rem.

Work 11 (11, 11, 11, 15, 19, 19) rnds in Yoke Color Sequence while working Rnds 1–4 of Slip-Stitch Patt, ending after Rnd 3 of Slip-Stitch Patt.

[Piece meas about 6¼ (6¾, 7¼, 7¼, 8¾, 9¾, 9¾)" (16 [17, 18.5, 18.5, 22, 25, 25] cm) from beg of yoke.]

Change to shorter, smallest cir or dpn.

Work 4 rnds in Yoke Color Sequence and Slip-Stitch Patt, ending after Rnd 3 of Slip-Stitch Patt.

COLLAR

Change to shorter, largest cir or dpn.

Work 25 rnds in Yoke Color Sequence and Slip-Stitch Patt, ending after Rnd 4 of Slip-Stitch Patt.

[Collar meas about 3" (7.5 cm).]

RNDS 1 AND 3: With color D, *k1, sl 1; rep from *.

RND 2: *P1, sl 1; rep from *.

RND 4: Knit.

Loosely BO all sts.

sleeves

Beg at center underarm, place 10 (12, 14, 16, 20, 22, 24) underarm sts from waste yarn onto largest dpn, transfer 30 (32, 32, 34, 36, 38, 40) sts from provisional CO onto 2 largest dpn, place 10 (12, 14, 16, 20, 22, 24) underarm sts from waste yarn onto fourth dpn—50 (56, 60, 66, 76, 82, 88) sts.

With color C, work Rnd 4 of Slip-Stitch Patt.

With color B, work Rnds 1 and 2 of Slip-Stitch Patt.

With color C, work 3 more rnds in Slip-Stitch Patt, ending after Rnd 1.

BO all sts.

Work second sleeve the same as the first.

finishing

Weave in loose ends. Block to measurements.

THE SHAWL IS worked from the neck down with a common increasing technique that creates a triangular shape. A simple slip-stitch pattern is used for the main portion of the shawl, and, at a certain point, stripes in a contrasting color are added. The last stripe is done in an eyelet pattern to transition to the border. A traditional and easy Orenburg-shawl border is knit separately and sewn to the main part to finish this striking shawl.

|| *designed by* **FAINA GOBERSTEIN**

bordo SHAWL

FINISHED SIZE

72" (182 cm) wide at upper edge and 35" (89 cm) tall at center after blocking.

YARN

Shown here: Claudia Hand Painted Yarns Oh Baby! Fingering 55 (55% silk, 45% merino wool; 175 yd [160 m]/1¾ oz [50 g]): silver shimmer (color A), 4 skeins; rubies playing (color B), 3 skeins.

NEEDLES

Size U.S. 8 (5 mm): 40" (101.5 cm) circular (cir).

Adjust needle size if necessary to obtain the correct gauge.

NOTIONS

Markers (m); sewing needle.

GAUGE

23 sts and 40 rows = 4" (10 cm) in stamen stitch (see Stitch Guide and chart) after blocking.

NOTES

Circular needle is used to accommodate large number of sts. Do not join; work back and forth in rows.

Slip stitches purlwise with yarn in back unless otherwise stated.

Slip first st of each row purlwise with yarn in front for selvedge.

TIPS

- Lightly block the main triangle and border separately to make it easier to sew the border to the shawl.
- After the border is attached to the shawl, use a strong thin nylon cord and tapestry needle to pull cord through each corner of the shawl. Wet the shawl and pin at the cord, not the shawl itself, to stretch to block.
- Change colors at the side.

STITCH GUIDE

STAMEN STITCH (FOR GAUGE ONLY)

(odd number of sts)

ROW 1 AND ALL RS ROWS: Knit.

ROW 2: (WS) K1, *sl1 wyb, k1; rep from *.

ROW 4: Sl1 wyb, *k1, sl1 wyb; rep from *.

Rep Rows 1–4 for patt.

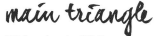

main triangle

With color A, CO 2 sts.

Knit 6 rows.

NEXT ROW: (RS) K2, rotate piece 90° clockwise and pick up and knit 1 st in next garter ridge, [pm for center, pick up and knit 1 st in next garter ridge] twice, then pick up and knit 1 st in each of 2 CO sts—7 sts.

Knit 1 WS row.

Work Rows 1–6 of Shawl Chart—17 sts; 5 sts between edging m and center m on each side.

Rep Rows 5 and 6 of Shawl Chart 78 times—329 sts; 161 sts between m on each side.

stripes

Cont to rep Rows 5 and 6 of Shawl Chart while working stripe sequence as foll:

ROWS 1–8: [2 rows color B, 2 rows color A] twice—345 sts; 169 sts between m on each side.

ROWS 9 AND 10: 2 rows color B—349 sts; 171 sts between m on each side.

ROWS 11–26: [4 rows color A, 4 rows color B] twice—381 sts; 187 sts between m on each side.

ROWS 27–32: 6 rows color A—393 sts; 193 sts between m on each side.

ROWS 33–38: 6 rows color B—405 sts; 199 sts between m on each side.

ROWS 39–44: 6 rows color A—417 sts; 205 sts between m on each side.

Cut color A yarn. Cont working with color B only as foll:

NEXT ROW: (RS) Sl 1 wyf, k2, sl m, yo, knit to center m, yo, sl m, k1, sl m, yo, knit to last 3 sts, yo, sl m, k3—419 sts; 207 sts between m on each side.

NEXT ROW: Sl 1 wyf, knit to end.

STAMEN

⅄	•	⅄	•	3
•	⅄	•		1

Legend:

☐	knit on RS, purl on WS
•	purl on RS, knit on WS
V	sl pwise wyf on WS
⅄	sl pwise wyf on RS, wyb on WS
o	yo
/	k2tog
⋀	sl2tog-k1-p2sso
⟍	ssk on WS
⅃	k1f&b on RS
⅃	k1f&b on WS
−	wrap and turn
▨	no stitch
☐	pattern repeat
∣	edging stitch marker
∣	center stitch marker

SHAWL

rep rows 5 and 6

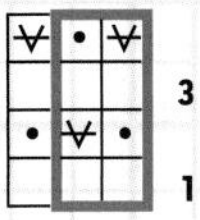

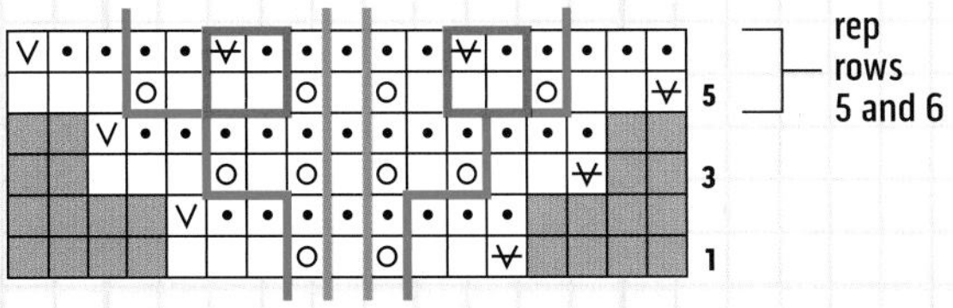

FIRST TAPERED CORNER

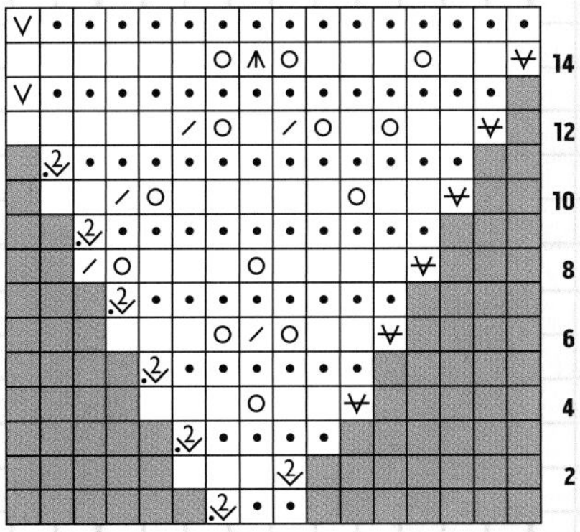

LAST TAPERED CORNER

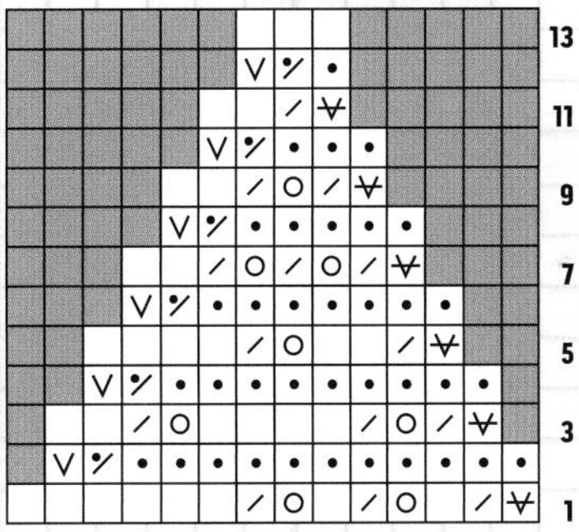

CORNER

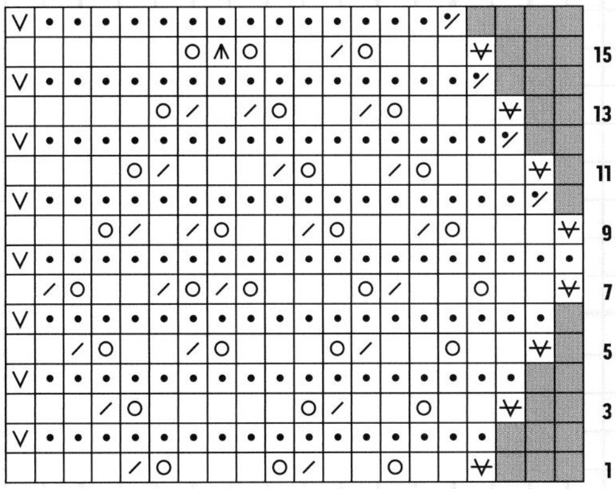

SHARP TURN (SHORT-ROW)

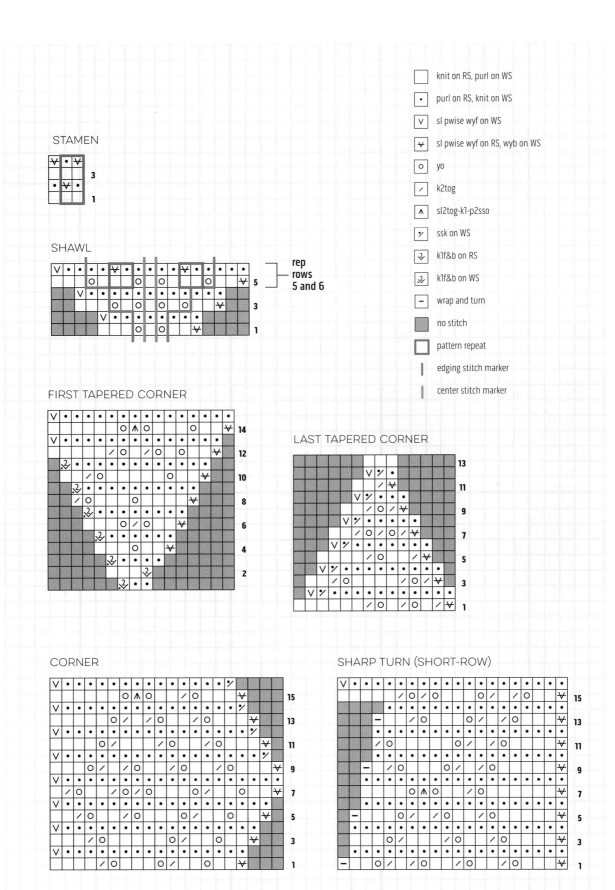

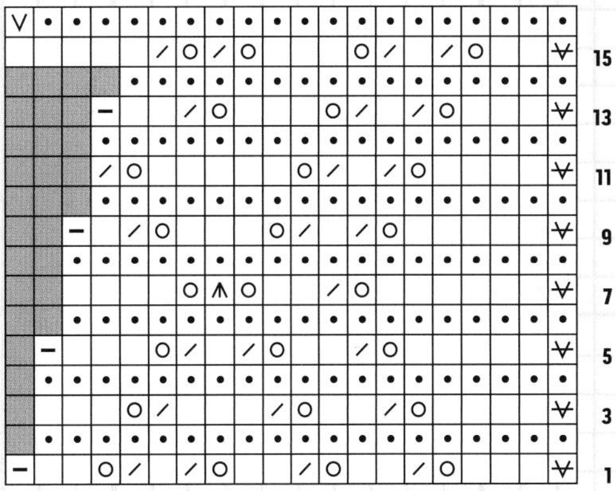

EYELET ROW: (RS) Sl 1 wyf, k2, sl m, yo, k1, yo, *k2tog, yo; rep from * to m, sl m, k1, sl m, **yo, k2tog; rep from ** to 1 st before m, yo, k1, yo, sl m, k3—423 sts; 209 sts between m on each side.

NEXT ROW: Sl 1 wyf, knit to end.

NEXT ROW: Sl 1 wyf, k2, sl m, yo, knit to center m, yo, sl m, k1, sl m, yo, knit to last 3 sts, yo, sl m, k3—427 sts; 211 sts between m on each side.

Loosely BO all sts.

LACE BORDER

Note: The border will be sewn along one side of shawl; at the center it makes a sharp turn and continues to the other side. Each patt repeat makes a corner.

With color B, CO 3 sts.

Work Rows 1–15 of First Tapered Corner Chart—16 sts.

Work Rows 1–16 of Corner Chart 18 times, then work Rows 1–8 once more—20 sts.

Work Rows 1–16 of Sharp Turn Chart twice.

Work Rows 9–16 of Corner Chart, then rep Rows 1–16 eighteen more times total, ending last row with k3tog instead of ssk—15 sts rem.

Work Rows 1–13 of Last Tapered Corner Chart—3 sts rem.

BO all sts.

finishing

Weave in ends. Block pieces, making sure that points along border are well defined. With RS of shawl and RS of border facing, beg at one corner, use color B to sew border to shawl, catching one side of sl st edge on border and one side of BO edge on shawl, aligning center sharp-turn point of border with center of shawl, and easing as necessary. Block seam.

MAKE IT YOURS

- The main pattern can be replaced with any 2- or 4-st repeat slip-stitch pattern.
- Work on a larger needle to create the look of an openwork pattern.
- Make a smaller size by stopping the increases at the spine of the shawl.
- Choose another border.
- Use more colors.
- Use multicolored yarn either for the triangle or for the border.

THIS JACKET, knitted in a beautiful silk-blend yarn, showcases traditional slip stitch in a very unexpected way. The allover slip-stitch pattern enables you to work a Fair Isle–looking pattern without any stranded work, making your stitching even and beautiful. The jacket is worked in a seamless construction to the underarms, then each front and back are finished separately and joined at the shoulder seam. Similarly, the sleeves are worked in the round to underarms, and sleeve caps are finished in rows.

|| *designed by* **SIMONA MERCHANT-DEST**

čekanka JACKET

FINISHED SIZE

About 35¾ (40, 44, 48¼, 52¼, 56½, 60¾)" (90.5 [101.5, 112, 122.5, 132.5, 143.5, 154.5 cm) bust circumference, with fronts meeting at center.

Jacket shown meas 35¾" (90.5 cm).

YARN

Aran weight (#4 Medium).

Shown here: Manos Silk Blend (70% merino wool, 30% silk; 150 yd [135 m]/1¾ oz [50 g]): #3069 hibiscus (color A), 4 (4, 5, 5, 5, 6, 6) skeins; #3203 tomato (color B), 2 (3, 3, 3, 3, 4, 4) skeins; #300C powder (color C), 2 (3, 3, 3, 3, 3, 4) skeins; #3068 citric (color D), 1 (1, 2, 2, 2, 2, 2) skeins.

NEEDLES

Body and Sleeves: Size U.S. 5 (3.75 mm): 32" (80 cm) circular (cir) and set of 5 double-pointed (dpn).

Waist: Size U.S. 4 (3.5 mm): 32" (80 cm) cir and set of 5 dpn.

Adjust needle sizes if necessary to obtain the correct gauge.

NOTIONS

Markers (m; two colors recommended); waste yarn of similar weight; spare cir needles of size 4 or smaller; tapestry needle; 2 medium hook-and-eye closures.

GAUGE

23 sts and 42 rows = 4" (10 cm) in slip-stitch patts with larger needles.

25 sts and 49 rows = 4" (10 cm) in slip-stitch patt with smaller needles.

23 sts and 28 rows = 4" (10 cm) in St st with smaller needles.

NOTES

For ease of shaping hips, waist, and bust, changing needle size is used to preserve continuity of the stitch pattern. Sleeve and armhole shaping is achieved with traditional decreases along edges.

The jacket's lower body is worked in one piece to underarms, then stitches are BO for armhole shaping. The back and fronts are finished separately to the shoulders. Sleeves are worked from lower cuff in the round to underarms; sleeve's cap is finished in rows. Set and sew in sleeves. Lastly, stitches are picked up along the neck to work the collar.

All slipped stitches are slipped purlwise with yarn carried on the WS of work.

STITCH GUIDE

PICOT

(multiple of 2 sts + 1)

ROW 1: (WS) Purl.

ROW 2: (RS) Knit.

ROW 3 (FOLD LINE): *P2tog, yo; rep from * to last st, p1.

ROW 4: Knit.

ROW 5: Purl.

STRIPE SEQUENCE

3 rnds in color B.

[2 rnds in color A, 2 rnds in color B] twice.

2 rnds in color D.

2 rnds in color A.

2 rnds in color B.

2 rnds in color A.

3 rnds in color D.

2 rnds in color C.

2 rnds in color B.

2 rnds in color A.

3 rnds in color D.

2 rnds in color C.

3 rnds in color B.

2 rnds in color C.

3X2 RIB

(multiple of 5 sts + 2)

ROW 1: (WS) K2, *p3, k2; rep from * to end.

ROW 2: K1, p1, *k3, p2; rep from * to last 5 sts, k3, p1, k1.

Rep Rows 1 and 2 for patt.

TIP

Use markers of different colors to set off the pattern repetitions for clarity if needed and another set of markers for front edges. Slip markers every row.

body

With color A and smaller cir needle, using a provisional cast-on method (see Glossary), CO 205 (229, 253, 277, 301, 325, 349) sts. Do not join; work back and forth in rows.

PICOT EDGING

Work 5 rows of picot (see Stitch Guide).

With WS together, fold fabric at fold line, transfer sts from provisional CO onto a third smaller needle.

NEXT ROW: (RS) *Picking 1 st from working needle and 1 st from provisional CO, k2tog; rep from * to end.

NEXT ROW: Knit. Break yarn.

FRONTS AND BACK

Note: Body (both fronts and back) are worked in 1 piece to underarms. The front edges are worked in color B at the same time as the body. If color B is not used on a row, twist the color B yarn used for the front edging around the color(s) used for the body of the row in the intarsia method (see Glossary). Use markers to separate the main body stitch pattern from front edges for clarity.

Join color B.

ROW 1: (RS) K1, p1, sl 1, k1, sl 1, p1, pm, (right front edge), knit to last 6 sts, pm, p1, sl 1, k1, sl 1, p1, k1 (left front edge).

ROW 2: K2, sl 1, p1, sl 1, k1, slip marker (sl m), purl to m, sl m, k1, sl 1, p1, sl 1, k2.

ROW 3: K1, p1, k1, sl 1, k1, p1, sl m, knit to m, sl m, p1, k1, sl 1, k1, p1, k1.

ROW 4: K2, p1, sl 1, p1, k1, sl m, purl to m, sl m, k1, p1, sl 1, p1, k2.

Note: Maintain these 4 rows over first and last 6 sts throughout for front edges.

Rep Rows 1 and 2 once more.

[Piece meas about 1¼" (3.2 cm) from fold of picot edging.]

Change to larger cir needle. Working front edges in patt as est, beg Swirls Slip-Stitch Chart.

ROW 1: (RS) Work 6 front edge sts as est, sl m, work Row 1 of Swirls Slip-Stitch Chart to m, sl m, and work 6 front edge sts as est.

ROW 2: Work 6 front edge sts as est, sl m, change to color D, work Row 2 of Swirls Slip-Stitch Chart to m, sl m,

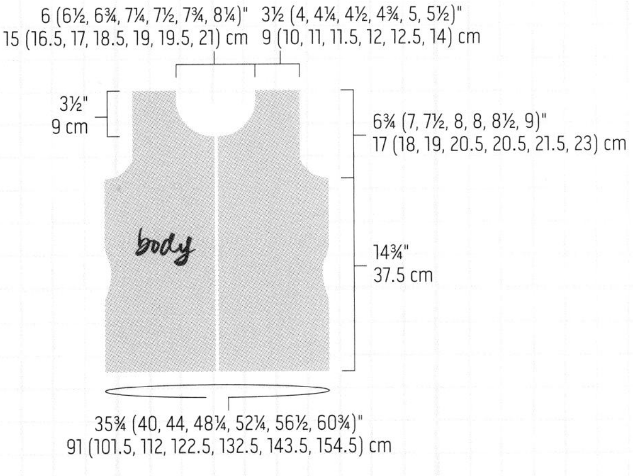

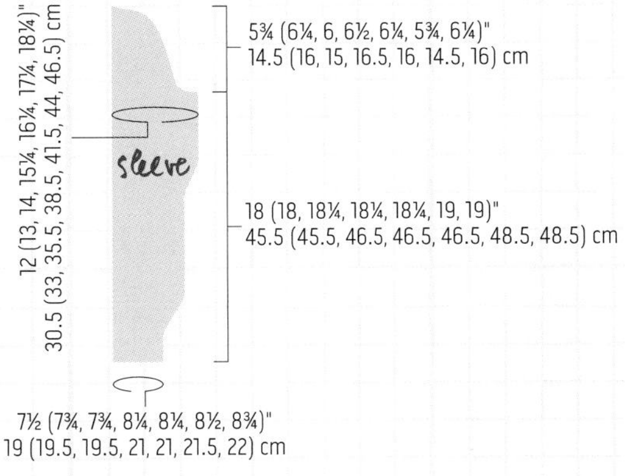

with A, knit on RS, purl on WS

with B, knit on RS, purl on WS

with C, knit on RS, purl on WS

with D, knit on RS, purl on WS

V sl pwise wyb on RS, sl pwise wyf on WS

pattern repeat

SWIRLS SLIP-STITCH

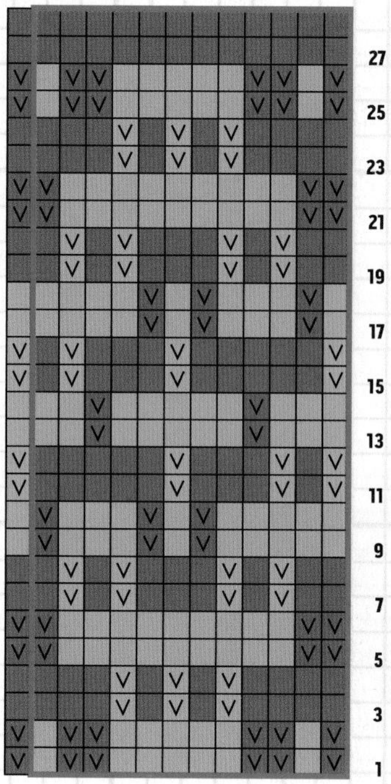

CLOVER SLIP-STITCH

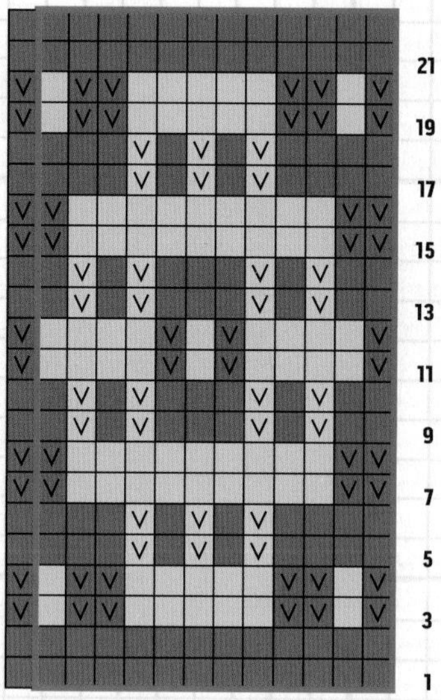

CHECKER SLIP-STITCH

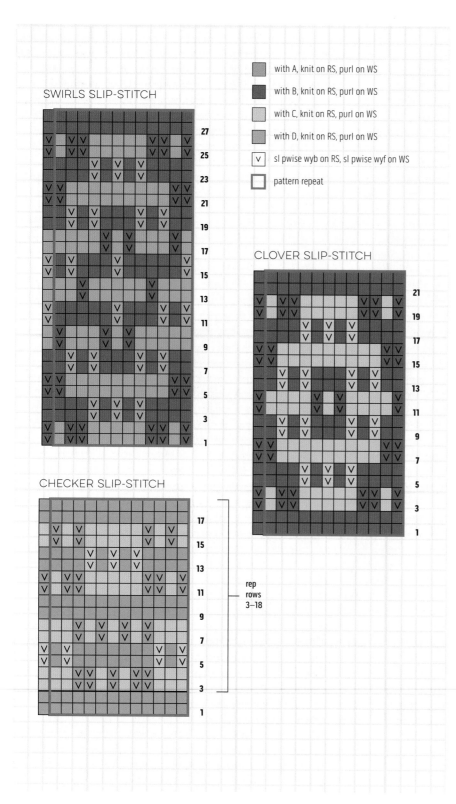

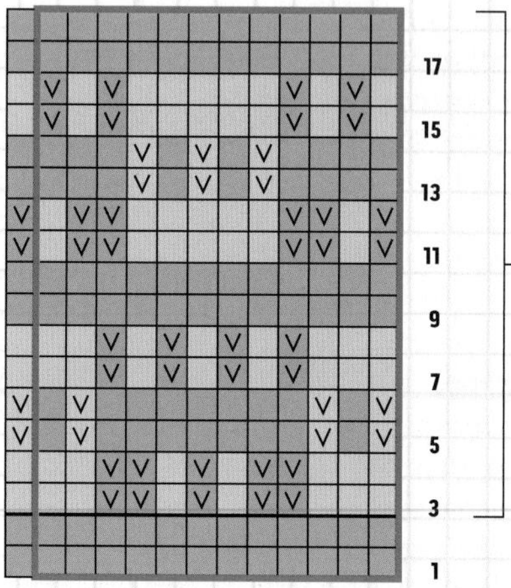

join color B and work 6 front edge sts as est.

Cont in patts as est, work Rows 3–28, then work Rows 1–22 again.

[Piece meas about 6" (15 cm) from fold of picot edging.]

WAIST

Change to smaller cir needle.

Working front edges in patt as est, work Rows 23–26 of Swirls Slip-Stitch Chart.

Working front edges in patt as est, beg Clover Slip-Stitch Chart as foll:

ROW 1: (RS) Work 6 front edge sts as est, sl m, work Row 1 of Clover Slip-Stitch Chart to m, sl m, work 6 front edge sts as est.

ROW 2: Work 6 front edge sts as est, sl m, work Row 2 of Clover Slip-Stitch Chart to m, sl m, work 6 front edge sts as est.

Working front edges in patt as est, work Rows 3–22 of Clover Slip-Stitch Chart.

Working front edges in color B as est, beg Checker Slip-Stitch Chart as foll:

ROW 1: (RS) Work 6 front edge sts as est, sl m, work Row 1 of Checker Slip-Stitch Chart to m, sl m, join a second ball of color B and work 6 front edge sts as est.

ROW 2: Work 6 front edge sts as est, sl m, work Row 2 of Checker Slip-Stitch Chart to m, sl m, work 6 front edge sts as est.

Working front edges in patt as est, work Rows 3–8 of Checker Slip-Stitch Chart.

[Piece meas about 8¾" (22 cm) from fold of picot edging.]

BUST

Change to larger cir needle.

Working front edges in patt as est, work Rows 9–18 of Checker Slip-Stitch Chart, then cont working Rows 3–18 for patt until piece meas 14¾"

(37.5 cm) from fold of picot edging, ending after a WS row.

DIVIDE FOR FRONTS AND BACK

Cont working in Checker Slip-Stitch Chart, while working as foll:

NEXT ROW: (RS) Work in patts as est over 51 (56, 61, 67, 72, 77, 82) sts for right front and place them onto st holder or waste yarn, BO 7 (9, 11, 11, 13, 15, 17) sts for right underarm, work in patt over 89 (99, 109, 121, 131, 141, 151) sts for back and place them onto st holder or waste yarn, BO 7 (9, 11, 11, 13, 15, 17) sts for left underarm, work in patt over rem 51 (56, 61, 67, 72, 77, 82) sts for left front and place them onto st holder or waste yarn.

back

Return 89 (99, 109, 121, 131, 141, 151) held back sts to larger needle and rejoin yarn preparing to work a WS row. Cont working in Checker Slip-Stitch Chart,while working as foll:

SHAPE ARMHOLES

BO 3 sts at beg of next 2 (2, 4, 4, 4, 4, 4) rows, then BO 2 sts at beg of foll 2 (2, 2, 2, 4, 4, 4) rows—79 (89, 93, 105, 111, 121, 131) sts rem.

NEXT ROW: (WS) P1 in color A, work in patt to last st, p1 in color A.

DEC ROW: K1 in color A, ssk, work in patt to last 3 sts, k2tog, k1 in color A —2 sts dec'd.

Rep last 2 rows 1 (2, 2, 5, 6, 9, 9) more time(s)—75 (83, 87, 93, 97, 101, 111) sts rem.

Cont even in patt, working selvedge sts as for last 2 rows until armhole meas 5¾ (6, 6½, 7, 7, 7½, 8)" (14.5 [15, 16.5, 18, 18, 19, 20.5] cm) from divide, ending after a RS row.

SHAPE NECK

NEXT ROW: (WS) Work in patt across 27 (30, 31, 33, 34, 35, 39) sts, place center 21 (23, 25, 27, 29, 31, 33) sts onto st holder or waste yarn, join new ball of yarn and work in patt to end—27 (30, 31, 33, 34, 35, 39) shoulder sts rem at each side. Maintaining first and last st in color A and working both sides at the same time, cont neck shaping as follows:

Note: Due to the nature of the slip-stitch pattern, join new ball of yarn per color used in upcoming row as needed.

ROW 1: (RS) For right shoulder: work in patt to end; for left shoulder: work 3 sts in patt, then place them onto a st holder or waste yarn, work in patt to end.

ROW 2: (WS) For left shoulder: work in patt to end; for right shoulder: work 3 sts in patt, then place them onto a st holder or waste yarn, work in patt to end—24 (27, 28, 30, 31, 32, 36) sts rem for each shoulder.

ROW 3: For right shoulder: work in patt to end; for left shoulder: work 2 sts in patt, then place them onto a st holder or waste yarn, work in patt to end.

ROW 4: For left shoulder: work in patt to end; for right shoulder: work 2 sts in patt, then place them onto a st holder or waste yarn, work in patt to end—22 (25, 26, 28, 29, 30, 34) sts rem for each shoulder.

ROW 5: For right shoulder: work in patt to end; for left shoulder: work 1 st, then place it onto a st holder or waste yarn, work in patt to end.

ROW 6: For left shoulder: work in patt to end; for right shoulder: work 1 st, then place it onto a st holder or waste yarn, work in patt to end—21 (24, 25, 27, 28, 29, 33) sts rem.

Rep Rows 5 and 6 once more—20 (23, 24, 26, 27, 28, 32) sts rem.

Maintaining first and last st in color A, cont working in patt as est until armhole meas 6¾ (7, 7½, 8, 8, 8½, 9)" (17 [18, 19, 20.5, 20.5, 21.5, 23] cm) from divide, ending after a WS row.

Place shoulder sts onto st holders or waste yarn, break yarn and set aside.

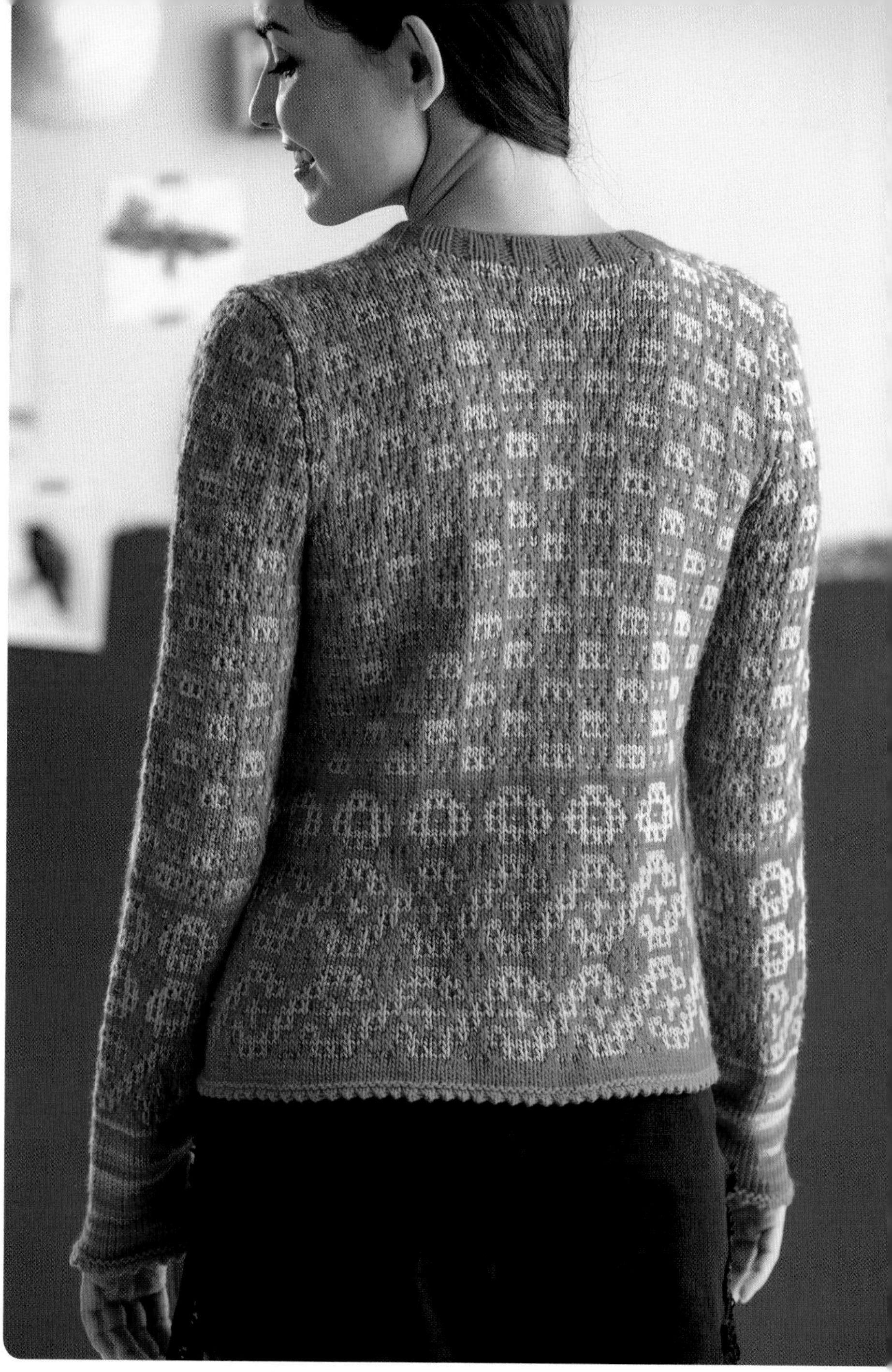

left front

Return 51 (56, 61, 67, 72, 77, 82) held left front sts to larger needle and rejoin yarn preparing to work a WS row. Cont working in Checker Slip-Stitch Chart, while working as foll:

Working front edges in patt as est, work 1 WS row even.

SHAPE ARMHOLE

NEXT ROW: (RS) Keeping in patt, BO 3 sts at beg of next 1 (1, 2, 2, 2, 2, 2) RS row(s), then BO 2 underarm edge sts at beg of foll 1 (1, 1, 1, 2, 2, 2) RS row(s)—46 (51, 53, 59, 62, 67, 72) sts rem.

NEXT ROW: (WS) Work 6 front edge sts as est, sl m, work in patt to last st, p1 in color A for selvedge.

DEC ROW: (RS) K1 in color A for selvedge, ssk, work in patt to m, sl m, work 6 front edge sts as est—1 st dec'd.

Rep last 2 rows 1 (2, 2, 5, 6, 9, 9) more time(s)—44 (48, 50, 53, 55, 57, 62) sts rem.

Working front edge and selvedge sts as for last 2 rows, cont in patt until armhole meas 3¼ (3½, 4, 4½, 4½, 5, 5½)" (8.5 [9, 10, 11.5, 11.5, 12.5, 14] cm) from divide, ending after a RS row. Break color D.

SHAPE NECK

Cont working in Checker Slip-Stitch Chart, while working as foll:

NEXT ROW: (WS) BO 12 (13, 14, 15, 16, 17, 18) sts removing front edge m, (if needed, rejoin color D) work in patt to last st, p1 in color A—32 (35, 36, 38, 39, 40, 44) sts rem.

NEXT ROW: K1 in color A, work in patt to last st, k1 in color A.

DEC ROW: (WS) BO 1 neck edge st, work in patt to last st, p1 in color A—1 st dec'd.

NEXT ROW: K1 in color A, work in patt to last st, k1 in color A.

Rep last 2 rows 11 more times—20 (23, 24, 26, 27, 28, 32) shoulder sts rem.

Maintaining first and last st in color A, cont working in patt as est until armhole meas 6¾ (7, 7½, 8, 8, 8½, 9)" (17 [18, 19, 20.5, 20.5, 21.5, 23] cm) from divide, ending after a WS row.

Place sts onto st holder or waste yarn, break yarn and set aside.

right front

Return 51 (56, 61, 67, 72, 77, 82) held right front sts to larger needle and rejoin yarn preparing to work a WS row. Cont working in front edges and Checker Slip-Stitch Patt as est, while working as foll:

SHAPE ARMHOLE

NEXT ROW: (WS) Keeping in patt, BO 3 armhole edge sts at beg of next 1 (1, 2, 2, 2, 2, 2) WS row(s), then BO 2 armhole edge sts at beg of foll 1(1, 1, 1, 2, 2, 2) WS row(s)—46 (51, 53, 59, 62, 67, 72) sts rem.

DEC ROW: (RS) Work 6 front edge sts as est, sl m, work in patt to last 3 sts, k2tog, k1 in color A for selvedge—1 st dec'd.

NEXT ROW: P1 in color A for selvedge, work in patt to m, sl m, work 6 front edge sts as est.

Rep last 2 rows 1 (2, 2, 5, 6, 9, 9) more time(s)—44 (48, 50, 53, 55, 57, 62) sts rem.

Working front edge and selvedge sts as for last 2 rows, cont in patt until armhole meas 3¼ (3½, 4, 4½, 4½, 5, 5½)" (8.5 [9, 10, 11.5, 11.5, 12.5, 14] cm) from divide row, ending after a WS row. Break color D.

SHAPE NECK

Cont working in Checker Slip-Stitch Chart, while working as foll:

NEXT ROW: (RS) BO 12 (13, 14, 15, 16, 17, 18) sts removing front edge m, (if needed, rejoin color D) work in patt to last st, k1 in color A—32 (35, 36, 38, 39, 40, 44) sts rem.

NEXT ROW: P1 in color A, work in patt to last st, p1 in color A.

DEC ROW: (RS) BO 1 neck edge st, work in patt to last st, k1 in color A—1 st dec'd.

NEXT ROW: P1 in color A, work in patt to last st, p1 in color A.

Rep last 2 rows 11 more times—20 (23, 24, 26, 27, 28, 32) shoulder sts rem.

Maintaining first and last st in color A, cont working in patt as est until armhole meas 6¾ (7, 7½, 8, 8, 8½, 9)" (17 [18, 19, 20.5, 20.5, 21.5, 23] cm) from divide, ending after a WS row.

Place sts onto st holder or waste yarn, break yarn and set aside.

sleeves

Note: The picot edge is worked in rows; then stitches are transferred onto dpn, and sleeves are worked in the rounds to underarms.

With color A and smaller cir needle, using a provisional cast-on method, CO 43 (45, 45, 47, 47, 49, 51) sts. Do not join; work back and forth in rows.

PICOT EDGING

Work 5 rows of picot.

With WS facing, fold fabric at fold line, transfer sts from provisional CO onto a third needle.

NEXT ROW: (RS) *Picking 1 st from working needle and 1 st from provisional CO, k2tog; rep from * to end.

NEXT ROW: Knit.

Divide sts evenly over 4 smaller dpn. Pm for beg of rnd. Join to work in rnds, being careful not to twist sts.

SHAPE SLEEVES

Note: Read through following instructions before proceeding. The Stripe Sequence is worked at the same time as the shaping of the sleeves.

Work 37 rnds of Stripe Sequence *and at the same time* shape sleeve as foll:

Work 14 (14, 10, 12, 12, 2, 4) rnds even in St st (knit every rnd), joining yarns as needed and carrying unused colors along the WS at the beg of rnd.

INC RND: K1, M1L, work in patt to last st, M1R, k1—2 sts inc'd.

Work 3 (3, 1, 1, 1, 1, 1) rnd(s) even.

Rep the last 4 (4, 2, 2, 2, 2, 2) rnds 2 (3, 13, 12, 12, 17, 16) more times—49 (53, 73, 73, 73, 85, 85) sts.

SIZES 35¾ (40)" ONLY:
[Rep inc rnd, then work 1 rnd even] 6 (4) times—61 sts.

ALL SIZES:
Cont working even until Stripe Sequence is completed.

[Piece meas about 4½" (11.5 cm) from fold of picot edging.]

BEGIN SWIRLS SLIP-STITCH CHART

Change to larger dpn.

Work Rnds 1–28 of Swirls Slip-Stitch Chart.

[Piece meas about 7¼" (18.5 cm) from fold of picot edging.]

BEGIN CLOVER SLIP-STITCH CHART

Work Rnds 3–22 of Clover Slip-Stitch Chart twice.

[Piece meas about 11" (28 cm) from fold of picot edging.]

BEGIN CHECKER SLIP-STITCH CHART

Work Rnds 1 and 2 of Checker Slip-Stitch Chart.

Cont working Rnds 3–18 of Checker Slip-Stitch Chart while shaping sleeve as foll:

Work next 16 (0, 16, 0, 0, 0, 0) rnds even in patt, ending after Rnd 18 (2, 18, 2, 2, 2, 2) of chart.

Note: Work first and last st of foll rnds in color A for underarm faux "seam" look.

INC RND: K1, M1L, work in patt as est to last st, M1R, k1—2 sts inc'd.

Work 5 (5, 5, 5, 3, 5, 3) rnds even.

Rep the last 6 (6, 6, 6, 4, 6, 4) rnds 3 (6, 3, 6, 9, 6, 9) more times—69 (75, 81, 87, 93, 99, 105) sts.

Cont working Checker Slip-Stitch Chart until piece meas 18 (18, 18¼, 18¼, 18¼, 19, 19)" (45.5 [45.5, 46.5, 46.5, 46.5, 48.5, 48.5] cm) from fold of picot edging, ending after an even-numbered rnd and ending last rnd 4 (5, 6, 6, 7, 8, 9) sts before m.

SHAPE CAP

NEXT RND: (odd-numbered rnd) BO 8 (10, 12, 12, 14, 16, 18) sts, removing m, work patt to end—61 (65, 69, 75, 79, 83, 87) sts rem.

Change to larger cir needle when comfortable to do so, and work back and forth in rows.

Beg with a WS row, cont in patt and BO 3 sts at beg of foll 2 (2, 4, 4, 4, 4, 4) rows, then BO 2 sts at beg of next 2 (2, 2, 2, 4, 4, 4) rows—51 (55, 53, 59, 59, 63, 67) sts rem.

Work 1 WS row even.

DEC ROW: (RS) K1, ssk, work to last 3 sts in patt, k2tog, k1—2 sts dec'd.

Work 3 rows even.

Rep the last 4 rows 11 (12, 11, 12, 10, 8, 9) more times—27 (29, 29, 33, 37, 45, 47) sts rem.

[Rep dec row, then work 1 WS row even] 0 (0, 0, 1, 2, 4, 4) times—27 (29, 29, 31, 33, 37, 39) sts rem.

BO 2 (2, 2, 3, 3, 3, 3) sts at beg of next 2 rows, then BO 2 (3, 3, 3, 3, 3, 3) sts at beg of next 2 rows, and then BO 3 sts at beg of next 2 rows—13 (13, 13, 13, 15, 19, 21) sts rem.

Work 1 more row even.

BO rem sts.

Make second sleeve the same as the first.

finishing

Block pieces to measurements.

JOIN SHOULDERS

Place 20 (23, 24, 26, 27, 28, 32) held left front shoulder sts on 1 needle and corresponding held left back shoulder sts onto another needle. Hold needles parallel with RS of fabric facing each other and WS facing out, using a three-needle bind-off method (see Glossary) to join all sts tog.

Rep for right shoulder.

SET IN SLEEVES

With yarn threaded on a tapestry needle, sew sleeves into armholes, matching center of sleeve cap to shoulder "seam."

NECKBAND

With smaller cir needle, color B and RS facing, pick up and knit 24 (25, 26, 27, 28, 29, 30) sts along right front neck edge BO sts, pick up and knit 7 (7, 8, 6, 6, 7, 7) sts along edge of right neck to held back sts, return 35 (37, 39, 41, 43, 45, 47) held back neck sts to empty needle then knit across, pick up and knit 7 (8, 8, 6, 7, 7, 8) sts edge of left neck, pick up and knit 24 (25, 26, 27, 28, 29, 30) along left front neck edge BO sts—97 (102, 107, 107, 112, 117, 122) sts.

Work in 3×2 rib until piece meas 1" (2.5 cm) from pick-up row, ending after a WS row.

BO all sts in pattern.

ATTACH CLOSURES

Mark placement for 2 hook-and-eye closures along left front as foll: one placed at the level of Row 2 and second at level of Row 21 of clover slip-stitch patt. Sew hook half of closures to WS of left front. Sew eye half of closures to corresponding position on right front so that the hook is concealed when the fronts are closed.

Weave in loose ends. Block again if desired.

THIS PROJECT EXPLORES the use of traditional stitch pattern placements. The body of the sweater is worked in a single color in stockinette stitch. The cuffs and front bands are worked in a two-color slip-stitch pattern. A different two-color slip-stitch pattern is placed at the hem around the body. Using slip-stitch patterns sparingly keeps them from overwhelming the design. || *designed by* **FAINA GOBERSTEIN**

kromka HOODIE

FINISHED SIZE

About 36½ (40, 43¾, 47½, 51, 54½, 57¼)" (92.5 [101.5, 111, 120.5, 129.5, 138.5, 145.5] cm) bust circumference, zipper closed, with positive ease about 2" (5 cm).

Hoodie shown measures 36½" (92.5 cm).

YARN

Worsted weight (#4 Medium).

Shown here: Lisa Souza Polwarth/Silk (85% Polwarth wool, 15% silk; 400 yd [366 m]/136 g): cameron (color A), 3 (4, 4, 5, 5, 5, 6) skeins; peacock (color B) and forbidden city (color C), 1 skein each.

NEEDLES

Size U.S. 6 (4 mm): 32" (80 cm) circular (cir) and set of 5 double-pointed (dpn).

Adjust needle size if necessary to obtain the correct gauge.

NOTIONS

Markers (m); removable markers; stitch holders or waste yarn; tapestry needle; waste yarn; zipper 20" (51 cm); sewing needle and matching thread.

GAUGE

22 sts and 27 rows = 4" (10 cm) in stockinette stitch.

NOTES

Slip all sts as if to purl with yarn in back, unless otherwise stated.

For a nice selvedge, work the first and last st of every row as foll: Sl 1 wyf, work to last st, k1.

STITCH GUIDE

STOCKINETTE STITCH

Worked Flat—Knit on RS, purl on WS.

Worked in the Rnd—Knit all sts, every rnd.

SEED STITCH

(even number of sts)

ROW 1: *K1, p1; rep from *.

ROW 2: *P1, k1; rep from *.

Rep Rows 1 and 2 for patt.

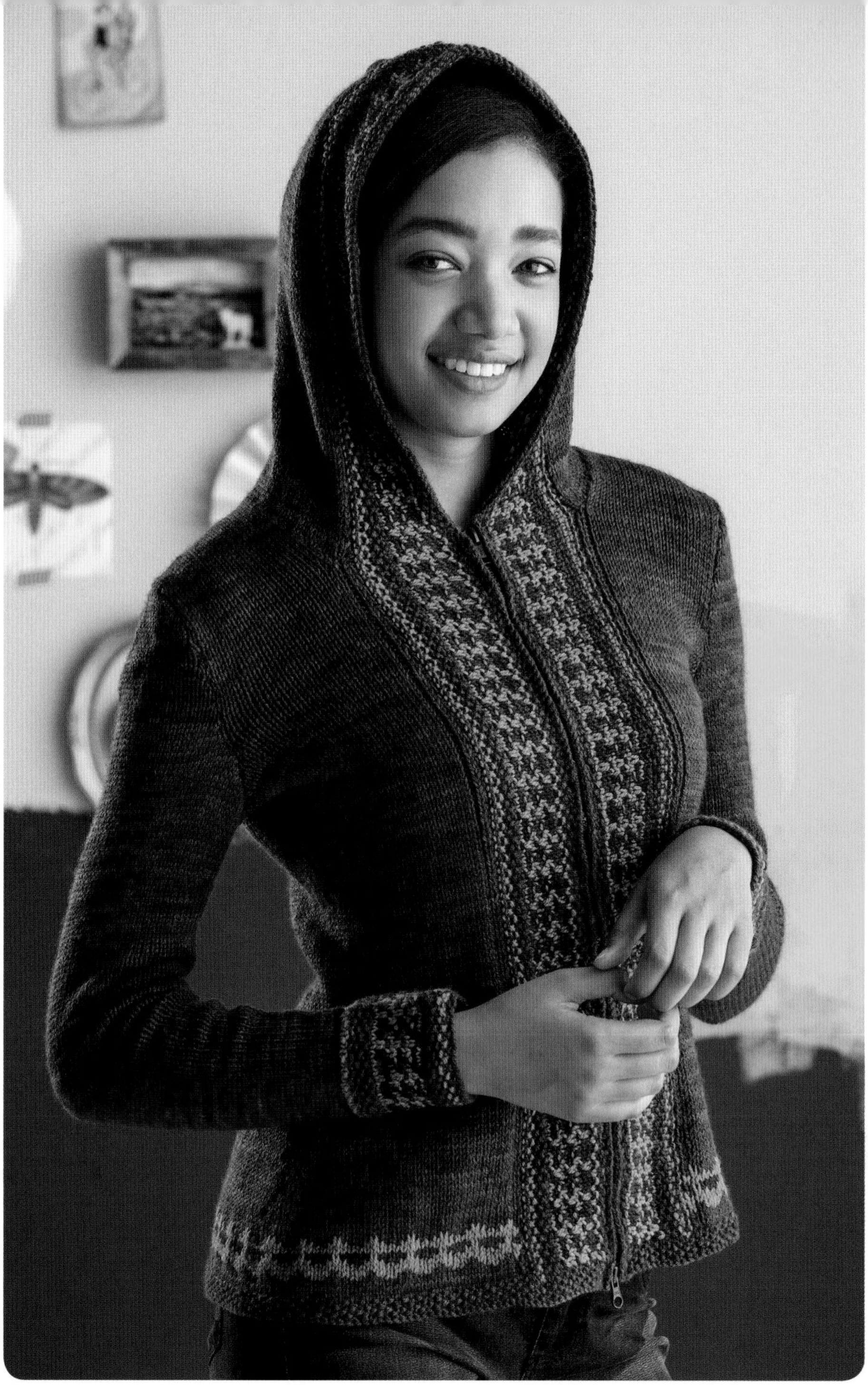

TIPS

- Place markers between the pattern repeats. Slip the markers every row as you come to them.
- Use different color markers for faux side seams.

body

With cir needle, color A, and using long-tail cast-on method (see Glossary), CO 182 (202, 222, 247, 267, 282, 297) sts. Do not join; work back and forth in rows.

SET-UP ROW: (WS) Sl 1 wyf, p1, k1, pm, purl to last 3 sts, pm, k1, p1, k1.

NEXT ROW: (RS) Sl 1 wyf, k1, p1, sl m, knit to last 3 sts, sl m, p1, k2.

Rep Set-Up Row 1 more time.

NEXT ROW: (RS) With color B, sl 1 wyf, k1, p1, sl m, work Color Print Chart to m, sl m, p1, k2.

Cont as est, working 9 more rows of Color Print Chart between markers and keeping 3 sts on each side as edging.

PLACE MARKERS FOR SIDES: (RS) With color A, sl 1 wyf, k1, p1, sl m, k35 (40, 45, 50, 55, 60, 65) for right front, pm (use a different colored m) for right "side seam," k106 (116, 126, 141, 151, 156, 161) for back, pm (use the same color m as for right "side seam") for left

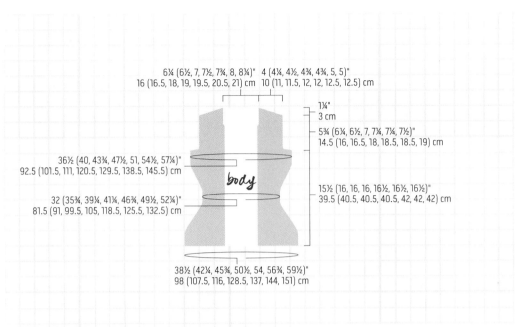

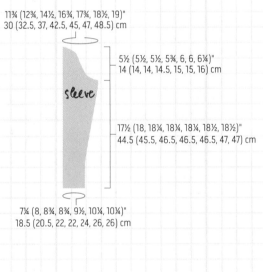

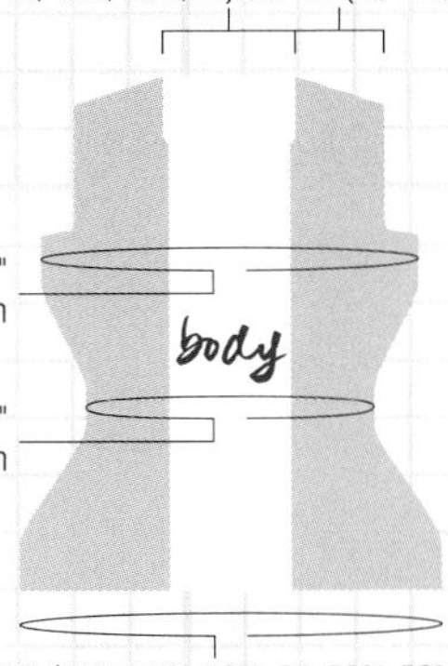

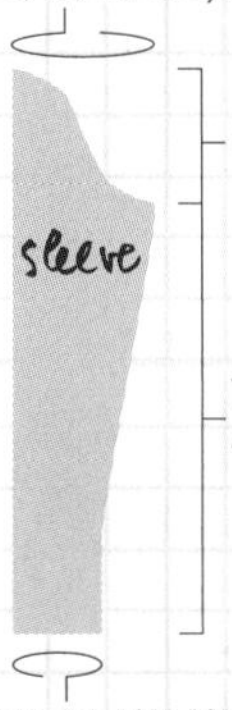

"side seam," k35 (40, 45, 50, 55, 60, 65) for left front, sl m, p1, k2.

Cont working with color A only, maintaining 3 edging sts at each edge and working St st between edging markers. When piece meas 2" (5 cm) from beg, end after a WS row.

SHAPE WAIST

SIZES 40 (43¾)" ONLY:

DEC ROW: (RS) Sl 1 wyf, k1, p1, sl m, *knit to 3 sts before side m, ssk, k1, sl m, k1, k2tog; rep from * 1 more time, knit to edging m, sl m, p1, k2—4 sts dec'd.

Work 5 rows even in patt.

Rep the last 6 rows 1 more time—194 (214) sts rem.

ALL SIZES:

DEC ROW: (RS) Sl 1 wyf, k1, p1, sl m, *knit to 3 sts before side m, ssk, k1, sl m, k1, k2tog; rep from * 1 more time, knit to edging m, sl m, p1, k2—4 sts dec'd.

Work 3 rows even in patt.

Rep the last 4 rows 8 (6, 6, 9, 9, 9, 9) more times—146 (166, 186, 207, 227, 242, 257) sts rem; 29 (34, 39, 43, 48, 53, 58) sts each front and 88 (98, 108, 121, 131, 136, 141) sts for back.

Work even in patt until piece meas 8¾ (9¼, 9¼, 9¼, 9¼, 9¼, 9¼)" (22 [23.5, 23.5, 23.5, 23.5, 23.5, 23.5] cm) from beg, ending after a WS row.

INC ROW: (RS) Sl 1 wyf, k1, p1, sl m, *knit to 1 st before side m, M1R (see Glossary), k1, sl m, k1, M1L (see Glossary); rep from * 1 more time, knit to edging m, sl m, p1, k2—4 sts inc'd.

Work 7 rows even in patt.

Rep the last 8 rows 3 (3, 2, 2, 1, 5, 5) more time(s)—162 (182, 198, 219, 235, 266, 281) sts; 33 (38, 42, 46, 50, 59, 64) sts each front and 96 (106, 114, 127, 135, 148, 153) sts for back.

[Rep inc row, then work 9 rows even in patt] 1 (1, 2, 2, 3, 0, 0) times, then rep inc row once more—170 (190, 210, 231, 251, 270, 285) sts; 35 (40, 45, 49, 54, 60, 65) sts each front and 100 (110, 120, 133, 143, 150, 155) for back.

Work even in patt until piece measures 15½ (16, 16, 16, 16½, 16½, 16½)" (39.5 [40.5, 40.5, 40.5, 42, 42, 42] cm) from beg, ending after a RS row.

DIVIDE FOR BACK AND FRONT

NEXT ROW: (WS) Sl 1 wyf, p1, k1, *purl to 5 (5, 6, 7, 8, 9, 10) sts before side m, removing side m BO 10 (10, 12, 14, 16, 18, 20) sts for underarm; rep from * 1 more time, purl to last st, k1 for right front—30 (35, 39, 42, 46, 51, 55) sts rem for each front and 90 (100, 108, 119, 127, 132, 135) sts rem for back.

Place sts for left and right fronts onto separate st holders or waste yarn. Cont working on back sts only.

back

Return 90 (100, 108, 119, 127, 132, 135) held back sts to needle and join yarn preparing to work a RS row.

SHAPE ARMHOLES

BO 3 sts at beg of next 2 (2, 2, 2, 4, 4, 4) rows, then BO 2 sts at the beg of foll 2 (4, 4, 6, 6, 6, 8) rows—80 (86, 94, 101, 103, 108, 107) sts rem.

DEC ROW: (RS) Sl 1 wyf, ssk, knit to last 3 sts, k2tog, k1—2 sts dec'd.

NEXT ROW: (WS) Sl 1 wyf, purl to last st, k1.

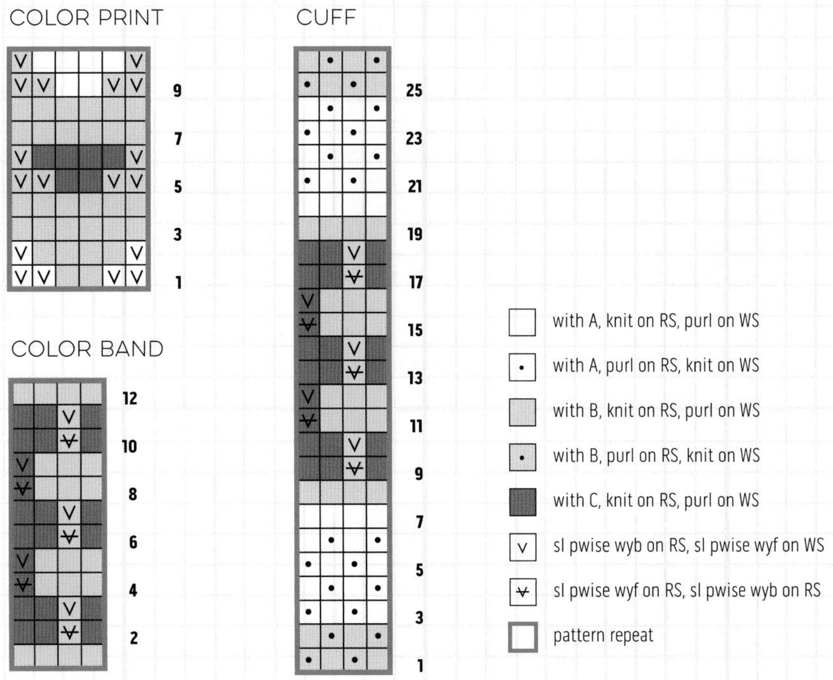

Rep the last 2 rows 0 (1, 3, 3, 3, 4, 3) more time(s)—78 (82, 86, 93, 95, 98, 99) sts rem.

Work even, keeping selvedge sts as est, until armholes measure 5¾ (6¼, 6½, 7, 7¼, 7¼, 7½)" (14.5 [16, 16.5, 18, 18.5, 18.5, 19] cm), ending after a RS row.

SHAPE SHOULDERS

Work in short-rows as foll:

SHORT-ROW 1: (RS) Sl 1 wyf, knit to last 6 sts, wrap next st, turn work.

SHORT-ROW 2: (WS) Purl to last 6 sts, wrap next st, turn work.

SHORT-ROWS 3 AND 4: Work to last 12 sts, wrap next st, turn work.

SHORT-ROWS 5 AND 6: Work to last 18 sts, wrap next st, turn work.

Next 2 rows: Work to end of row, working wraps together with wrapped sts when you come to them.

Break yarn. Place 22 (23, 24, 26, 26, 27, 27) sts onto st holder or waste yarn for right shoulder, place next 34 (36, 38, 41, 43, 44, 45) sts onto a second st holder or waste yarn for neck, place rem 22 (23, 24, 26, 26, 27, 27) sts onto a third st holder or waste yarn for left shoulder.

right front

SHAPE ARMHOLE

Return 30 (35, 39, 42, 46, 51, 55) held right front sts to needle and rejoin yarn preparing to work RS row.

NEXT ROW: (RS) Sl 1 wyf, k1, p1, sl m, knit to end.

NEXT ROW: (WS) BO 3 sts, purl to last st, k1—3 sts dec'd.

Rep the last 2 rows 0 (0, 0, 0, 1, 1, 1) more time(s)—27 (32, 36, 39, 40, 45, 49) sts rem.

NEXT ROW: Sl 1 wyf, k1, p1, sl m, knit to end.

NEXT ROW: BO 2 sts, purl to last st, k1—2 sts dec'd.

Rep the last 2 rows 0 (1, 1, 2, 2, 2, 3) more time(s)—25 (28, 32, 33, 34, 39, 41) sts rem.

Work 1 RS row even.

DEC ROW: (WS) Sl 1 wyf, p2tog, work to last st, k1—1 st dec'd.

NEXT ROW: (RS) Sl 1 wyf, k1, p1, sl m, knit to end.

Rep the last 2 rows 0 (1, 3, 3, 3, 4, 3) more time(s)—24 (26, 28, 29, 30, 34, 37) sts rem.

Maintaining edges as est, work even until armhole meas 3 (3½, 4, 4½, 4¾, 5, 5¼)" (7.5 [9, 10, 11.5, 12, 12.5, 13.5] cm) from divide, ending after a WS row. Place removable (locking) m in center front edge (beg of RS row) to mark end of zipper.

SHAPE NECK

Remove edging markers as you work the first row as foll:

NEXT ROW: (RS) BO 2 sts, knit to end—2 sts dec'd.

NEXT ROW: (WS) Sl 1 wyf, purl to end.

Rep the last 2 rows 0 (0, 0, 0, 1, 1, 2) time(s)—22 (24, 26, 27, 26, 30, 31) sts.

SIZES 40 (43¾, 47½, 54½, 57¼)" ONLY:

DEC ROW: (RS) Sl 1 wyf, ssk, knit to end—1 st dec'd.

NEXT ROW: Sl 1 wyf, purl to last st, k1.

Rep the last 2 rows 0 (1, 0, 2, 3) more time(s)—22 (23, 24, 26, 26, 27, 27) sts.

ALL SIZES:

Maintaining edges as est, work even until armhole meas 5¾ (6¼, 6½, 7, 7¼, 7¼, 7½)" (14.5 [16, 16.5, 18, 18.5, 18.5, 19] cm) from divide, ending after a WS row.

SHAPE SHOULDER

Work in short-rows (see Glossary) as foll:

SHORT-ROW 1: (RS) Sl 1 wyf, knit to last 6 sts, wrap next st, turn work.

NEXT ROW: (WS) Purl to last st, k1.

SHORT-ROW 2: Sl 1 wyf, knit to last 12 sts, wrap next st, turn work.

NEXT ROW: Purl to last st, k1.

SHORT-ROW 3: Sl 1 wyf, knit to last 18 sts, wrap next st, turn work.

NEXT ROW: Purl to last st, k1.

NEXT ROW: (RS) Sl 1 wyf, knit to end of row, working wraps together with wrapped sts when you come to them.

Break yarn and place sts onto st holder or waste yarn for right shoulder.

left front

Return 30 (35, 39, 42, 46, 51, 55) held left front sts to needle and rejoin yarn preparing to work a RS row.

SHAPE ARMHOLE

NEXT ROW: (RS) BO 3 sts, knit to edging m, sl m, p1, k2—3 sts dec'd.

NEXT ROW: (WS) Sl 1 wyf, p1, k1, sl m, purl to end.

Rep the last 2 rows 0 (0, 0, 0, 1, 1, 1) more time(s)—27 (32, 36, 39, 40, 45, 49) sts rem.

NEXT ROW: BO 2 sts, knit to edging m, sl m, p1, k2—2 sts dec'd.

NEXT ROW: Sl 1 wyf, p1, k1, sl m, purl to end.

Rep the last 2 rows 0 (1, 1, 2, 2, 2, 3) more time(s)—25 (28, 32, 33, 34, 39, 41) sts rem.

DEC ROW: (RS) Sl 1 wyf, ssk, knit to edging m, sl m, p1, k2—1 st dec'd.

NEXT ROW: (WS) Sl 1 wyf, p1, k1, sl m, purl to last st, k1.

Rep the last 2 rows 0 (1, 3, 3, 3, 4, 3) more time(s)—24 (26, 28, 29, 30, 34, 37) sts rem.

Maintaining edges as est, work even until armhole meas 3 (3½, 4, 4½, 4¾, 5, 5¼)" (7.5 [9, 10, 11.5, 12, 12.5, 13.5] cm) from divide, ending after a RS row. Place removable (locking) m in center front

edge (end of RS row) to mark end of zipper.

SHAPE NECK

Remove edging markers as you work the first row as foll:

NEXT ROW: (WS) BO 2 sts, purl to last st, k1—2 sts dec'd.

NEXT ROW: (RS) Sl 1 wyf, knit to end.

Rep the last 2 rows 0 (0, 0, 0, 1, 1, 2) more time(s)—22 (24, 26, 27, 26, 30, 31) sts rem.

SIZES 40 (43¾, 47½, 54½, 57¼)" ONLY:

NEXT ROW: (RS) Sl 1 wyf, knit to end.

DEC ROW: (WS) Sl 1 wyf, ssp, purl to last st, k1—1 st dec'd.

Rep the last 2 rows 0 (1, 0, 2, 3) more time(s)—22 (23, 24, 26, 26, 27, 27) sts.

ALL SIZES:

Maintaining edges as est, work even until armhole meas 5¾ (6¼, 6½, 7, 7¼, 7¼, 7½)" (14.5 [16, 16.5, 18, 18.5, 18.5, 19] cm) from divide, ending after a RS row.

SHAPE SHOULDER

Work in short-rows as foll:

SHORT-ROW 1: (WS) Sl 1 wyf, purl to last 6 sts, wrap next st, turn work.

NEXT ROW: (RS) Knit to end.

SHORT-ROW 2: Purl to last 12 sts, wrap next st, turn work.

NEXT ROW: Knit to end.

SHORT-ROW 3: Purl to last 18 sts, wrap next st, turn work.

NEXT ROW: Knit to end.

NEXT ROW: (WS) Sl 1 wyf, purl to end of row, working wraps together with wrapped sts when you come to them.

Break yarn and place sts onto st holder or waste yarn for left shoulder.

sleeves

With color A, CO 40 (44, 48, 48, 52, 56, 56) sts. Distribute sts evenly over dpn. Pm for beg of rnd and join for working in rnds, being careful not to twist sts.

Work Rnds 1–26 of Cuff Chart.

Cont working with color A only, in St st. Knit 1 rnd.

SHAPE SLEEVE

INC RND: K1, M1R, work in patt to last st, M1L, k1—2 sts inc'd.

Knit 7 (7, 5, 5, 5, 5, 3) rnds.

Rep the last 8 (8, 6, 6, 6, 6, 4) rnds 7 (5, 13, 1, 0, 0, 22) more time(s)—56 (56, 76, 52, 54, 58, 102) sts rem.

[Rep inc rnd, then knit 5 (5, 3, 3, 3, 3, 1) rnds] 4 (7, 2, 20, 22, 22, 1) time(s)—64 (70, 80, 92, 98, 102, 104) sts rem.

Work even until piece meas 17½ (18, 18¼, 18¼, 18¼, 18½, 18½)" (44.5 [45.5, 46.5, 46.5, 46.5, 47, 47] cm) from beg, ending last rnd 5 (5, 6, 7, 8, 9, 10) sts before end of rnd.

SHAPE CAP

NEXT RND: BO 10 (10, 12, 14, 16, 18, 20) sts removing m, knit to end—54 (60, 68, 78, 82, 84, 84) sts rem.

Change to working back and forth in rows.

Beg with a WS row, BO 3 sts at beg of next 2 (2, 2, 2, 4, 4, 4) rows, then BO 2 sts at the beg of foll 2 (4, 4, 6, 6, 6, 8) rows—44 (46, 54, 60, 58, 60, 56) sts rem.

NEXT ROW: (WS) Sl 1 wyf, purl to last st, k1.

DEC ROW: (RS) Sl 1 wyf, ssk, knit to last 3 sts, k2tog, k1—2 sts dec'd.

Rep the last 2 rows 2 (3, 7, 9, 9, 9, 9) more times—38 (38, 38, 40, 38, 40, 36) sts rem.

[Work 3 rows even, slipping the first st of each row, then rep dec row] 5 (4, 2, 1, 1, 1, 1) time(s)—28 (30, 34, 38, 36, 38, 34) sts rem.

BO 2 (2, 2, 3, 2, 3, 2) sts at beg of next 2 rows, then BO 2 (2, 3, 3, 3, 3, 2) sts at beg of foll 2 rows, and then BO 2 (3, 3, 3, 3, 3, 3) sts at beg of foll 2 rows—16 (16, 18, 20, 20, 20, 20) sts rem.

NEXT ROW: (WS) Sl 1 wyf, purl to last st, k1.

BO all sts.

finishing

Carefully block all pieces to measurements.

JOIN SHOULDERS

Return 22 (23, 24, 26, 26, 27, 27) held sts from right front and back shoulders onto separate dpn. Holding RS's together, join sts together using three-needle bind-off (see Glossary). Rep for left shoulder.

HOOD

With RS facing, beg at right front neck edge, join color A and pick up and knit 2 (2, 2, 2, 4, 4, 6) sts along neck BO, 24 sts along right neck edge, 3 sts at right shoulder seam, 34 (36, 38, 40, 42, 44, 46) sts along back neck, 3 sts at left shoulder seam, 24 sts along left neck edge, 2 (2, 2, 2, 4, 4, 6) sts along left neck BO—92 (94, 96, 98, 104, 106, 112) sts.

Work even in St st until hood measures 11½" (29 cm) from pick-up row, ending after a WS row.

SHAPE TOP OF HOOD

Note: Left and right sides of hood are shaped separately. Short-row stitch count is done on half of total hood sts.

NEXT ROW: (RS) K46 (47, 48, 49, 52, 53, 56), pm to center hood, work to end.

SHAPE LEFT SIDE OF HOOD

SHORT-ROW SET 1: (WS) Work to last 6 sts before m, wrap next st, turn; work back.

SHORT-ROW SET 2: Work to last 12 sts before m, wrap next st, turn; work back.

SHORT-ROW SET 3: Work to last 18 sts before m, wrap next st, turn; work back.

SHORT-ROW SET 4: Work to last 24 sts before m, wrap next st, turn; work back.

SHORT-ROW SET 5: Work to last 30 sts before m, wrap next st, turn; work back.

NEXT ROW: Work to end of row, hiding wraps as you come to them.

Place 46 (47, 48, 49, 52, 53, 56) sts on a holder for left-side hood.

SHAPE RIGHT SIDE OF HOOD

With WS facing, join yarn at center of hood and p46 (47, 48, 49, 52, 53, 56). Work short-row sets as for left side of hood, beg each set with RS facing.

Place 46 (47, 48, 49, 52, 53, 56) sts on a holder for right-side hood.

With RS tog and three-needle bind-off (see Glossary), join both sides of hood.

FRONT BAND

With RS facing and color A, beg at right side of hem pick up and knit 102 (108, 108, 108, 112, 112, 114) sts along right front to neck shaping, pm for beg of zipper, 72 sts along right side of hood, 72 sts along left side of hood, pm for zipper, 102 (108, 108, 108, 112, 112, 114) sts along left front—348 (360, 360, 360, 368, 368, 372) sts.

With color B, knit 1 WS row.

Work Row 1 of seed stitch (see Stitch Guide).

With color A, work 4 more rows of seed stitch, ending after a RS row.

With color B and color C, work 12 rows of Color Band Chart.

With color A, work 4 rows of seed stitch.

BO all sts loosely, changing markers to removable markers.

HEM BORDER

With color A and RS facing, join yarn at left front band, pick up and knit 12 sts along selvedge edge of left band, 182 (202, 222, 246, 266, 282, 296) sts along CO edge of body and 12 sts for right band—206 (226, 246, 270, 290, 306, 320) sts.

Work 4 rows of seed stitch. BO all sts loosely.

ZIPPER

With zipper closed and RS facing, beg at hem, baste both sides of zipper to WS of fronts. Separate zipper.

With RS facing, sew one side of zipper to edge of front using backstitch (see Glossary) and leaving enough room for a slider to go through. Rep for second side.

Set in sleeves.

Weave in loose ends. Block again if desired.

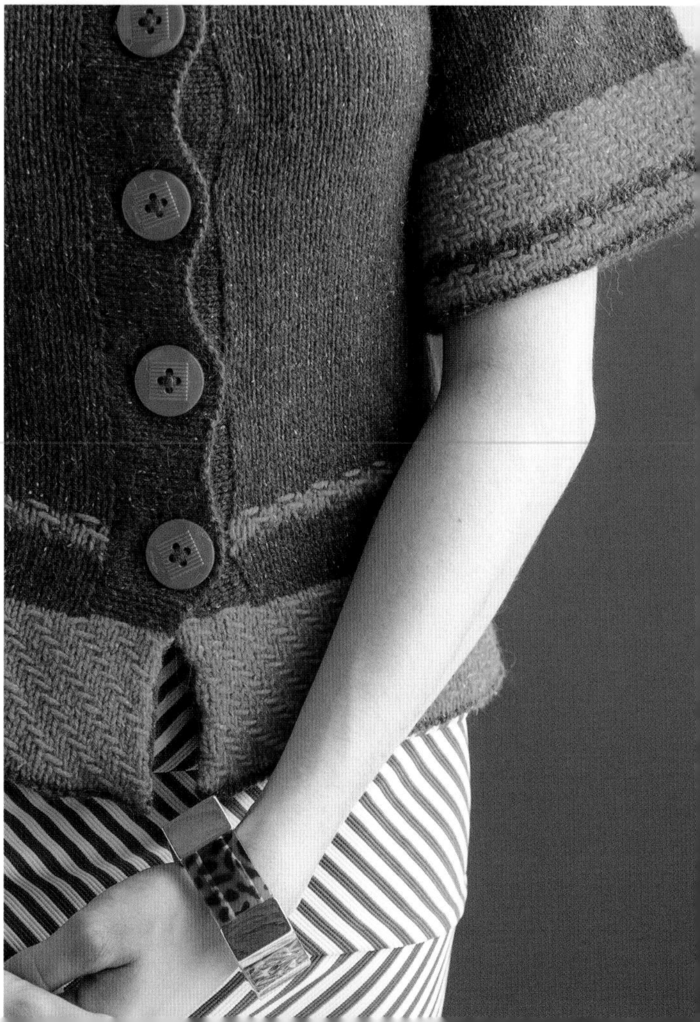

CHAPTER 3

woven SLIP-STITCH PATTERNS

THIS CHAPTER INCLUDES our favorite slip-stitch patterns: patterns that in their structure and appearance are reminiscent of woven fabric. These patterns heavily use front floats to build the texture. Floats vary in length and direction. Some patterns use both front and back floats. Practically all of these stitches are reversible.

The more you work with these stitches, the more you'll find yourself thinking: "What if I make a float shorter or change direction later . . . ?" You'll probably want to experiment with them more than other stitches because it's so easy to make significant changes.

Mainly, these stitches are worked with floats placed on top of the right side of stockinette stitch. It's very clear where the floats go as you work the stitch pattern. Knitting in the round using these stitches is more convenient than flat because you can see and control the placement of floats along the right side of the work. Another thing to notice about working in the round with woven stitches is that there is no visible jog at the beginning of the round because the float covers the jog. It's one less thing to worry about (see Spiral Hat on page 94).

Make sure that the float tension is just right. Check the length of the float at the point you are working the next stitch. You will still be able to tug or loosen the float at this time. Woven stitches are dense and can be loosened by choosing a bigger needle size. Mostly, though, these stitches tend to be used in the projects where holding the shape is important. If you want softer fabric with more drape, use soft yarns such as alpaca or silk blends.

There are ten woven stitch patterns in this chapter. Some of them are in multiple colors, but we mostly included solid-color swatches to show the texture in its glory. There are so many variations of these stitches it's almost mind-boggling. We're thrilled to have a chance to show these stitches in the way they deserve.

woven
STITCHES
DICTIONARY

MULTIDIRECTIONAL WEAVE
(MULTIPLE OF 10 STS)

ROW 1: (RS) *K1, sl 3 wyf, k3, sl 3 wyf; rep from *.

ROW 2: *(P1, sl 3 wyb) twice, p2; rep from *.

ROW 3: *K5, sl 3 wyf, k2; rep from *.

ROW 4: *P3, sl 3 wyb, p4; rep from *.

ROW 5: *K3, sl 3 wyf, k1, sl 3 wyf; rep from *.

ROW 6: *Sl 2 wyb, p3, sl 3 wyb, p1, sl 1 wyb; rep from *.

ROW 7: *Sl 2 wyf, k7, sl 1 wyf; rep from *.

ROW 8: *P7, sl 3 wyb; rep from *.

Rep Rows 1–8 for patt.

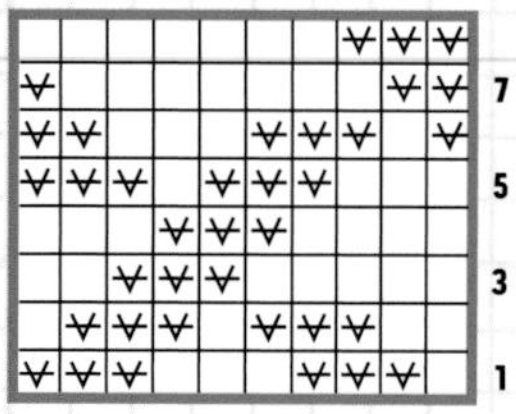

knit on RS, purl on WS

sl pwise wyf on RS, wyb on WS

pattern repeat

VERTICAL RIBS
(MULTIPLE OF 13 STS + 2)

– Reversible.

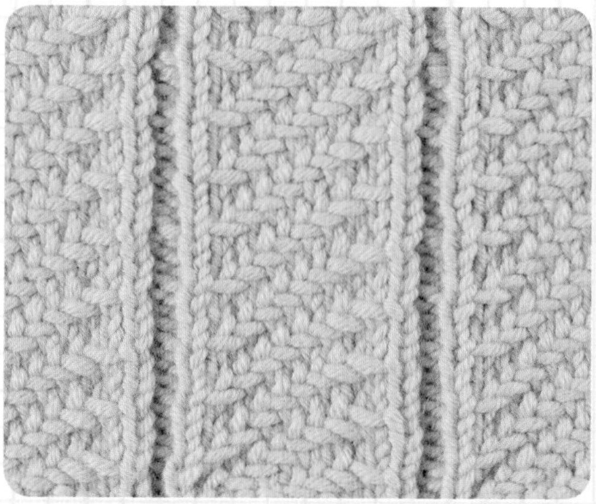

ROW 1: (RS) *P2, k4, sl 2 wyf, k2, sl 2 wyf, k1; rep from * to last 2 sts, p2.

ROW 2: K2, *(p2, sl 2 wyb) twice, p3, k2; rep from *.

ROW 3: *P2, (k2, sl 2 wyf) twice, k3; rep from * to last 2 sts, p2.

ROW 4: K2, *p4, sl 2 wyb, p2, sl 2 wyb, p1, k2; rep from *.

Rep Rows 1–4 for patt.

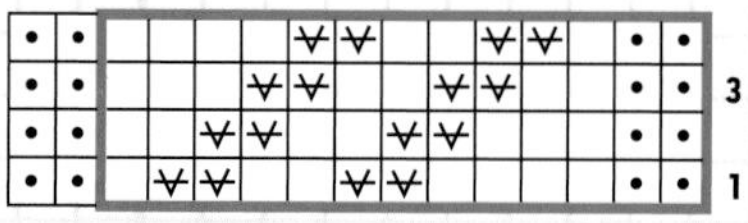

knit on RS, purl on WS

purl on RS, knit on WS

sl pwise wyf on RS, wyb on WS

pattern repeat

BUTTES

(MULTIPLE OF 10 STS)

- Solid color shows pattern best.
- Dense fabric.
- Reversible.

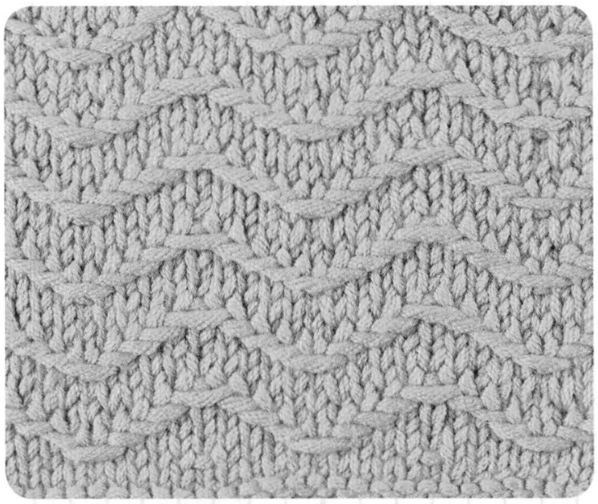

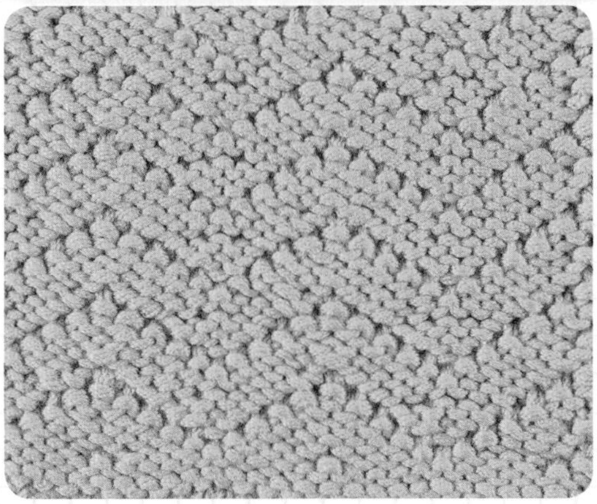

ROW 1: (RS) *K4, sl 1 wyf; rep from *.

ROW 2: *P4, sl 3 wyb, p3; rep from *.

ROW 3: *K2, sl 2 wyf, k1, sl 2 wyf, k3; rep from *.

ROW 4: *P2, sl 2 wyb, p3, sl 2 wyb, p1; rep from *.

ROW 5: *Sl 2 wyf, k5, sl 2 wyf, k1; rep from *.

ROW 6: *Sl 2 wyb, p7, sl 1 wyb; rep from *.

Rep Rows 1–6 for patt.

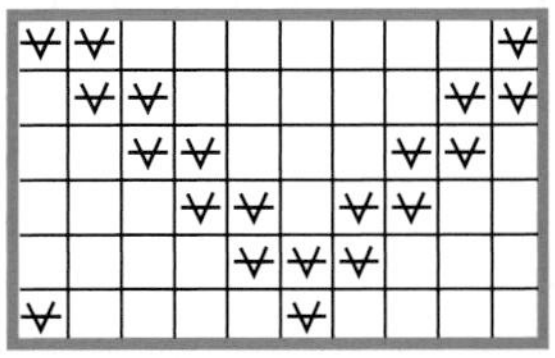

knit on RS, purl on WS

sl pwise wyf on RS, wyb on WS

pattern repeat

WOVEN DIAGONALS

(MULTIPLE OF 4 STS)

- Dense woven-looking fabric.
- This stitch is reversible. Great for scarves.
- Change needle size for different thickness.

ROW 1: (RS) *K2, sl 2 wyf; rep from *.

ROW 2 AND ALL WS ROWS: Purl.

ROW 3: *Sl 1 wyf, k2, sl 1, wyf; rep from *.

ROW 5: * Sl 2 wyf, k2; rep from *.

ROW 7: *K1, sl2 wyf, k1; rep from *.

ROW 8: Purl.

Rep Rows 1–8 for patt.

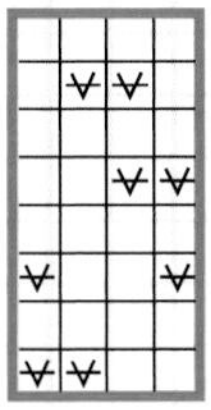

knit on RS, purl on WS

sl pwise wyf on RS, wyb on WS

pattern repeat

HORIZONTAL CHAINS

(MULTIPLE OF 8 STS)

ROW 1: (RS) *K7, sl 1 wyf; rep from *.

ROW 2: *Sl 2 wyb, p5, sl 1 wyb; rep from *.

ROW 3: *Sl 2 wyf, k3, sl 2 wyf, k1; rep from *.

ROW 4: *P2, (sl 2 wyb, p1) twice; rep from *.

ROW 5: *K2, sl 3 wyf, k3; rep from *.

ROW 6: *P4, sl 1 wyb, p3; rep from *.

ROW 7: Rep Row 5.

ROW 8: Rep Row 4.

ROW 9: Rep Row 3.

ROW 10: Rep Row 2.

ROW 11: Rep Row 1.

ROW 12: Purl.

ROW 13: *K2, sl 2 wyf; rep from *.

ROW 14: *Sl 2 wyb, p2; rep from *.

ROW 15: Knit.

ROW 16: Purl.

Rep Rows 1–16 for patt.

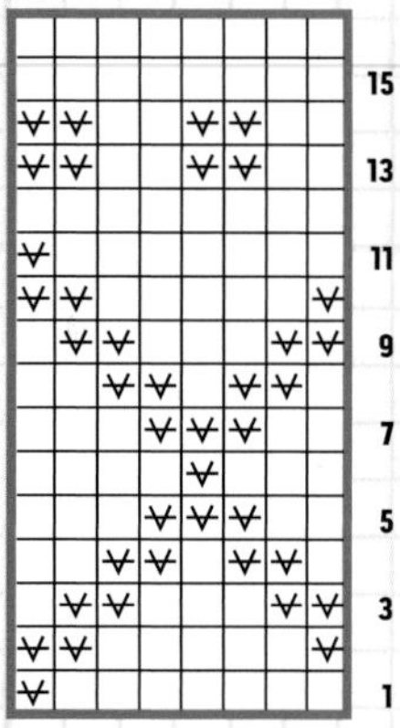

knit on RS, purl on WS

sl pwise wyf on RS, wyb on WS

pattern repeat

LINEN STITCH

(MULTIPLE OF 2 STS + 1)

– Three-color swatch. Brown is named A, orange is named B, and gray is named C. Each color is worked for 1 row.

– Dense fabric with reversible pattern.

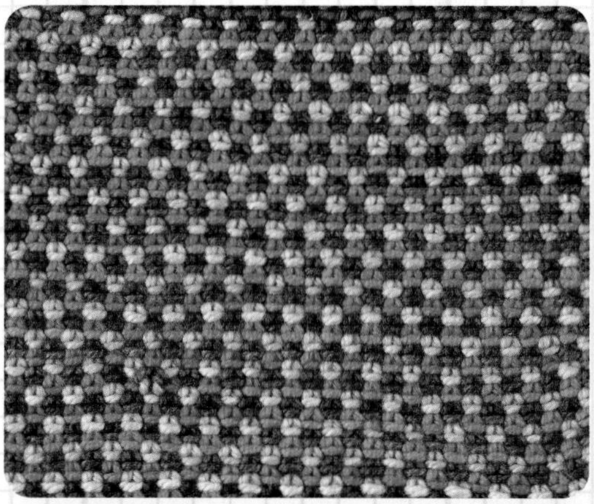

ROW 1: (RS) With A, *k1, sl 1 wyf; rep from * to last st, k1.

ROW 2: With B, sl 1 wyb, *p1, sl 1, wyb; rep from *.

ROW 3: With C, rep Row 1.

ROW 4: With A, rep Row 2.

ROW 5: With B, rep Row 1.

ROW 6: With C, rep Row 2.

Rep Rows 1–6 for patt.

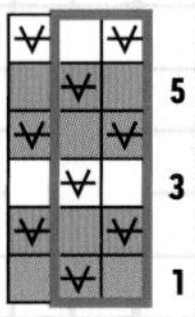

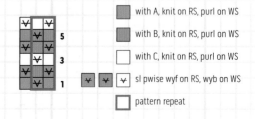

with A, knit on RS, purl on WS

with B, knit on RS, purl on WS

with C, knit on RS, purl on WS

sl pwise wyf on RS, wyb on WS

pattern repeat

STAMEN STITCH

(MULTIPLE OF 2 STS + 1)

– Solid-colored yarn shows this pattern best.

– Using larger size needles keeps the integrity of the pattern while making the fabric softer and almost lacelike.

– Reversible.

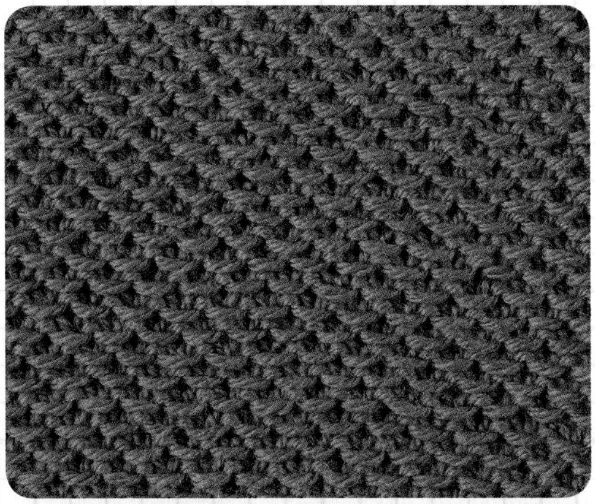

ROWS 1 AND 3: (RS) Knit.

ROW 2: P1, *sl 1 wyf, p1; rep from *.

ROW 4: Sl 1 wyf, *p1, sl 1 wyf; rep from *.

Rep Rows 1–4 for patt.

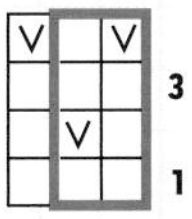

knit on RS, purl on WS

sl pwise wyb on RS, wyf on WS

pattern repeat

CHECKS TO STRIPES

(MULTIPLE OF 4 STS)

– Very dense fabric.

– Reversible.

ROW 1: (RS) *Sl 2 wyf, p2; rep from *.

ROW 2: *K2, sl 2 wyb; rep from *.

ROW 3: *P2, sl 2 wyf; rep from *.

ROW 4: *Sl 2 wyb, k2; rep from *.

Rep Rows 1–4 for patt.

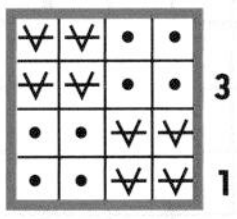

purl on RS, knit on WS

sl pwise wyf on RS, wyb on WS

pattern repeat

WOVEN WAVES

(MULTIPLE OF 12 STS)

- Three-color swatch. Brown is named A, orange is named B, and gray is named C.
- Reversible.
- The fabric is bulked up on the RS, but it is not very dense.

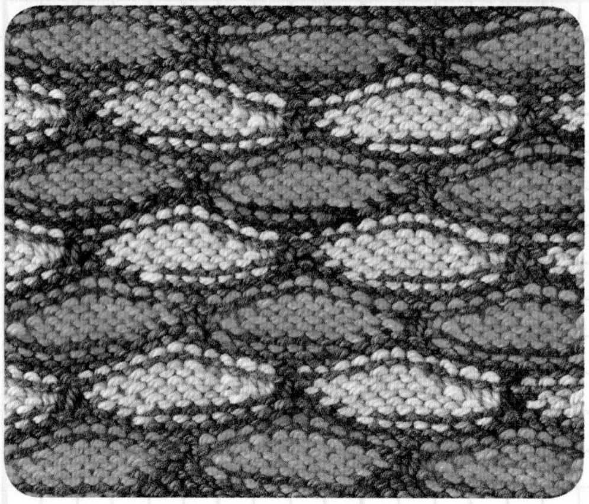

ROW 1: (RS) With A, knit.

ROW 2: Purl.

ROW 3: With B, *sl 4 wyf, k8; rep from *.

ROW 4: *P7, sl 4 wyb, p1; rep from *.

ROW 5: *K2, sl 4 wyf, k6; rep from *.

ROW 6: *P5, sl 4 wyb, p3; rep from *.

ROW 7: With A, knit.

ROW 8: Purl.

ROW 9: With C, *k8, sl 4 wyf; rep from *.

ROW 10: *P1, sl 4 wyb, p7; rep from *.

ROW 11: *K6, sl 4 wyf, k2; rep from *.

ROW 12: *P3, sl 4 wyb, p5; rep from *.

Rep Rows 1–12 for patt.

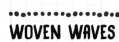

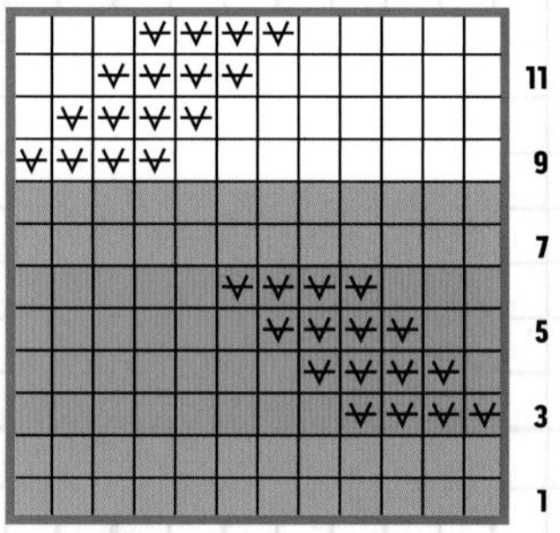

- with A, knit on RS, purl on WS
- with B, knit on RS, purl on WS
- with C, knit on RS, purl on WS
- sl pwise wyf on RS, wyb on WS
- pattern repeat

WOVEN CHEVRONS

(MULTIPLE OF 8 STS)

– Reversible.

ROW 1: (RS) Knit.

ROW 2: Purl.

ROW 3: *K2, sl 1 wyf, k2, sl 3 wyf ; rep from *.

ROW 4: *P1, sl 3 wyb, p2, sl 1 wyb, p1; rep from *.

ROW 5: *Sl 1 wyf, k2, sl 3 wyf, k2; rep from *.

ROW 6: *Sl 1 wyb, p2, sl 3 wyb, p2; rep from *.

ROW 7: *K1, sl 3 wyf, k2, sl 1 wyf, k1; rep from *.

ROW 8: *P2, sl 1 wyb, p2, sl 3 wyb; rep from *.

ROW 9: *Sl 2 wyf, (k2, sl 1 wyf) twice; rep from *.

ROW 10: *Sl 2 wyb, (p2, sl 1 wyb) twice; rep from *.

ROW 11: Rep Row 9.

ROW 12: Rep Row 8.

ROW 13: Rep Row 7.

ROW 14: Rep Row 6.

ROW 15: Rep Row 5.

ROW 16: Rep Row 4.

ROW 17: Rep Row 3.

ROW 18: Purl.

Rep Rows 1–18 for patt.

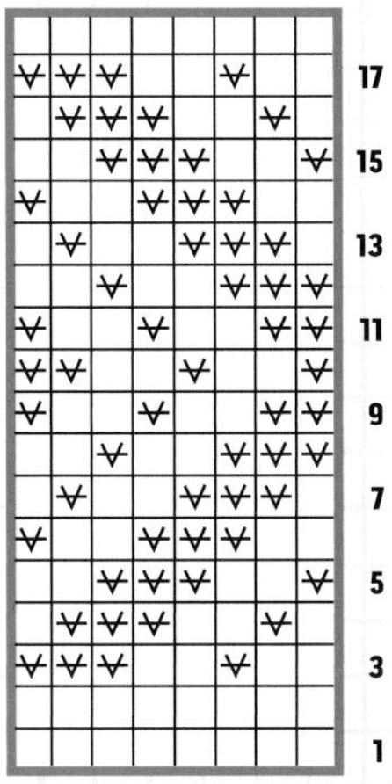

knit on RS, purl on WS

sl pwise wyf on RS, wyb on WS

pattern repeat

THIS CHEERFUL BAG is as beautiful as it is functional. The oval bottom in little herringbone pattern is knit at a tight gauge to make it sturdy, and then a round of single crochet is worked along the outer edge of the oval to provide a foundation for picking up stitches for the sides of the bag. The chart has bands of Fair Isle and zigzag weaving patterns that are repeated in different color combinations. The solid-color top border is worked in a stitch commonly used for sock heels. || *designed by* **FAINA GOBERSTEIN**

gobelen BAG

FINISHED SIZE
About 17" (43 cm) wide, 13½" (34.5 cm) tall, and 6¼" (16 cm) deep.

YARN
Worsted weight (#4 Medium).

Shown here: HiKoo Simpliworsted (55% merino superwash, 28% acrylic, 17% nylon; 140 yd [128 m]/100 g): #038 Seattle sky (A, dark gray), 3 skeins; #045 edgy eggplant (B, burgundy), #006 citronella (C, lemon yellow), and #037 gun metal grey (D, medium gray), 1 skein each.

NEEDLES
Size U.S. 5 (3.75 mm): straight and 24" (60 cm) circular (cir).

Adjust needle size if necessary to obtain the correct gauge.

NOTIONS
Markers (m); tapestry needle; size H/8 (5 mm) crochet hook; two 26" (66 cm) leather handles (handle shown is Budapest Floral leather handle with tabs by JUL Designs [juldesigns.com]); 13½" (34.5 cm) Pellon Peltex #71 extra-firm stabilizer with adhesive on one side; ¾ yd (68.5 cm) Pellon #911FF fusible interfacing; about 1 yd (1 m) lining fabric; sharp-point sewing needle or sewing machine and matching thread for sewing lining; sharp scissors.

GAUGE
36 sts and 24 rows = 4" (10 cm) in little herringbone patt.

22 sts = 4" (10 cm) wide, and 29 rnds average 3" (7.5 cm) high in Zigzag Weave Chart.

NOTES
Make generously sized swatches, not only for gauge calculation but also for practicing the stitch patterns.

The needles called for in this project are deliberately smaller than needles typically used with worsted-weight yarn to produce a tight, durable fabric.

The tension of the floats in the zigzag sections must be just right—tight enough to hold the strands tidily against the face of the fabric without drooping, loose enough that the strands still provide three-dimensional texture, but not so tight that the fabric puckers.

On some rounds, the woven strands of the zigzag weave travel across the end-of-round. Just continue to follow the chart pattern. It makes a very smooth transition between rounds.

Knitted I-cords or strips of dense, felted knitted fabric can be substituted for the purchased handles.

Slip all slipped sts purlwise (pwise).

STITCH GUIDE

P2TOG-P1 IN SAME 2 STS

P2tog but do not remove the sts from the left needle, purl the first st again, then slip both sts from needle—2 sts made from 2 sts.

SL 1-K1-PSSO-K1TBL

Sl 1 wyb, k1, use the left needle tip to lift the slipped st up and over the k1 as if to pass the slipped stitch over (psso), but do not drop the passed-over st from the left needle. Insert the right needle tip into the passed-over st on the left needle, knit it through its back loop (tbl), and then drop the passed-over st from the left needle—2 sts made from 2 sts.

LEFT TWIST (LT)

Bring right needle behind first st to knit into the back of the 2nd st on left needle, then knit the first st, then slip both sts from left needle together.

LITTLE HERRINGBONE

(odd number of sts)

ROW 1: (WS) Sl 1 wyf, *p2tog-p1 in same 2 sts (see Stitch Guide); rep from * to last 2 sts, p1, k1.

ROW 2: (RS) Sl 1 wyf, *sl 1-k1-psso-k1tbl (see Stitch Guide); rep from * to last 2 sts, k2.

Rep Rows 1 and 2 for patt.

HEEL STITCH

(even number of sts)

RND 1: Knit.

RND 2: *Sl 1 pwise wyb, k1; rep from *.

Rep Rnds 1 and 2 for patt.

base

With color A and straight needles, CO 93 sts.

Work Rows 1 and 2 of little herringbone patt (see Stitch Guide), ending after a RS row.

INCREASE BASE

INC ROW 1: (WS) Sl 1 wyf, M1 (see Glossary), *p2tog-p1 in same 2 sts; rep from * to last 2 sts, p1, M1, k1—2 sts inc'd.

INC ROW 2: (RS) Sl 1 wyf, M1, k1, *sl 1-k1-psso-k1tbl; rep from * to last st, M1, k1—2 sts inc'd.

Rep the last 2 rows 5 more times—117 sts.

[Piece meas 2¼" (5.5 cm) from beg.]

Work even in little herringbone patt until piece meas 3¾" (9.5 cm) from beg, ending after a WS row.

DECREASE BASE

DEC ROW 1: (RS) Sl 1 wyf, k2tog, *sl 1-k1-psso-k1tbl; rep from * to last 2 sts, k2tog—2 sts dec'd.

DEC ROW 2: (WS) Sl 1 wyf, p2tog, p1, *p2tog-p1 in same 2 sts; rep from * to last 3 sts, p2tog, k1—2 sts dec'd.

Rep the last 2 rows 5 more times—93 sts rem.

[Piece meas about 5¾" (14.5 cm) from beg.]

BO ALL STS AS FOLL: (RS) *BO 3 sts (1 st on right needle after 3rd BO), k2tog, pass st on right needle over k2tog to BO 1 st; rep from * until 3 sts rem on left needle, BO last 3 sts—1 st rem on right needle after last BO. Do not cut yarn.

sides

Transfer rem st to crochet hook. With RS still facing, work 1 rnd of single crochet (sc; see Glossary for crochet instructions) as foll: 22 sc along shaped selvedge at end of RS rows, 52 sc along CO edge, 22 sc along other shaped selvedge, and 52 sc along BO edge—148 sc total.

With RS still facing, transfer last loop on crochet hook to cir needle. Skipping the first sc, pick up and knit 1 st in the back half of each sc of previous rnd—148 sts. Pm and join for working in rnds. Break color A.

CHAIN RND 1: With color B, LT (see Stitch Guide), *slip the first st on right needle to left needle, pull yarn to tighten st, LT; rep from *.

JOIN THE ENDS OF THE CHAIN JUST COMPLETED AS FOLL: Slip the last st on right needle to left needle, then slip it kwise back to right needle to change its st mount. Insert the right needle tip into the fabric from front to back into the center of the first chain of the rnd, wrap yarn around needle as if to knit and draw up a loop onto the right

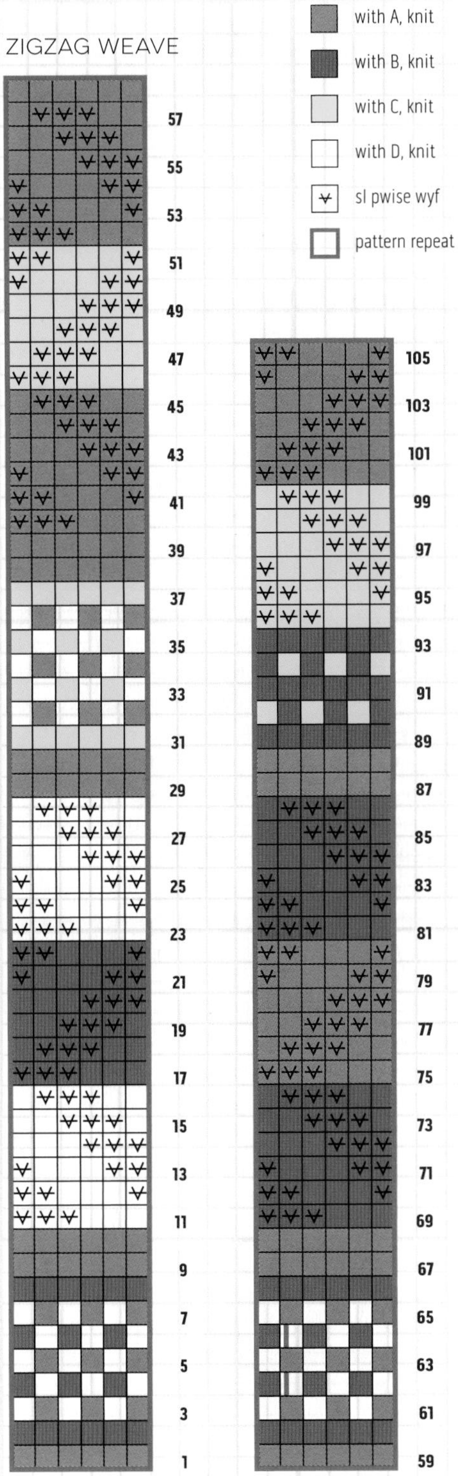

needle. Pass the last st of the rnd over the new loop. Break B and bring tail to WS of work.

CHAIN RND 2: With C, knit the first st of the rnd, then slip it to the left needle, LT, *slip the first st on right needle to left needle, pull yarn to tighten st, LT; rep from *.

Join the ends of the chain as in Chain Rnd 1. Break C and bring tail to WS.

CHAIN RND 3: With A, knit the first st of the rnd, then return it to the left needle, LT, *return the first st on right needle to left needle, pull yarn to tighten st, LT; rep from * to end of rnd.

Join the ends of the chain as in Chain Rnd 1. Do not cut yarn.

NEXT RND: With A, knit *and at the same time* inc 38 sts evenly spaced—186 sts.

[Piece meas about ¾" (2 cm) from pick-up rnd.]

Work Rnds 1–105 of Zigzag Weave Chart (see Notes).

[Piece meas about 11½" (29 cm) from pick-up rnd.]

Cont working with color A only as foll:

Knit 1 rnd.

Work heel st (see Stitch Guide) for 1½" (3.8 cm).

[Rep Chain Rnd 1 as on previous page, join ends of chain, but do not cut yarn] twice.

[Piece meas 13½" (34.5 cm) from pick-up rnd.]

BO ALL STS AS FOLL: *K2tog-tbl, slip st on right needle to left needle; rep from * until 1 st rem. Fasten off last st.

finishing

Weave in loose ends. Stuff bag with towels to hold its shape, lightly steam-block, and allow to air-dry thoroughly before removing towels.

LINING

Trace the oval bottom of the bag on the extra-firm stabilizer and cut a piece the shape of the bottom of the bag. Lay the stabilizer on the lining fabric to use as a template and cut a piece of bottom lining 1" (2.5 cm) larger all the way around than the stabilizer for a seam allowance. Fuse the stabilizer in the center of the WS of the lining piece.

Cut another piece of lining 36" × 17" (91.5 × 43 cm). Cut piece of fusible interfacing 34" × 12" (86.5 x 30.5 cm). Lay the lining WS up with the 36" (91.5 cm) edges running across the top and bottom. Position the interfacing on top of the lining 4" (10 cm) down from the top long side and 1" (2.5 cm) in from the edges on the other three sides, and fuse in place. Cut a piece of extra-firm stabilizer 34" × 2" (86.5 × 5 cm), position it on top of the lining 2" (5 cm) down from the top and 1" (2.5 cm) in from each short side, and fuse in place.

Fold the lining in half with right sides touching and use a sewing machine or sharp-point sewing needle and thread to sew the short sides together with a 1" (2.5 cm) seam allowance, forming a cylinder. Press the seam open. Sew the cylinder to the bottom lining piece with a 1" (2.5 cm) seam allowance.

Insert lining into bag with wrong sides of bag and lining touching and right side of lining showing on the inside of the bag. Using a sharp-point sewing needle and thread, tack the bottom of the lining to the bottom of the bag along the bottom seam. Fold the top of the lining 2" (5 cm) to the WS, and carefully tack the lining in place around the top of the bag, just below the last 2 chain rnds.

Attach handles according to manufacturer's instructions (for other options, see Notes).

THIS VERSATILE CARDIGAN is worked top down in one piece. A great addition to any wardrobe, you can dress it up or dress it down. The collar, cuffs, and hem are double-sided; it looks as beautiful on the inside as on the outside, so wear it unbuttoned or with the collar turned down. || *designed by* **SIMONA MERCHANT-DEST**

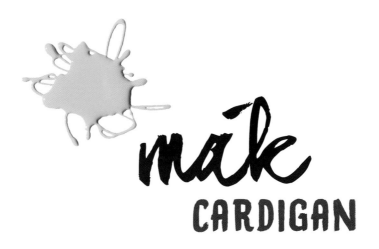

make CARDIGAN

FINISHED SIZE

About 31¾ (35¾, 39¾, 43¾, 47¾, 51¾, 55¾, 59¾)" (80.5 [90.5, 101, 111, 121.5, 131.5, 141.5, 152] cm) bust circumference, with fronts closed.

Jacket shown measures 35¾" (90.5 cm).

YARN

Worsted weight (#4 Medium).

Shown here: Hikoo Kenzie (50% New Zealand merino, 25% nylon, 10% angora, 10% alpaca, 5% silk noils; 160 yd [146 m]/1 ¾ oz [50 g]): #1004 beetroot (color A), 7 (8, 9, 9, 10, 11, 11, 12) skeins; #1005 bayberry (color B), 3 (3, 3, 3, 3, 3, 4, 4) skeins.

NEEDLES

Size U.S. 5 (3.75 mm): 32" (80 cm) circular (cir), and 16" (40 cm) cir or set of 5 double-pointed (dpn).

Adjust needle sizes if necessary to obtain the correct gauge.

NOTIONS

Markers (m); stitch holders or waste yarn; tapestry needle; seven 1⅜" (3.4 cm) buttons.

GAUGE

20 sts and 33 rows = 4" (10 cm) in St st.

20 sts and 44 rows = 4" (10 cm) in Woven Diagonals patt.

NOTES

The slightly oversized jacket is constructed from the top down in one piece and shaped along raglan lines. At the underarms it is divided for sleeves, fronts, and back. Sleeves are placed on holders. Body is worked back and forth in rows in one piece to beg of hem. Sleeves are worked in rounds to cuffs. After buttonband and buttonhole bands are knitted onto the fronts, stitches are picked up along the lower edges to finish lower edge hem.

All slipped stitches are slipped purlwise with the yarn float carried on the right side of the fabric.

Circular needle is used to accommodate large number of sts on body. Do not join; work back and forth in rows.

Change to color A and cont next 6 rows in patt, ending after a WS row.

Change to color B and cont next 6 rows in patt, ending after a WS row.

[Piece meas 3½" (9 cm) from beg.]

TURNING ROWS: Change to color A and knit 3 rows, ending after a RS row.

OUTER COLLAR

Change to color B.

Work next 3 rows in St st (knit on RS, purl on WS), ending after a WS row.

Work 6 rows in Woven Diagonals patt.

Change to color A and cont next 6 rows in patt, ending after a WS row.

Change to color B and work in patt until piece meas 7¼" (18.5 cm) from beg, ending after a RS row.

collar

With color B and longer cir, CO 98 (98, 102, 106, 110, 114, 118, 126) sts. Do not join; work back and forth in rows.

COLLAR FACING

Purl 1 WS row.

Work Woven Diagonals patt (worked in rows; see chart on page 92) until piece meas 2½" (6.5 cm) from beg, ending after a WS row.

yoke

SET-UP ROW: (WS) Change to color A and p13 (13, 14, 15, 16, 17, 17, 19) for right front, place marker (pm), p20 for right sleeve, pm, p32 (32, 34, 36, 38, 40, 44, 48) for back, pm, p20 for left sleeve, pm, p13 (13, 14, 15, 16, 17, 17, 19) for left front.

SHAPE RAGLAN

INC ROW: (RS) *Knit to 2 sts before m, M1R (see Glossary), k2, sl m, k2, M1L (see Glossary); rep from * 3 more times, knit to end—8 sts inc'd.

NEXT ROW: (WS) Purl.

Rep the last 2 rows 21 (23, 25, 26, 28, 29, 31, 32) more times—274 (290, 310, 322, 342, 354, 374, 390) sts; 35 (37, 40, 42, 45, 47, 49, 52) sts for each front, 64 (68, 72, 74, 78, 80, 84, 86) sts for each sleeve, and 76 (80, 86, 90, 96, 100, 108, 114) sts for back.

DIVIDE FOR BODY AND SLEEVES

DIVIDING ROW: (RS) Work 35 (37, 40, 42, 45, 47, 49, 52) left front sts, remove m, put next 64 (68, 72, 74, 78,

80, 84, 86) sleeve sts onto st holder or waste yarn, remove m, use the knitted method (see Glossary) to CO 1 (4, 6, 9, 11, 14, 16, 18) underarm sts, pm for side "seam," CO 1 (4, 6, 9, 11, 14, 16, 18) more underarm sts, work 76 (80, 86, 90, 96, 100, 108, 114) back sts, remove m, put next 64 (68, 72, 74, 78, 80, 84, 86) sleeve sts onto st holder or waste yarn, remove m, CO 1 (4, 6, 9, 11, 14, 16, 18) underarm sts, pm for side "seam," CO 1 (4, 6, 9, 11, 14, 16, 18) more underarm sts, work 35 (37, 40, 42, 45, 47, 49, 52) right front sts—150 (170, 190, 210, 230, 250, 270, 290) sts total; 36 (41, 46, 51, 56, 61, 65, 70) sts each front, 78 (88, 98, 108, 118, 128, 140, 150) back sts.

body

Work in St st until piece meas 1" (2.5 cm) from divide, ending after a WS row.

SHAPE WAIST

DEC ROW: (RS) *Knit to 7 sts before side "seam" m, k2tog, knit to m, sl m, k5, ssk; rep from * once more, knit to end—4 sts dec'd.

Work 5 rows even.

Rep the last 6 rows 2 more times—138 (158, 178, 198, 218, 238, 258, 278) sts rem; 33 (38, 43, 48, 53, 58, 62, 67) sts each front and 72 (82, 92, 102, 112, 122, 134, 144) sts for back.

[Rep dec row, then work 3 rows even] 3 times—126 (146, 166, 186, 206, 226, 246, 266) sts rem; 30 (35, 40, 45, 50, 55, 59, 64) sts each front and 66 (76, 86, 96, 106, 116, 128, 138) sts for back.

Work even in St st until piece meas 7½" (19 cm) from divide, ending after a WS row.

SHAPE HIPS

HIP INC ROW: (RS) *Knit to 6 sts before side "seam" m, M1R, knit to m, sl m, k6, M1L; rep from * once more, knit to end—4 sts inc'd.

Work 1 row even.

Rep the last 2 rows 2 more times—138 (158, 178, 198, 218, 238, 258, 278) sts total; 33 (38, 43, 48, 53, 58, 62, 67) sts each front and 72 (82, 92, 102, 112, 122, 134, 144) sts for back.

[Rep Hip Inc Row, then work 3 rows even] twice—146 (166, 186, 206, 226, 246, 266, 286) sts total; 35 (40, 45, 50, 55, 60, 64, 69) sts each front and 76 (86, 96, 106, 116, 126, 138, 148) sts for back.

Cont working even in St st until piece meas 9¾" (25 cm) from divide, ending after a WS row.

Change to color B. Work Rows 1–4 of Woven Diagonals patt.

Change to color A. Work Rows 5 and 6 of Woven Diagonals patt.

Change to St st and work Hip Inc Row, work 3 rows even, then rep Hip Inc Row once more—154 (174, 194, 214, 234, 254, 274, 294) sts total; 37 (42, 47, 52, 57, 62, 66, 71) sts each front, 80 (90, 100, 110, 120, 130, 142, 152) sts for back.

Cont working even in St st until piece meas 11½" (29 cm) from divide, ending after WS row. Place all sts onto st holder or waste yarn.

sleeves

Return 64 (68, 72, 74, 78, 80, 84, 86) held sts from 1 sleeve to shorter cir or dpn. With color A, beg at center of underarm CO sts, pick up and knit 1 (4, 6, 9, 11, 14, 16, 18) sts along first half of CO sts, M1 (see Glossary) in corner between CO sts and held sts, knit to end of held sts, M1 in corner between held sts and CO sts, pick up and knit 1 (4, 6, 9, 11, 14, 16, 18) sts along other half of CO sts—68 (78, 86, 94, 102, 110, 118, 124) sts total. Pm and join for working in rnds.

DEC RND: K0 (3, 5, 8, 10, 13, 15, 17), k2tog, knit to last 2 (5, 7, 10, 12, 15,

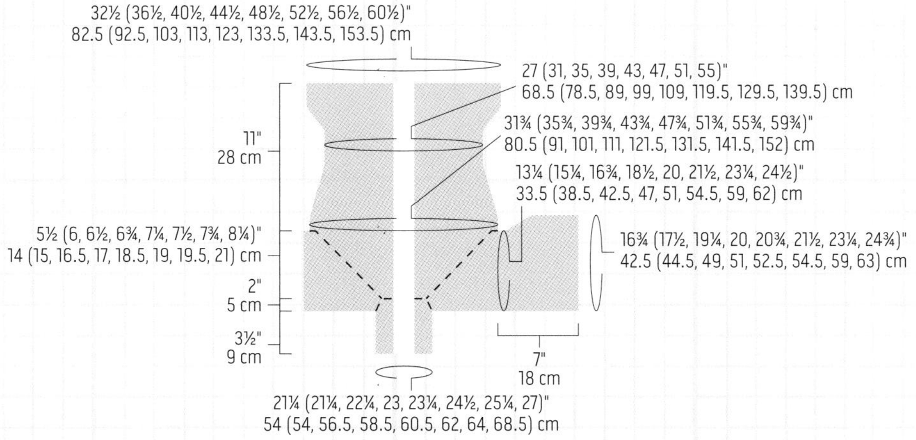

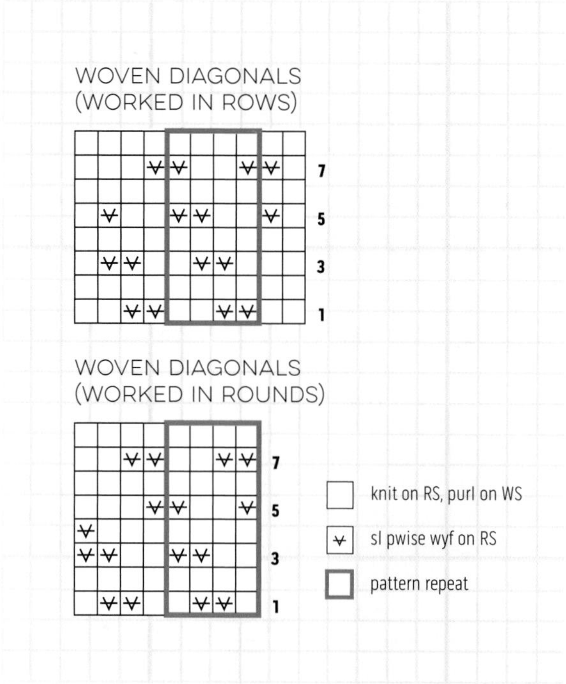

17, 19) sts ssk, knit to end if necessary—66 (76, 84, 92, 100, 108, 116, 122) sts total.

SHAPE SLEEVE

SIZES 31¾ (35¾, 39¾, 43¾, 47¾, 59¾)" ONLY:

Knit 2 (4, 4, 6, 12, 12) rnds.

INC RND: K1, M1L, knit to last 2 sts, M1R, k1—2 sts inc'd.

Knit 1 (3, 3, 5, 11, 11) rnds.

Rep the last 2 (4, 4, 6, 12, 12) rnds 5 (5, 5, 3, 1, 0) more time(s)—78 (88, 96, 100, 104, 124) sts.

SIZE 31¾" ONLY:
[Rep inc rnd, then knit 3 rnds] 3 times—84 sts.

ALL SIZES:
Work even in St st (knit all sts, every rnd) until piece meas 4" (10 cm) from divide.

SLEEVE HEM

Change to color B and knit 1 rnd.

Work in Woven Diagonals patt (worked in rnds) until sleeve edge meas about 2" (5 cm).

Change to color A, cont in patt for next 4 rnds.

Change to color B, cont in patt for next 6 rnds.

Hem meas about 3" (7.5 cm) to here.

Change to color A and knit 1 rnd.

HEM FACING

TURNING RND: Purl.

Cont in St st until hem facing meas 3" (7.5 cm) from turning rnd.

BO all sts.

Fold facing to WS along fold line and, with yarn threaded on a tapestry needle, whipstitch (see Glossary) in place.

Work second sleeve the same as the first.

finishing

JOIN COLLAR

With WS facing, fold collar along turning row and, with yarn threaded on a tapestry needle, whipstitch in place. Block piece to measurements.

BUTTONBAND

With longer cir needle, color A and RS facing, beg at turning row of left front collar, pick up and knit 126 (128, 128, 134, 136, 136, 142, 142) sts evenly spaced along left front edge and collar.

Beg with a WS row, work 12 rows in St st, ending after a RS row.

[Band meas about 1¾" (4.5 cm) from pick-up row.]

TURNING ROW: (WS) Knit.

Work 12 rows in St st, ending after a WS row.

BO all sts.

Fold facing to WS along turning row and with yarn threaded on a tapestry needle, whipstitch in place.

BUTTONHOLE BAND

Mark placement of 7 buttonholes on right front, the top buttonhole

1" (2.5 cm) down from upper collar edge, another ¾" (2 cm) down from neck edge, the lower buttonhole ¾" (2 cm) up from lower edge, and the rem 4 evenly spaced in between along front edge.

With longer cir needle, color A and RS facing, beg at lower edge of right front, pick up and knit 126 (128, 128, 134, 136, 136, 142, 142) sts evenly spaced along right front edge and collar.

Beg with WS, work 5 rows in St st, ending after a WS row.

BUTTONHOLE ROW: (RS) Knit to end and *at the same time* use the one-row method (see Glossary) to make a 3-st buttonhole opposite each marked buttonhole position.

Work 6 more rows in St st, ending after a WS row.

[Band measures about 1¾" (4.5 cm) from pick-up row.]

TURNING ROW: (RS) Purl.

Work 5 rows in St st, ending after a WS row.

Work Buttonhole Row same as before.

Work 5 rows in patt, ending after a WS row.

BO all sts.

Fold facing to WS along fold line and, with yarn threaded on a tapestry needle, whipstitch in place.

LOWER HEM

With longer cir needle, color B and RS facing, beg at turning row of left front buttonband, pick up and knit 13 sts along the buttonband edge, work 37 (42, 47, 52, 57, 62, 66, 71) held left front sts, 80 (90, 100, 110, 120, 130, 142, 152) back sts, and 37 (42, 47, 52, 57, 62, 66, 71) held right front sts, pick up and knit 13 sts along the buttonhole-band edge—180 (200, 220, 240, 260, 280, 300, 320) sts total.

Purl 1 WS row.

Work Woven Diagonals patt (worked in rows) until hem meas about 3" (7.5 cm) from pick-up row, ending after a WS row. Break yarn.

Change to color A and knit 1 row.

TURNING ROW: (WS) Knit.

Cont in St st until hem facing meas 3" (7.5 cm) from turning row, ending after a WS row.

BO all sts.

Fold facing to WS along fold line and, with yarn threaded on a tapestry needle, whipstitch in place.

Weave in loose ends. Block again if desired. Sew buttons to buttonband, opposite buttonholes.

THE SIMPLE woven slip-stitch pattern forms a spiral effect as it goes through color changes all the way to this hat's crown. This and another small slip-stitch pattern at the brim make this hat interesting and at the same time an opportunity to learn new stitches and to adapt them for working in the round. || *designed by* **FAINA GOBERSTEIN**

Spiral HAT

FINISHED SIZE

18 (20, 21½)" (45.5 [51, 54.5] cm) circumference at band, slightly stretched, and 9¾" (25 cm) long.

Hat shown meas 20" (51 cm) circumference.

YARN

Worsted weight (#4 Medium).

Shown here: Anzula Cricket (80% superwash merino 10% cashmere, 10% nylon; 250 yd [228 m]/3½ oz [100 g]): moss (color A), seaside (color B), and persimmon (color C), 1 skein each.

NEEDLES

Hat: Size U.S. 5 (3.75 mm): 16" (40.5 cm) circular (cir) and set of 5 double-pointed (dpn).

Ribbing: Size U.S. 3 (3.25 mm): 16" (40.5 cm) cir.

Adjust needle sizes if necessary to obtain the correct gauge.

NOTIONS

Marker (m); tapestry needle.

GAUGE

26 sts and 44 rnds = 4" (10 cm) in diagonal weave patt (see Stitch Guide or chart), on larger needle.

NOTES

Stitch patterns are written for working in the round. For best results, make a gauge swatch in the round.

On some rounds, the woven strands of the diagonal weave travel across the end-of-round. Just continue to follow the pattern. It makes a very smooth transition between rounds.

One extra stitch is added at the beg of Rnd 2 of the first repeat of diagonal weave. Because the pattern is moving on a spiral, it "loses" 1 stitch at beg of second rnd. The extra stitch will help to keep 6 knit stitches between all sets of slipped stitches.

STITCH GUIDE

K1, P1 RIB

(multiple of 2 sts)

RND 1: *K1, p1; rep from *.

Rep Rnd 1 for patt.

DIAGONAL WEAVE PATTERN

(multiple of 9 sts + 1)

RND 1: Sl1 wyf, *K6, sl3 wyf; rep from *.

RND 2: K1, *k5, sl 3, k1; rep from *.

RND 3: K1, *k4, sl3 wyf, k2; rep from *.

RND 4: K1, *k3, sl3 wyf, k3; rep from *.

RND 5: K1, *k2, sl3 wyf, k4; rep from *.

RND 6: K1, *k1, sl3 wyf, k5; rep from *.

RND 7: K1, *sl3 wyf, k6; rep from *.

RND 8: Sl1 wyf, *sl2 wyf, k6, sl1 wyf; rep from *.

RND 9: Sl1 wyf, *sl1 wyf, k6, sl2 wyf; rep from *.

Rep Rnds 1–9 for patt.

TIPS

- The tension of the floats must be just right—tight enough to hold the strands tidily against the face of the fabric without drooping, loose enough that the strands still provide three-dimensional texture, but not so tight that the fabric puckers.
- It helps to put your finger on a float while you slip the sts behind the float.

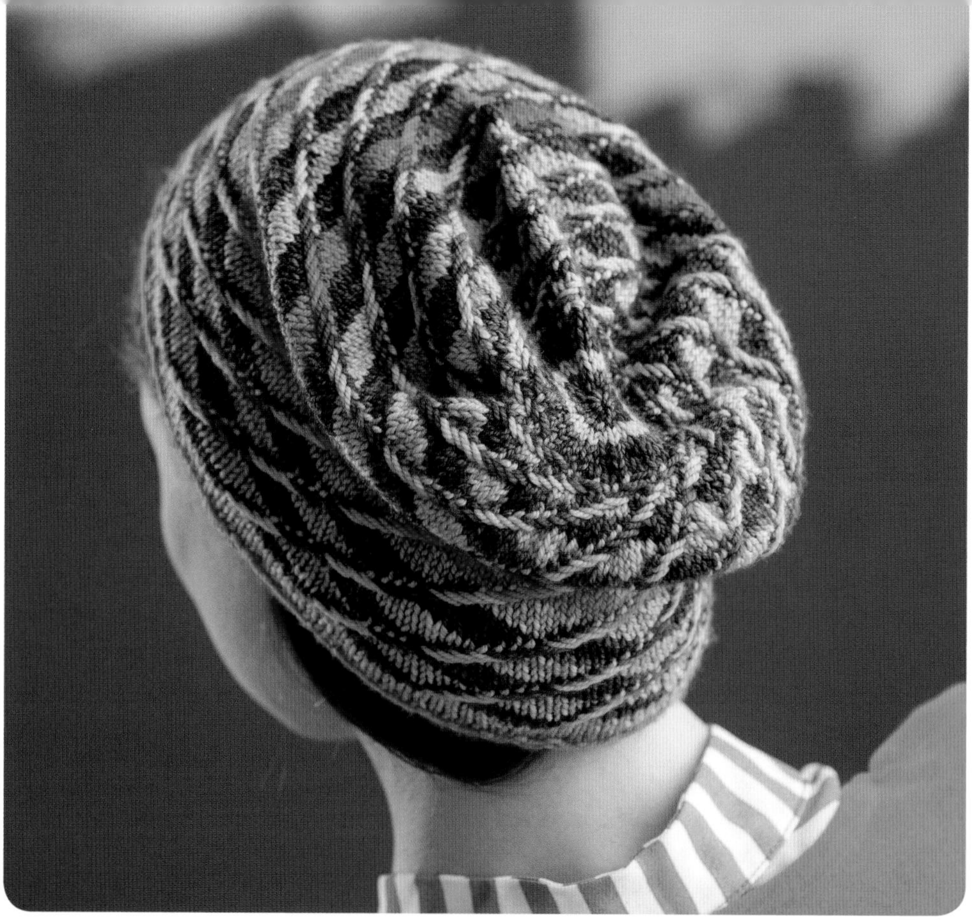

hat

With color B and smaller needle, CO 116 (126, 136) sts. Pm for beg of rnd, and join for working in the rnd, being careful not to twist sts.

Change to color A and work 6 rnds of k1, p1 rib.

Change to larger needle and color B.

Knit 3 rnds.

RND 1: With color C, *p1, sl 1 wyf; rep from * to end.

RND 2: Knit.

RND 3: Rep Rnd 1.

With color B, knit 3 rnds, and inc 10 (9, 8) sts evenly spaced on the last rnd—126 (135, 144) sts.

With color A, knit 2 rnds.

[Piece meas about 2" (5 cm) to here.]

Work diagonal weave patt (see Stitch Guide or chart) continually, changing colors every 4 rnds as foll:

With color B, rep the 9 sts in the red rep box on chart (or after the * of written instructions in Stitch Guide) to end.

INC RND 2: M1, rep the 9 sts in the red rep box on chart (or after the * of written instructions in Stitch Guide) to end—127 (136, 145) sts.

Work Rnds 3 and 4.

With color A, work Rnds 5–8.

With color B, work Rnds 9, 1, 2, and 3.

With color A, work Rnds 4–7.

With color B, work Rnds 8, 9, 1, and 2.

With color C, work Rnds 3–6.

With color B, work Rnds 7, 8, 9, and 1.

With color A, work Rnds 2–5.

With color B, work Rnds 6–9.

With color A, work Rnds 1–4.

With color C, work Rnds 5–8.

With color A, work Rnds 9, 1, 2, and 3.

With color B, work Rnds 4–7.

With color A, work Rnds 8, 9, 1, and 2.

With color B, work Rnds 3–6.

With color A, Rnds 7, 8, 9, and 1.

With color B, work Rnds 2–5.

[Piece meas about 8¼" [21 cm] from beg.]

DIAGONAL WEAVE

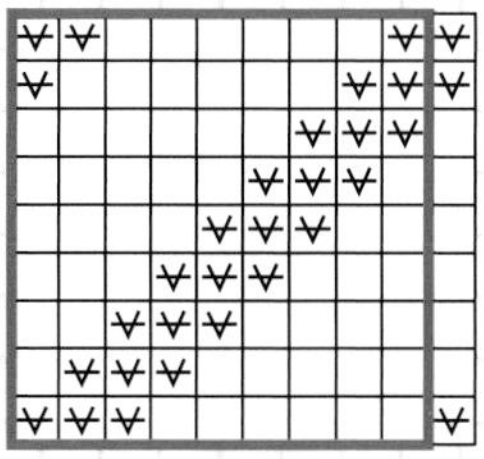

knit

sl pwise wyf

pattern repeat

CROWN SHAPING

Note: The beg of rnd is shifted 1 st to the right at the end of each rnd to keep the slipped sts as the first 3 sts of each rnd. Change to dpn when sts no longer fit comfortably on cir needle.

Remove beg of rnd m, k2, replace m.

DEC RND 1: With color A, *sl 3 wyf, k3, k2tog, k1; rep from * to last st, sl last st to right needle, remove beg of rnd m, return slipped st to left needle and replace m—113 (121, 129) sts.

RND 2: *Sl 3 wyf, k5; rep from * to last st, sl last st to right needle, remove beg of rnd m, return slipped st to left needle and replace m.

DEC RND 3: *Sl 3 wyf, k2, k2tog, k1; rep from * to last st, sl last st to right needle, remove beg of rnd m, return slipped st to left needle and replace m—99 (106, 113) sts.

RND 4: *Sl 3 wyf, k4; rep from * to last st, sl last st to right needle, remove beg of rnd m, return slipped st to left needle and replace m.

DEC RND 5: With color B, *sl 3 wyf, k1, k2tog, k1; rep from * to last st, sl last st to right needle, remove beg of rnd m, return slipped st to left needle and replace m—85 (91, 97) sts.

RND 6: *Sl 3 wyf, k3; rep from * to last st, sl last st to right needle, remove beg of rnd m, return slipped st to left needle and replace m.

DEC RND 7: *Sl 3 wyf, k1, k2tog; rep from * to last st, sl last st to right needle, remove beg of rnd m, return slipped st to left needle and replace m—71 (76, 81) sts.

RND 8: *Sl 3 wyf, k2; rep from * to last st, sl last st to right needle, remove beg of rnd m, return slipped st to left needle and replace m.

DEC RND 9: With color A, *sl 3 wyf, k2tog; rep from * to last st, sl last st to right needle, remove beg of rnd m, return slipped st to left needle and replace m—57 (61, 65) sts.

RND 10: *Sl 3 wyf, k1; rep from *.

RND 11: Knit.

DEC RND 12: *K2, k2tog; rep from *—43 (46, 49) sts.

RND 13: Knit.

DEC RND 14: With color B, *k1, k2tog; rep from * to end—29 (31, 33) sts.

RND 15: Knit.

DEC RND 16: With color A, k2tog, knit to end—28 (30, 32) sts.

DEC RND 17: *K2tog; rep from *—14 (15, 16) sts.

RND 18: Knit.

Break yarn, leaving about 8" (20.5 cm) tail.

Draw yarn tail through rem sts. Secure tail to WS.

finishing

Weave in loose ends. Block piece to measurements.

MAKE IT YOURS

- To make a beanie instead of a slouch, the depth at beginning of crown needs to be 4½ (5½, 6)" (11.5 [14, 15] cm) from beg or desired height. Continue with crown shaping as written.
- Choose your own colors or color sequence.
- This stitch pattern can be modified very easily. Within 9 st-repeat, instead of 3 work 2 or 4 slipped sts (e.g., k7, sl 2 wyf; or k5, sl 4 wyf).
- Change rib to a twisted rib pattern to give a different look.

THE ASYMMETRICAL placement of border patterns and use of color give a freehand artistic feel to this scarf, which was inspired by the painting *Lake George* by Georgia O'Keeffe. This scarf is worked sideways in three colors. The woven waves pattern is the center of attention and is reminiscent of waves in a lake. The side edges are finished by a simple crochet chain pattern. || *designed by* **FAINA GOBERSTEIN**

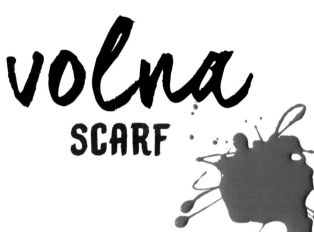

volna SCARF

FINISHED SIZE
About 6" (15 cm) wide and 60" (152.5 cm) long.

YARN
DK weight (#3 Light).

Shown here: Manos del Uruguay Silk Blend (70% merino, 30% silk; 150 yd [135 m]; 1¾ oz [50 g]): #3014 natural (A), #3214 oxygen (B), and #3029 steel (C), 1 skein each.

NEEDLE
Size U.S. 8 (5 mm): 32" circular (cir).

Adjust needle size if necessary to obtain the correct gauge.

NOTIONS
Size I-9 (5.5 mm) crochet hook; tapestry needle.

GAUGE
21 sts and 48 rows = 4" (10 cm) in woven waves after blocking.

NOTES
Scarf is worked sideways.

Circular needle is used to accommodate large number of sts. Do not join; work back and forth in rows.

Slip sts purlwise wyb or wyf as indicated in the pattern.

When slipping multiple sts at once, make sure that float is not too tight.

All stitch patterns begin with Row 1 worked with the WS facing.

STITCH GUIDE

SEED STITCH

(even number of sts)

ROW 1: (WS) *K1, p1; rep from *.

ROW 2: *P1, k1; rep from *.

Rep Rows 1 and 2 for patt.

WOVEN CHECKS PATTERN

(multiple of 4 sts + 8)

ROW 1: (WS) K4, *sl2 wyb, p2; rep from * to last 4 sts, k4.

ROW 2: (RS) K4,*k2, sl2 wyf; rep from * to last 4 sts, k4.

ROW 3: K4, *p2, sl2 wyb; rep from * to last 4 sts, k4.

ROW 4: K4, *sl2 wyf, k2; rep from * to last 4 sts, k4.

Rep Rows 1–4 for patt.

TIPS

- To ensure the right length of front float, keep your finger on the float before working next stitch.
- Slip selvedge stitch with previous color and change color on the next st. The new color sinks between first and second sts for flawless effect.

scarf

With color A and using long-tail method (see Glossary), CO 308 sts. Do not join; work back and forth in rows.

Work 2 rows of seed st (see Stitch Guide), ending after a RS row.

With color B, knit 2 rows, ending after a RS row.

Change to color A and work Rows 1 and 2 of woven checks patt (see Stitch Guide or chart).

Change to color C and work Rows 3 and 4 of woven checks patt.

NEXT ROW: With color B, k4, purl to last 4 sts, k4.

NEXT ROW: Knit.

Change to color A and work Rows 1–6 of right woven wave patt.

[Change to color C and work Rows 1–6 of left woven wave patt. Change to color B and work Rows 1–6 of right woven wave patt] 3 times.

Change to color A and work Rows 1–6 of right woven wave patt.

NEXT ROW: (WS) With color B, k4, purl to last 4 sts, k4.

NEXT ROW: Knit.

Change to color C and work Rows 3 and 4 of woven checks patt.

Change to color A and work Rows 1 and 2 of woven checks patt.

Change to color B and work Rows 3 and 4 of woven checks patt.

Change to color C and work Rows 1 and 2 of woven checks patt.

Change to color A and work Rows 3 and 4 of woven checks patt.

NEXT ROW: (WS) With C, k4, purl to last 4 sts, k4.

Work 3 rows of seed st.

BO all sts in patt.

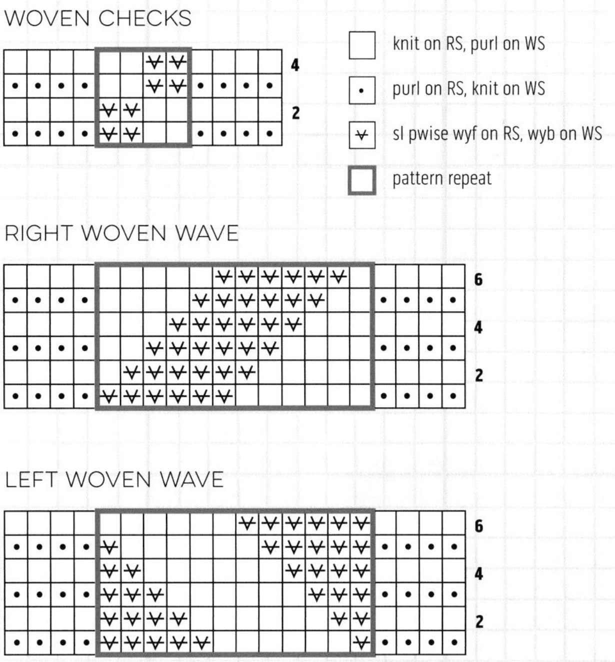

finishing

Block scarf to measurements.

SIDE EDGE TRIM

With RS facing and colors A, B, and C held together, beg at right edge of short end of scarf.

Insert hook from front to back at corner of scarf, pull yarns through to front, sl st (see Glossary for crochet terms) to secure yarns.

*Ch2, skip about ½" (1.3 cm), sl st into edge; rep from * to end, sl st to secure. Fasten off.

Rep for the other short edge of scarf.

Weave in loose ends.

MAKE IT YOURS

- Choose different small slip-stitch patterns for the border.
- Change the color sequence.
- The Woven Waves Chart can be modified very easily. Keep the same number of sts that are slipped and not slipped. If floats are too long, they will sag. Swatch your version to see if they hold in place.
- Make a different edge trim.

CHAPTER 4

Fancy SLIP-STITCH PATTERNS

IN THIS CHAPTER, we introduce some unknown, redesigned, and other rather unexpected slip-stitch patterns that we find really intriguing. There are so many fascinating possibilities, we wish we could have fit more of them into this book. With some, you would never guess they're slip-stitch patterns.

Any slip-stitch pattern that is combined with other knitting techniques such as lace or cables is classified here as a fancy stitch pattern. Many of these stitches are reversible.

Some of these stitches were reengineered from old patterns we found in European books. You can also experiment with these and other stitches in this book by changing the number of rows you slip stitches over, adding or removing yarnovers, stacking stitches on top of each other, or adding extra purl or knit stitches between the slip stitches to change the look of the original stitches.

Many of the fancy stitch patterns are ideal for light knitwear such as shawls, scarves, and summer tops. We have included four designs in this chapter. Each of them is worked in a different fancy slip-stitch pattern. We hope to pass on to you our excitement about generating more interesting stitches for your future projects.

fancy STITCHES DICTIONARY

STITCH GUIDE

1/1 RC
Sl 1 st onto cn and hold in back, k1, k1 from cn.

1/1 LC
Sl 1 st onto cn and hold in front, k1, k1 from cn.

1/2 RC
Sl 2 sts onto cn and hold in back, k1, k2 from cn.

1/2 LC
Sl 1 st onto cn and hold in front, k2, k1 from cn.

SL2TOG-K1-P2SSO
Sl 2 sts tog as if to knit, k1, pass 2 sl sts over.

SL 1 WYON (Slip one with yarn over needle)
Slip 1 stitch purlwise carrying yarn float over the needle from front to back (see page 10).

COMBO TUCK ST (for Blue Ridge Mountain)
P1tog with yon from Row 2 and float from Row 1.

PT3-YON (for Alternating Tracks and Dainty Silk)
P1tog with all 3 floats on needle.

3SL-ST-CROSSING-DEC
Sl 1 st onto cn and hold in front, sl 3 sts onto second cn and hold in back, k1 (the left elongated st), sl2tog-k1-p2sso from back cn, k1 from front cn (the right elongated st).

5SL-ST-CROSSING-DEC
Sl 2 sts onto cn and hold in back, sl 1 st onto second cn and hold in front, sl 1 more st onto back cn (3 sts on the back cn), k1 (the left elongated st), return 3 sts from back cn to left needle, k1, sl2tog-k1-p2sso, k1, k1 (the right elongated st) from front cn.

DEC-1/2RC
Sl 1 st onto cn and hold in front, p2, return st on cn to left needle and ssk—1 st dec'd.

FANCY FERN

(MULTIPLE OF 7 STS)

– Reversible.

– Very light and open fabric.

ROW 1: (WS) Purl.

ROW 2: *K1, sl 1 wyb, k3, sl 1 wyb, k1; rep from *.

ROW 3: *P1, sl 1 wyf, p3, sl 1 wyf, p1; rep from *.

ROW 4: *K1, yo, 3Sl-St-Crossing-Dec (see Stitch Guide), yo, k1; rep from *.

ROW 5: Purl.

Rep Rows 2–5 for patt.

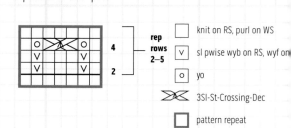

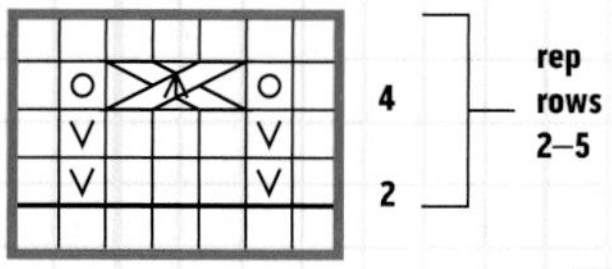

- knit on RS, purl on WS
- sl pwise wyb on RS, wyf on WS
- yo
- 3Sl-St-Crossing-Dec
- pattern repeat

ALTERNATING TRACKS
(MULTIPLE OF 4 STS + 2)

— Use smaller needles for more dense fabric.

— Use bigger needles for thinner fabric.

ROWS 1 AND 3: (WS) Sl 2 wyon, *k2, sl 2 wyon; rep from *.

ROW 2: *Sl 2 wyon, p2; rep from * to last 2 sts, sl 2 wyon.

ROW 4: *(PT3-yon) twice (see Stitch Guide), p2; rep from * to last 2 sts, (pT3-yon) twice.

ROWS 5 AND 7: K2, *sl 2 wyon, k2; rep from *.

ROW 6: *P2, sl 2 wyon; rep from * to last 2 sts, p2.

ROW 8: *P2, (pT3-yon) twice; rep from * to last 2 sts, p2.

Rep Rows 1—8 for patt.

•	•	T3	T3	•	•	**8**
•	•	∩	∩	•	•	
•	•	∩	∩	•	•	**6**
•	•	∩	∩	•	•	
T3	T3	•	•	T3	T3	**4**
∩	∩	•	•	∩	∩	
∩	∩	•	•	∩	∩	**2**
∩	∩	•	•	∩	∩	

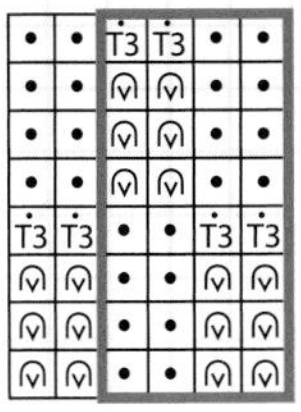

•	purl on RS, knit on WS
T3	pT3-yon
∩	sl 1 wyon
☐	pattern repeat

SLIP-STITCH ARGYLE
(MULTIPLE OF 6 STS)

— Good for accents or allover patterning.

ROWS 1 AND 3: (RS) *Sl 1 wyb, k4, sl 1 wyb; rep from *.

ROWS 2 AND 4: *Sl 1 wyf, p4, sl 1 wyf; rep from *.

ROW 5: *1/2 LC (see Stitch Guide), 1/2 RC (see Stitch Guide); rep from *.

ROW 6: Purl.

ROWS 7 AND 9: *K2, sl 2 wyb, k2; rep from *.

ROWS 8 AND 10: *P2, sl 2 wyf, p2; rep from *.

ROW 11: *1/2 RC, 1/2 LC; rep from *.

ROW 12: Purl.

Rep Rows 1—12 for patt.

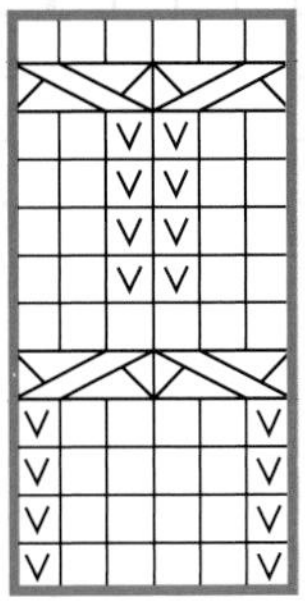

☐	knit on RS, purl on WS
v	sl pwise wyb on RS, wyf on WS
⧄	1/2 RC
⧅	1/2 LC
☐	pattern repeat

STRANDED PEARLS

(MULTIPLE OF 6 STS)

– Reversible.

– Creates light fabric.

– Use larger needles with lightweight yarn for lace imitation.

– Use heavier yarn for exaggerated texture.

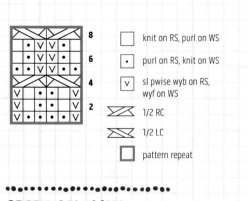

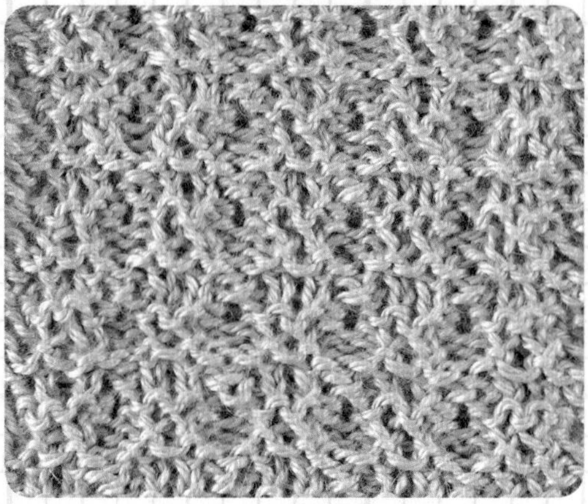

ROW 1: (WS) *Sl 1 wyf, k4, sl 1 wyf; rep from *.

ROW 2: *Sl 1 wyb, k1, p2, k1, sl 1 wyb; rep from *.

ROW 3: *Sl 1 wyf, p1, k2, p1, sl 1 wyf; rep from *.

ROW 4: *1/2 LC (see Stitch Guide), 1/2 RC (see Stitch Guide); rep from *.

ROW 5: *K2, sl 2 wyf, k2; rep from *.

ROW 6: *K1, p1, sl 2 wyb, p1, k1; rep from *.

ROW 7: *P1, k1, sl 2 wyf, k1, p1; rep from *.

ROW 8: *1/2 RC, 1/2 LC; rep from *.

Rep Rows 1–8 for patt.

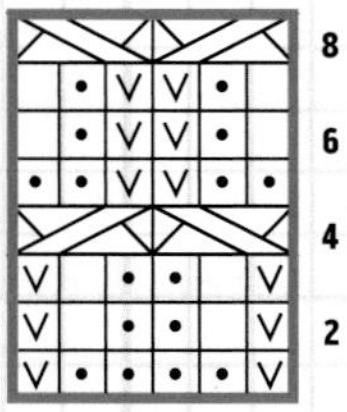

- knit on RS, purl on WS
- purl on RS, knit on WS
- sl pwise wyb on RS, wyf on WS
- 1/2 RC
- 1/2 LC
- pattern repeat

GREEK COLUMNS

(MULTIPLE OF 8 STS + 1)

– Light and open fabric.

ROW 1: (RS) Knit.

ROW 2: Purl.

ROWS 3 AND 5: *K3, sl 1 wyb, k1, sl 1 wyb, k2; rep from * to last st, k1.

ROWS 4 AND 6: P1, *p2, sl 1 wyf, p1, sl 1 wyf, p3; rep from *.

ROW 7: *K1, yo, 5Sl-St-Crossing-Dec (see Stitch Guide), yo; rep from * to last st, k1.

ROW 8: Purl.

Rep Rows 3–8 for patt.

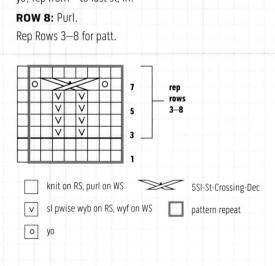

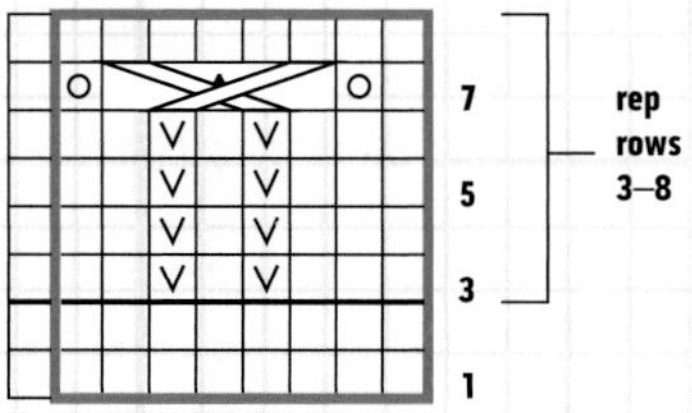

- knit on RS, purl on WS
- sl pwise wyb on RS, wyf on WS
- yo
- 5Sl-St-Crossing-Dec
- pattern repeat

BLUE RIDGE MOUNTAINS

(MULTIPLE OF 7 STS + 2)

– Reversible.

– Light and lacy fabric.

– Good for garments or accessories.

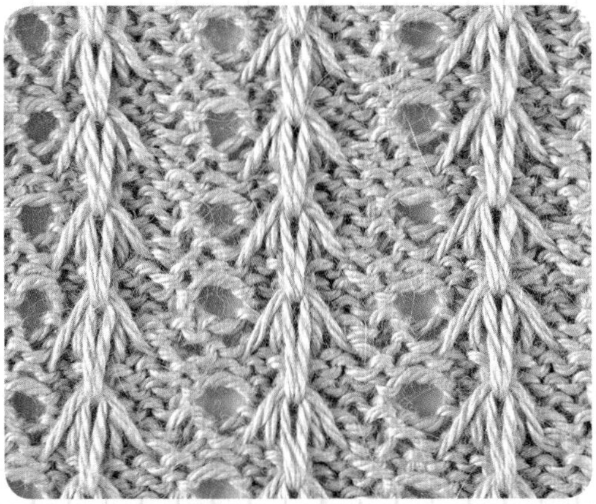

ROW 1: (RS) *K2, sl 5 wyf; rep from * to last 2 sts, k2.

ROW 2: K2, *k2, sl 1 wyon (see Stitch Guide), k4; rep from *.

ROW 3: *P4, sl 1 wyb (slipping together with yon from Row 2), p2; rep from * to last 2 sts, p2.

ROW 4: K2tog, yo, *k2, sl 1 wyf (slipping together with yon from Row 2), k2, k2tog, yo; rep from *.

ROW 5: Rep Row 3.

ROW 6: K2, *k2, combo tuck stitch (see Stitch Guide), k4; rep from *.

Rep Rows 1–6 for patt.

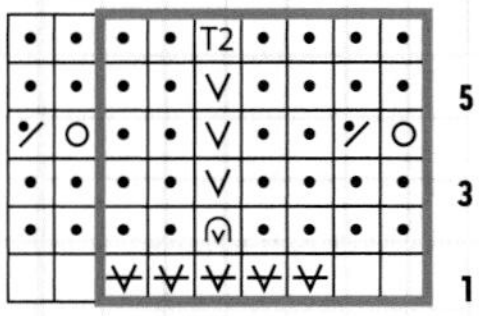

- knit on RS, purl on WS
- purl on RS, knit on WS
- sl pwise wyb on RS, wyf on WS (include yon if necessary)
- sl pwise wyf on RS, wyb on WS
- T2 combo tuck st (see Stitch Guide)
- sl 1 wyon
- yo
- k2tog on WS
- pattern repeat

TRAVELING STREAMS

(MULTIPLE OF 7 STS)

– Can be worked with yarn of any weight.

ROW 1: (RS) *(K1, p2) twice, k1; rep from *.

ROW 2: *(P1, k2) twice, p1; rep from *.

INC ROW 3: *K1, p2, RLI (see Glossary), k1, p2, k1; rep from *—1 st inc'd per each repeat.

ROWS 4, 6, AND 8: *P1, k2, sl 1 wyf, p1, k2, p1; rep from *.

ROWS 5 AND 7: *K1, p2, k1, sl 1 wyb, p2, k1; rep from *.

DEC ROW 9: *K1, p2, k1, Dec-1/2 RC (see Stitch Guide); rep from *—1 st dec'd per each repeat.

ROW 10: Rep Row 2.

INC ROW 11: *RLI, (k1, p2) twice, k1; rep from *—1 st inc'd per each repeat.

ROWS 12, 14, AND 16: *(P1, k2) twice, sl 1 wyf, p1; rep from *.

ROWS 13 AND 15: *K1, sl 1 wyb, (p2, k1) twice; rep from *.

DEC ROW 17: K1, Dec-1/2 RC, p2, k1; rep from *—1 st dec'd per each repeat.

ROW 18: Rep Row 2.

Rep Rows 3–18 for patt.

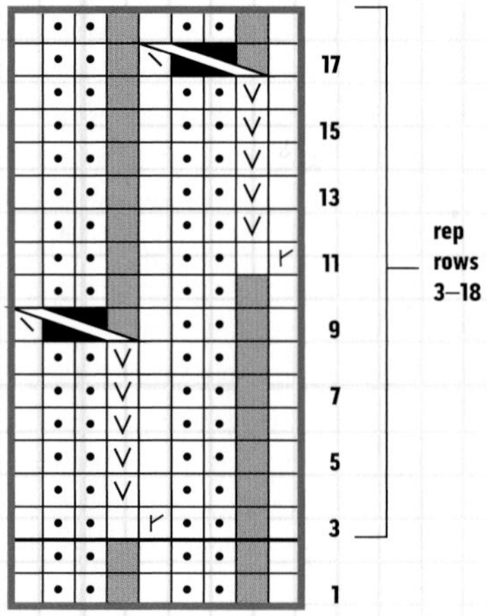

- knit on RS, purl on WS
- purl on RS, knit on WS
- sl pwise wyb on RS, wyf on WS
- RLI (see Glossary)
- no stitch
- Dec-1/2 RC
- pattern repeat

DAINTY SILK STITCH
(MULTIPLE OF 10 STS)

— Reversible.

— Light and open fabric.

— Great for shawls and scarves.

ROW 1: (RS) *K5, p5; rep from *.

ROW 2: *Yo, p2tog-tbl, p1, p2tog, yo, k5; rep from *.

ROW 3: *P2, sl 1 wyon (see Stitch Guide), p2, k1, yo, sl2tog-k1-p2sso (see Stitch Guide), yo, k1; rep from *.

ROW 4: *P2tog, yo, p1, yo, p2tog-tbl, k2, sl 1 wyon, k2; rep from *.

ROW 5: *P2, sl 1 wyon, p2, k5; rep from *.

ROW 6: *P5, k2, pT3-yon (see Stitch Guide), k2; rep from *.

ROW 7: *P5, k5; rep from *.

ROW 8: *K5, yo, p2tog-tbl, p1, p2tog, yo; rep from *.

ROW 9: *K1, yo, sl2tog-k1-p2sso, yo, k1, p2, sl 1 wyon, p2; rep from *.

ROW 10: *K2, sl 1 wyon, k2, p2tog, yo, p1, yo, p2tog-tbl; rep from *.

ROW 11: *K5, p2, sl 1 wyon, p2; rep from *.

ROW 12: *K2, pT3-yon, k2, p5; rep from *.

Rep Rows 1–12 for patt.

•	•	T3	•	•						
•	•	⋒	•	•						**11**
•	•	⋒	•	•	∕	o		o	∖	
•	•	⋒	•	•		o	⋏	o		**9**
•	•	•	•	•	o	∖		∕	o	
					•	∖	•	∕	•	**7**
					•	•	T3	•	•	
					•	•	⋒	•	•	**5**
∕	o		o	∖	•	•	⋒	•	•	
	o	⋏	o		•	•	⋒	•	•	**3**
o	∖		∕	o	•	•	•	•	•	
•	•	•	•	•						**1**

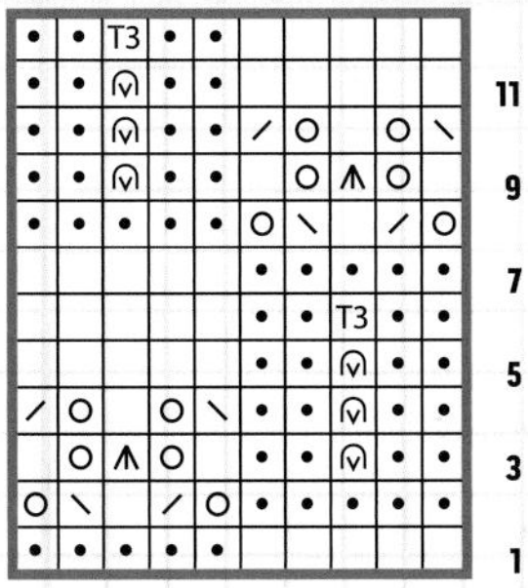

☐	knit on RS, purl on WS
•	purl on RS, knit on WS
T3	pT3-yon on WS
⋒	sl 1 wyon
o	yo
∕	k2tog on RS, p2tog on WS
∖	ssk on RS, p2tog-tbl on WS
⋏	sl2tog-k1-p2sso (see Stitch Guide)
☐	pattern repeat

WATER LILY

(MULTIPLE OF 7 STS + 3)

- Choose two yarns of different weights for a bolder effect.
- Two-color swatch. Green is named A, white is named B.

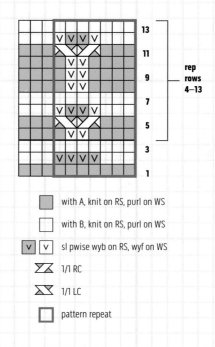

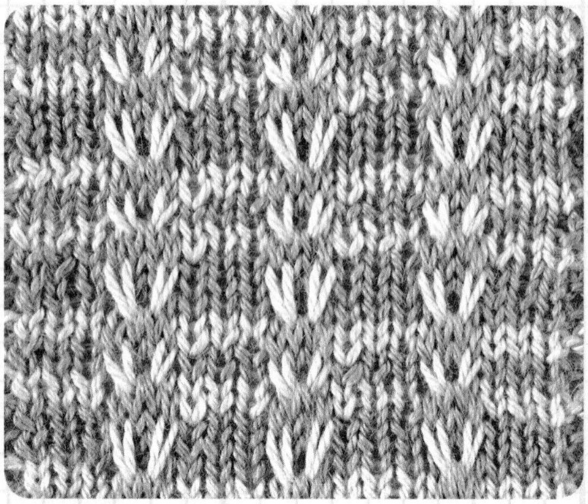

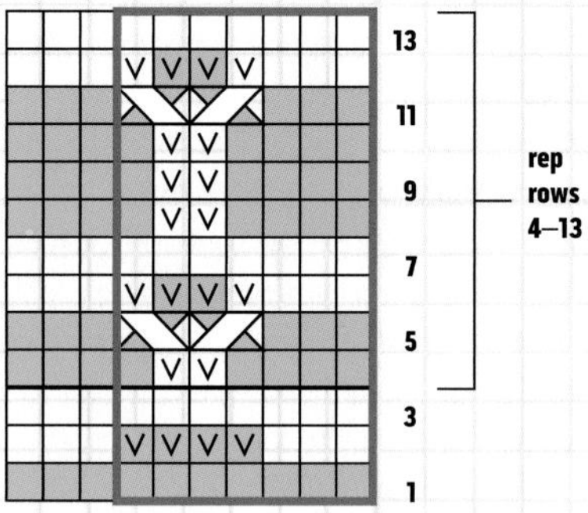

with A, knit on RS, purl on WS

with B, knit on RS, purl on WS

sl pwise wyb on RS, wyf on WS

1/1 RC

1/1 LC

pattern repeat

ROW 1: (RS) With A, knit.

ROW 2: With B, *p3, sl 4 wyf; rep from * to last 3 sts, p3.

ROW 3: With B, knit.

ROWS 4, 8, AND 10: With A, p3, *p1, sl 2 wyf, p4; rep from *.

ROWS 5 AND 11: With A, *k3, 1/1 RC (see Stitch Guide), 1/1 LC (see Stitch Guide); rep from * to last 3 sts, k3.

ROWS 6 AND 7: Rep Rows 2 and 3.

ROW 9: With A, *k4, sl 2 wyb, k1; rep from * to last 3 sts, k3.

ROWS 12 AND 13: Rep Rows 2 and 3.

Rep Rows 4–13 for patt.

FLOWING RIBBONS

(MULTIPLE OF 36 STS)

– Reversible.

– Solid-color yarn shows pattern best.

– Not bulky fabric.

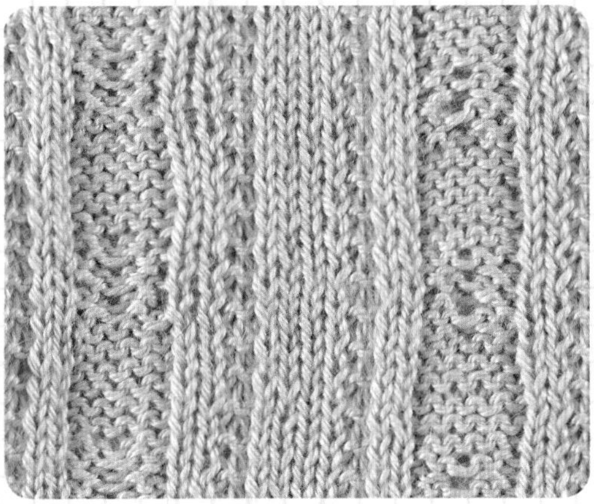

ROWS 1, 3, AND 11: (RS) *P2, sl 2 wyf, p2, k6, (p2, sl 2 wyf, p2) twice, k6, p2, sl 2 wyf, p2; rep from *.

ROW 2: *K2, p2, k2, p6, (k2, p2, k2) twice, p6, k2, p2, k2; rep from *.

ROWS 4, 6, AND 8: *K2, p2, k2, p2, sl 2 wyf, p2, (k2, p2, k2) twice, sl 1 wyf, p4, sl 1 wyf, k2, p2, k2; rep from *.

ROWS 5, 7, AND 9: *P2, sl 2 wyf, p2, 1/2 LC (see Stitch Guide), 1/2 RC (see Stitch Guide), (p2, sl 2 wyf, p2) twice, 1/2 RC, 1/2 LC, p2, sl 2 wyf, p2; rep from *.

ROWS 10 AND 12: Rep Row 2.

Rep Rows 1–12 for patt.

- knit on RS, purl on WS
- purl on RS, knit on WS
- sl 1 wyf on WS
- sl pwise wyf on RS
- 1/2 RC
- 1/2 LC
- pattern repeat

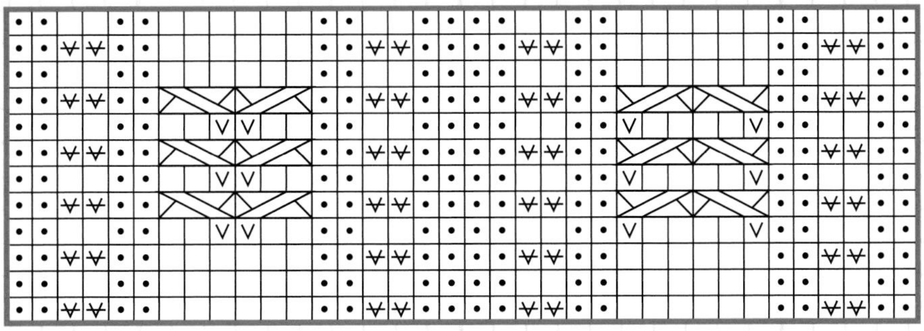

THE SWEATER is worked in a classic top-down raglan construction with a carefully placed slip-stitch cable panel at center front and a slipped checks pattern on sleeves. The sweater is fitted, and its hourglass silhouette is achieved by decreases for waist and consequently increases for hips. The neckline and borders for sleeves and hemline are worked in a slipped rib pattern. || *designed by* **FAINA GOBERSTEIN**

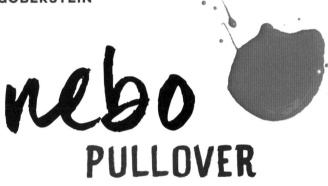

nebo PULLOVER

FINISHED SIZES
34¾ (38, 42½, 46¼, 50¾, 53, 55¾, 57½)" (88.5 [96.5, 108, 117.5, 129, 134.5, 141.5, 146] cm) bust.

Sweater shown measures 34¾" (88.5 cm).

YARN
Sportweight (#2 Fine).

Shown here: Bijou Basin Ranch Lhasa Wilderness (75% yak down, 25% bamboo; 250 yd [228 m]/2.7 oz [76 g]): skye, 4 (5, 5, 6, 6, 7, 8, 8) skeins.

NEEDLES
Body and Sleeves: Size U.S. 4 (3.5 mm): 32" (81.5 cm) circular (cir) and set of 5 double-pointed (dpn).

Ribbing: Size U.S. 3 (3.25 mm): 16" (40.5 cm) cir and set of 4 or 5 dpn.

Adjust needle sizes if necessary to obtain the correct gauge.

NOTIONS
Markers (m); stitch holders or waste yarn; tapestry needle.

GAUGE
23 sts and 32 rows = 4" (10 cm) in St st with larger needle.

25 sts and 34 rows = 4" (10 cm) in slipped check pattern with larger needle.

35 sts and 36 rows = 4" (10 cm) in slipped cable pattern with larger needle.

NOTES
Piece is worked top down, beginning at neckline. Yoke is worked back and forth in rows then joined at the neck and worked in the round to underarms.

At underarms, the sleeves are separated from body and placed onto stitch holders; the front and back are joined to work in the round to the hem.

Sleeves are finished by working in the round.

Body is worked in St st throughout with Front Panel Chart at center front. Sleeves are worked in slipped checks pattern.

Markers are placed at the beginning of the round (the left side of body), to mark raglan armholes and at outer edges of Front Panel Chart; slip markers (sl m) as you come to them.

Stitch count differs for back and front to accommodate for the stitch gauge of Front Panel Chart.

STITCH GUIDE

SLIPPED RIB

(multiple of 3 sts)

RND 1: *Sl 1, p2; rep from *.

RND 2: *K1, p2; rep from *.

Rep Rnds 1 and 2 for patt.

TIPS

- Use markers in three different colors; one color for the beginning of the round at left back/sleeve and left side of body, a second color for the raglan armholes, and third to indicate placement of Front Panel Chart.
- Keep floats of slipped sts relaxed.

yoke

Using larger cir, CO 2 (2, 4, 4, 6, 8, 8, 8) sts for right front, pm, 1 st for raglan, pm, 15 (15, 15, 15, 15, 15, 17, 19) sts for right sleeve, pm, 1 st for raglan, pm, 36 (40, 42, 44, 46, 46, 46, 48) sts for back neck, pm, 1 st for raglan, pm, 15 (15, 15, 15, 15, 15, 17, 19) sts for left sleeve, pm, 1 st for raglan, pm, 2 (2, 4, 4, 6, 8, 8, 8) sts for left front—74 (78, 84, 86, 92, 96, 100, 106) sts. Do not join; work back and forth in rows.

SHAPE RAGLAN

NEXT ROW: (WS) Purl.

INC ROW: (RS) *Knit to m, M1R (see Glossary), sl m, k1, sl m, M1L (see Glossary), work Row 1 of slipped checks patt to next m, M1R, sl m, k1, sl m, M1L; rep from * once more, knit to end—8 sts inc'd.

Rep the last 2 rows 5 more times—122 (126, 132, 134, 140, 144, 148, 154) sts; 8 (8, 10, 10, 12, 14, 14, 14) sts each front, 27 (27, 27, 27, 27, 27, 29, 31) sts each sleeve, and 48 (52, 54, 56, 58, 58, 58, 60) sts for back.

SHAPE RAGLAN AND NECK

Note: The following rows gradually introduce the front panel without using the chart, while continuing to inc raglan.

ROW 1: (RS) K1 f&b, work inc row to last st, k1 f&b—10 sts inc'd.

ROW 2: (WS) P1, k1, work in est patt to last 2 sts, k1, p1.

ROW 3: K1 f&b, p1, work inc row to last 2 sts, p1, k1 f&b—10 sts inc'd.

ROW 4: P1, k2, work in est patt to last 3 sts, k2, p1.

ROW 5: K1 f&b, p2, work inc row to last 3 sts, p2, k1 f&b—10 sts inc'd.

ROW 6: P2, k2, work in est patt to last 4 sts, k2, p2.

ROW 7: K1 f&b, sl 1 wyb, p2, work inc row to last 4 sts, p2, sl 1 wyb, k1 f&b—10 sts inc'd.

ROW 8: P1, k1, p1, k2, work in est patt to last 5 sts, k2, p1, k1, p1.

ROW 9: K1 f&b, p1, sl 1 wyb, p2, work inc row to last 5 sts, p2, sl 1 wyb, p1, k1 f&b—10 sts inc'd.

ROW 10: P2, k1, p1, k2, work in est patt to last 6 sts, k2, p1, k1, p2.

ROW 11: K1 f&b, (sl 1 wyb, p1) twice, p1, work inc row to last 6 sts, p1, (p1, sl 1 wyb) twice, k1 f&b—10 sts inc'd.

ROW 12: (P1, k1) 3 times, k1, pm of a different color for Front Panel Chart, work in est patt to last 7 sts, pm of a different color for Front Panel Chart, k1, (k1, p1) 3 times.

Cont increasing 10 sts every RS row as est 1 (1, 1, 2, 3, 3, 4, 4) more time(s) and working new sts in St st, and ending after a WS row—192 (196, 202, 214, 230, 234, 248, 254) sts; 22 (22, 24, 26, 30, 32, 34, 34) sts each front, 41 (41, 41, 43, 45, 45, 49, 51) sts each sleeve, and 62 (66, 68, 72, 76, 76, 78, 80) sts for back.

NEXT ROW: (RS) K1 (1, 1, 2, 3, 3, 4, 4), p2, sl 1 wyb, p1, sl 1 wyb, p2, work inc row to last 8 (8, 8, 9, 10, 10, 11, 11) sts, p2, sl 1 wyb, p1, sl 1 wyb, p2, k1 (1, 1, 2, 3, 3, 4, 4), use backward loop method (see Glossary) to CO 30 (30, 30, 28, 26, 26, 24, 24) sts for front neck. Join for working in the rnd—230 (234, 240, 250, 264, 268, 280, 286) sts; 76 (76, 80, 82, 88, 92, 94, 94) sts for front, 43 (43, 43, 45, 47, 47, 51, 53) sts each sleeve and 64 (68, 70, 74, 78, 78, 80, 82) sts for back.

SHIFT BEG OF RND: K1 (1, 1, 2, 3, 3, 4, 4), p2, k1, p1, k1, p2, knit to 2 sts before next m, pm with third colored m for beg of rnd. Beg of rnd m is on the left front.

BODY

NEXT RND: Knit left front sts to m, sl m, k1, sl m, work left sleeve sts in slipped checks patt as est to next m, sl m, k1, sl m, knit across back sts to next m, sl m, k1, sl m, work right sleeve sts in slipped checks patt as est to next m, sl m, k1, sl m, knit across right front sts to next m, sl m, work Rnd 1 of front panel to next m, sl m, knit rem left front sts to end of rnd.

SHAPE RAGLAN

INC RND: *Work in est patt to m, M1R, sl m, k1, sl m, M1L; rep from * 3 more times, work in est patt to end of rnd—8 sts inc'd.

NEXT RND: Work even in est patt.

Rep the last 2 rnds 12 (14, 16, 19, 20, 21, 25, 26) more times—334 (354, 376, 410, 432, 444, 488, 502) sts; 102 (106, 114, 122, 130, 136, 146, 148) sts for front, 69 (73, 77, 85, 89, 91, 103, 107) sts each sleeve, and 90 (98, 104, 114, 120, 122, 132, 136) sts for back.

SEPARATE SLEEVES FROM BODY

NOTE: Raglan sts are added to front and back.

Remove beg of rnd m.

NEXT RND: Knit left front sts to m, remove m, k1, remove m, place next 69 (73, 77, 85, 89, 91, 103, 107) sts on st holder or waste yarn for left sleeve, remove raglan m, use twisted backward loop method to CO 5 (7, 10, 11, 14, 15, 14, 15) sts, pm for left side and new beg of rnd, CO another 5 (7, 10, 11, 14, 15, 14, 15) sts, k1, remove m, knit across back to raglan m, remove m, k1, remove m, place next 69 (73, 77, 85, 89, 91, 103, 107) sts on st holder or waste yarn for right sleeve, CO 5 (7, 10, 11, 14, 15, 14, 15) sts, pm in for right side, CO another 5 (7, 10, 11, 14, 15, 14, 15) sts, remove m, k1, remove m, work across front sts in est patt to new beg of rnd m—216 (234, 260, 282, 308, 320, 336, 346) sts; 114 (122, 136, 146, 160, 168, 176, 180) sts for front and 102 (112, 124, 136, 148, 152, 160, 166) sts for back.

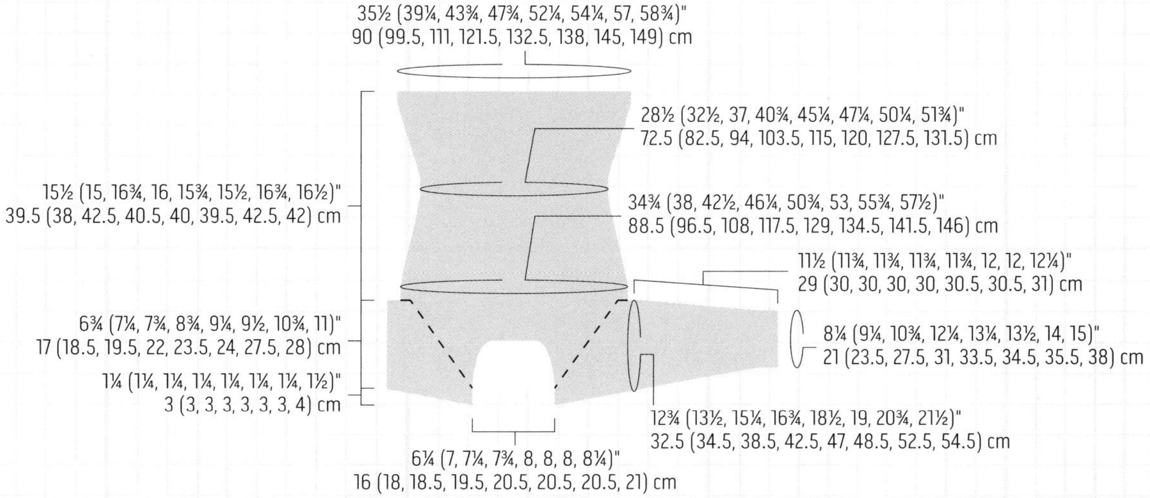

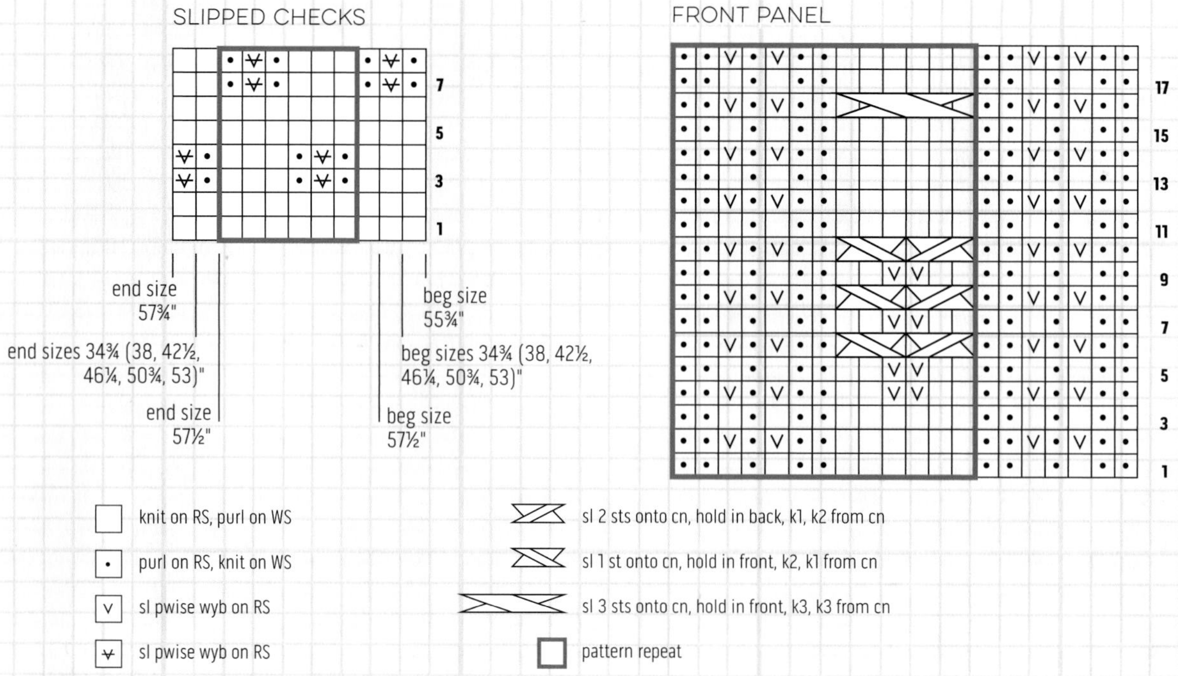

body

NEXT RND: Knit to front panel m, sl m, work Front Panel Chart to next m, sl m, knit to end.

Rep the last rnd 7 (7, 7, 5, 5, 5, 5, 5) more times.

SHAPE WAIST

DEC RND: *K1, ssk, work in patt as est to 3 sts before m, k2tog, k1 sl m; rep from * once more—4 sts dec'd.

Work 5 rnds even in patt.

Rep the last 6 rnds 8 (4, 4, 5, 4, 4, 4, 5) more times—180 (214, 240, 258, 288, 300, 316, 322) sts rem; 96 (112, 126, 134, 150, 158, 166, 168) sts for front and 84 (102, 114, 124, 138, 142, 150, 154) sts for back.

[Rep dec rnd, then work 7 rnds even in patt] 0 (3, 3, 2, 3, 3, 3, 2) times—180 (202, 228, 250, 276, 288, 304, 314) sts rem; 96 (106, 120, 130, 144, 152, 160, 164) sts for front and 84 (96, 108, 120, 132, 136, 144, 150) sts for back.

Work even in patt until piece meas 9" (23 cm) from underarm divide.

SHAPE HIPS

INC RND: *K1, M1R, work in patt as est to 1 st before m, M1L, k1 sl m; rep from * once more—4 sts inc'd.

Work 3 rnds even in patt.

Rep the last 4 rnds 6 (8, 3, 4, 5, 6, 2, 3) more times—208 (238, 244, 270, 300, 316, 316, 330) sts; 110 (124, 128, 140, 156, 166, 166, 172) sts for front and 98 (114, 116, 130, 144, 150, 150, 158) sts for back.

[Rep inc rnd, then work 5 rnds even in patt] 3 (1, 6, 5, 4, 3, 7, 6) time(s)—220 (242, 268, 290, 316, 328, 344, 354) sts; 116 (126, 140, 150, 164, 172, 180, 184) sts for front and 104 (116, 128, 140, 152, 156, 164, 170) sts for back.

Work even in patt until piece meas about 14¾ (14¼, 14¾, 15¼, 15, 14¾, 16, 15¾)" (37.5 [36, 37.5, 38.5, 38, 37.5, 40.5, 40] cm) from underarm divide, ending after Rnd 2 of Front Panel Chart.

INC RND: Work in patt as est and inc 4 (2, 1, 4, 3, 1, 0, 0) sts evenly spaced across back—224 (244, 269, 294, 319, 329, 344, 354) sts; 116 (126, 140, 150, 164, 172, 180, 184) sts for front and 108 (118, 129, 144, 155, 157, 164, 170) sts for back.

HEM

Remove beg of rnd m, k0 (0, 3, 3, 1, 2, 3, 1), pm for new beg of rnd, shifting beg of rnd to the left. On the following rnd, remove side m as you pass it.

SET-UP RND: *Sl 1, p1, sl 1, p2; rep from * to 3 sts before front panel m, sl 1, p1, sl 1, sl m, p2, sl 1, p1, sl 1, p2, sl 1, p2tog, [(sl 1, p1, sl 1, p2) twice, sl 1, p2tog] twice, **sl 1, p1, sl 1, p2; rep from ** to end—221 (241, 266, 291, 316, 326, 341, 351) sts rem.

RND 1: *K1, p1, k1, p2; rep from * to 3 sts before front panel m, k1, p1, k1, sl m, p2, k1, p1, k1, p2, k1, p1, [(k1, p1, k1, p2) twice, k1, p1] twice, **k1, p1, k1, p2; rep from ** to end.

RND 2: *Sl 1, p1, sl 1, p2; rep from * to 3 sts before front panel m, sl 1, p1, sl 1, sl m, p2, sl 1, p1, sl 1, p2, sl 1, p1, [(sl 1, p1, sl 1, p2) twice, sl 1, p1] twice, **sl 1, p1, sl 1, p2; rep from ** to end.

Rep the last 2 rnds once, then work Rnd 1 once more.

Loosely BO in patt.

SLEEVES

Place 69 (73, 77, 85, 89, 91, 103, 107) held sts from one sleeve onto larger dpn. With RS facing, beg at center of underarm CO sts, join new ball of yarn, pick up and knit 5 (6, 9, 10, 13, 14, 13, 14) sts along first half of underarm CO sts, work in patt as est over sleeve sts, pick up and knit 5 (6, 9, 10, 13, 14, 13, 14) sts along rem underarm sts—79 (85, 95, 105, 115, 119, 129, 135) sts. Join to work in rnds, pm for beg of rnd

Work even in est patt for 1" (2.5 cm).

SHAPE SLEEVE

DEC RND: K1, k2tog, work in patt to last 3 sts, ssk, k1—2 sts dec'd.

Work 3 (3, 3, 3, 3, 3, 1, 1) rnd(s) even in patt.

Rep the last 4 (4, 4, 4, 4, 4, 2, 2) rnds 3 (2, 2, 2, 8, 10, 2, 1) more time(s)—71 (79, 89, 99, 97, 97, 123, 131) sts rem.

[Rep dec rnd, then work 5 (5, 5, 5, 5, 5, 3, 3) rnds even] 9 (10, 10, 10, 6, 5, 17, 18) times, then rep dec rnd once more—51 (57, 67, 77, 83, 85, 87, 93) sts rem.

Work even in patt until sleeve meas 10¾ (11, 11, 11, 11, 11¼, 11¼, 11½)" (27.5 [28, 28, 28, 28, 28.5, 28.5, 29] cm) from underarm.

DEC RND: Dec 0 (0, 1, 2, 2, 1, 0, 0) sts evenly around—51 (57, 66, 75, 81, 84, 87, 93) sts.

Switch to smaller dpn.

NEXT RND: *Sl 1, p2; rep from * to end.

NEXT RND: *K1, p2; rep from * to end.

Rep the last 2 rnds 2 more times.

BO all sts in patt using larger needle.

Work second sleeve the same as the first.

finishing

Block to measurements.

NECKBAND

With smaller cir and RS facing, beg at right back raglan line, pick up and knit 37 (41, 43, 45, 47, 47, 47, 49) sts along back neck, 17 (17, 17, 17, 17, 17, 19, 21) along left sleeve, 18 (21, 20, 23, 24, 24, 25, 25) sts along left neck, 31 (30, 30, 28, 27, 27, 24, 24) sts across front panel, 18 (21, 20, 23, 24, 24, 25, 25) sts along right neck, and 17 (17, 17, 17, 17, 17, 19, 21) sts along right sleeve—138 (147, 147, 153, 156, 156, 159, 165) sts total. Pm and join to work in the rnd.

Work slipped rib for 6 rnds. BO all sts in patt. Weave in ends.

MAKE IT YOURS

- Make the sleeves shorter by using the same decrease sequence and stopping at your desired length.
- Make the sleeves wider by skipping all decreases.
- Change the front panel to any other stitch pattern or combination of patterns. Make sure that the 46-st panel of your choice is 5¼" (13.5 cm) wide.
- Change neckline rib to a rolled edge.

THIS IS A perfect beginners' project because there's almost no shaping involved. The rectangular vest is worked sideways from the right front edge across back to the left front edge, casting off and then casting on stitches for armhole openings.

// designed by **SIMONA MERCHANT-DEST**

káva VEST

FINISHED SIZE

About 32 (36, 40, 44, 48, 52, 56)" (81.5 [91.5, 101.5, 112, 122, 132, 142] cm) bust circumference.

Vest shown measures 36" (91.5 cm).

YARN

Chunky weight (#5 Bulky).

Shown here: Cascade Ecological Wool (100% natural Peruvian wool; 478 yd [437 m]/1¾ oz [250 g]): tarnish 8049, 1 (2, 2, 2, 2, 2, 2) skeins.

NEEDLES

Size U.S. 9 (5.5 mm): 32" (80 cm) circular (cir).

Adjust needle size if necessary to obtain the correct gauge.

NOTIONS

Markers (m); tapestry needle; stitch holders or waste yarn.

GAUGE

13 sts and 20 rows = 4" (10 cm) in St st.

12.5 sts and 26 rows = 4" (10 cm) in slip-stitch patt. *Note: When blocking swatch in slip-stitch pattern, stretch your fabric lengthwise (vertically) to ensure the opened look of the slip-stitch pattern.*

16 sts and 20 rows = 4" (10 cm) in 3x2 rib.

NOTES

As you work the project, measure lengths of blocked fabric to ensure that you will end up with correct circumference measurements. If measuring unblocked fabric, measure in number of rows per inch to ensure correct measurement after blocking.

Unless otherwise specified, all slipped stitches are slipped purlwise with yarn carried over the needle as if to make a yarnover (wyon). In the following row, the slipped stitch and the yarn float are worked together as one stitch.

The slip-stitch pattern used here has a smaller gauge (fewer stitches per inch) than stockinette stitch, so we need to change the number of stitches between these two patterns to keep the width of the fabric the same.

Vest is reversible. Shown on page 123 (left) as knit; reverse side shown opposite.

STITCH GUIDE

SL 1 WYON (SLIP ONE WITH YARN OVER NEEDLE)

Slip 1 stitch purlwise carrying yarn float over the needle from front to back (see Glossary).

T1-YON

Knit 1 stitch together with the yarn float carried over the needle in previous row.

PT1-YON

Purl 1 stitch together with the yarn float carried over the needle in previous row.

3X2 RIB

(multiple of 5 sts + 3)

ROW 1: (WS) *P3, k2; rep from * to last 3 sts, p3.

ROW 2: *K3, p2; rep from * to last 3 sts, k3.

Rep Rows 1 and 2 for patt.

SLIP-STITCH PATT

(multiple of 2 sts + 1)

ROW 1: (RS) *Sl 1 wyon, p1; rep from * to last st, sl 1 wyon.

ROW 2: *T1-yon, sl 1 wyon; rep from * to last st, k1tog-w-float.

ROW 3: *Sl 1 wyon, pT1-yon; rep from * to last st, sl 1 wyon.

ROW 4: *T1-yon, sl 1 wyon; rep from * to last st, k1tog-w-float.

Rep Rows 3 and 4 for patt.

right front

With cir needle, CO 118 (118, 118, 123, 123, 123, 123) sts. Do not join; work back and forth in rows.

FRONT BAND

Work 7 rows in 3×2 rib, ending after a WS row. Piece meas about 1½" (3.8 cm) from beg.

BEGIN STOCKINETTE ST

DEC ROW: (RS) K3, p1, pm, knit and dec 23 (22, 20, 24, 23, 22, 20) sts evenly spaced across to last 4 sts, pm, p1, k3—95 (96, 98, 99, 100, 101, 103) sts rem.

NEXT ROW: (WS) K1, p2, k1, sl m, purl to last 4 sts, sl m, k1, p2, k1.

NEXT ROW: K3, p1, knit to m, p1, k3.

Rep last 2 rows until piece meas 2½ (2¾, 3, 3¼, 3½, 3¾, 4)" (6.5 [7, 7.5, 8.5,

9, 9.5, 10] cm) from beg, ending after a RS row.

DEC ROW: (WS) K1, p2, k1, remove m, purl and dec 8 (7, 7, 8, 7, 8, 8) sts evenly across to last 4 sts, remove m, k1, p2, k1—87 (89, 91, 91, 93, 93, 95) sts rem.

BEGIN SLIP-STITCH PATT

ROW 1: (RS) K2, sl 1 wyb, pm, work Row 1 of slip-stitch patt to last 3 sts, pm, sl 1 wyb, k2.

ROW 2: K1, p1, sl 1 wyf, sl m, work Row 2 of slip-stitch patt to last 3 sts, sl m, sl 1 wyf, p1, k1.

ROW 3: K1, sl 1 wyb, k1, sl m, work Row 3 of slip-stitch patt to m, sl m, k1, sl 1 wyb, k1.

ROW 4: P1, sl 1 wyf, p1, sl m, work Row 4 of slip-stitch patt to m, sl m, p1, sl 1 wyf, p1.

ROW 5: K2, sl 1 wyb, pm, work Row 3 of slip-stitch patt to m, sl m, sl 1 wyb, k2.

ROW 6: K1, p1, sl 1 wyf, sl m, work Row 4 of slip-stitch patt to m, sl m, sl 1 wyf, p1, k1.

Rep the last 4 rows until piece meas 5 (5½, 6, 6½, 7, 7½, 8)" (12.5 [14, 15, 16.5, 18, 19, 20.5] cm) from beg, ending after a WS row.

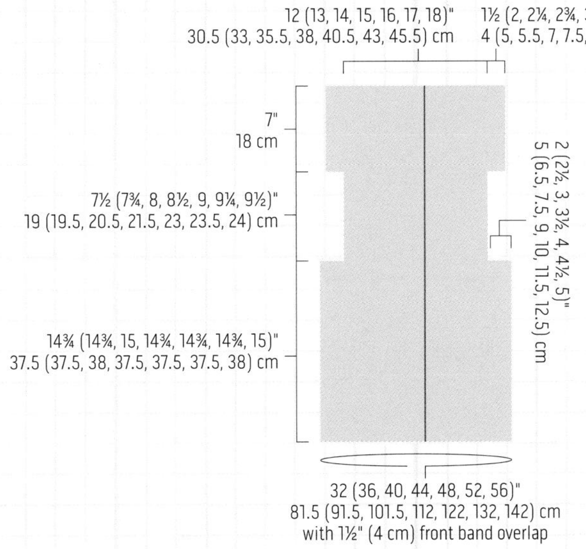

BEGIN STOCKINETTE ST

INC ROW: (RS) K3, remove m, p1, pm, knit and inc 8 (7, 7, 8, 7, 8, 8) sts evenly spaced across to last 4 sts, pm, p1, remove m, k3—95 (96, 98, 99, 100, 101, 103) sts.

NEXT ROW: K1, p2, k1, sl m, purl to last 4 sts, sl m, k1, p2, k1.

NEXT ROW: K3, p1, knit to m, p1, k3.

Rep the last 2 rows until piece meas 6¾ (7¼, 7¾, 8¼, 8¾, 9¼, 9¾)" (17 [18.5, 19.5, 21, 22, 23.5, 25] cm) from beg, ending after a WS row.

SHAPE RIGHT ARMHOLE

NEXT ROW: (RS) K3, p1, sl m, k19 for collar, BO 24 (25, 26, 28, 29, 30, 31) sts, knit to last 4 sts, sl m, p1, k3—23 collar sts rem and 48 (48, 49, 48, 48, 48, 49) body sts rem.

Place first 23 sts onto st holder or waste yarn for collar. Cont working body sts as foll:

right body

Cont in patt as est over last 48 (48, 49, 48, 48, 48, 49) sts until piece meas 10¾ (12¼, 13¾, 15¼, 16¾, 18¼, 19¾)" (27.5 [31, 35, 38.5, 42.5, 46.5, 50] cm) from beg, and 4 (5, 6, 7, 8, 9, 10)" (10 [12.5, 15, 18, 20.5, 23, 25.5] cm) from armhole BO edge, ending after a RS row. Place sts onto st holder or waste yarn and set aside, keeping yarn attached.

right collar

Return 23 held collar sts to needle and join yarn preparing to work a WS row. Work in patt as est until piece meas 3 (4, 4½, 5½, 6, 6½, 7)" (7.5 [10, 11.5, 14, 15, 16.5, 18] cm) from armhole BO edge, ending after a RS row. Break yarn.

Return 48 (48, 49, 48, 48, 48, 49) held right body sts to needle holding the right collar sts, and with WS facing cont as foll:

JOINING ROW: (WS) Work in patt over 48 (48, 49, 48, 48, 48, 49) body sts, turn to RS and use knitted method (see Glossary) to CO 24 (25, 26, 28, 29, 30, 31) sts for armhole, turn to WS, work in patt over 23 collar sts to end—95 (96, 98, 99, 100, 101, 103) sts.

back

Work in patt until piece meas 12½ (14, 15½, 17, 18½, 20, 21½)" (31.5 [35.5, 39.5, 43, 47, 51, 54.5] cm) from beg, and 1¾" (4.5 cm) from right armhole CO edge, ending after a RS row.

DEC ROW: (WS) K1, p2, k1, remove m, purl and dec 8 (7, 7, 8, 7, 8, 8) sts evenly across to last 4 sts, remove m, k1, p2, k1—87 (89, 91, 91, 93, 93, 95) sts rem.

BEGIN SLIP-STITCH PATT

ROW 1: (RS) K2, sl 1 wyb, pm, work Row 1 of slip-stitch patt to last 3 sts, pm, sl 1 wyb, k2.

ROW 2: K1, p1, sl 1 wyf, sl m, work Row 2 of slip-stitch patt to last 3 sts, sl m, sl 1 wyf, p1, k1.

ROW 3: K1, sl 1 wyb, k1, sl m, work Row 3 of slip-stitch patt to m, sl m, k1, sl 1 wyb, k1.

ROW 4: P1, sl 1 wyf, p1, sl m, work Row 4 of slip-stitch patt to m, sl m, p1, sl 1 wyf, p1.

ROW 5: K2, sl 1 wyb, pm, work Row 3 of slip-stitch patt to m, sl m, sl 1 wyb, k2.

ROW 6: K1, p1, sl 1 wyf, sl m, work Row 4 of slip-stitch patt to m, sl m, sl 1 wyf, p1, k1.

Rep the last 4 rows until piece meas 21 (23½, 26, 28½, 31, 33½, 36)" (53.5 [59.5, 66, 72.5, 79, 85, 91.5] cm) from beg, and 10¼ (11¼, 12¼, 13¼, 14¼, 15¼, 16¼)" (26 [28.5, 31, 33.5, 36, 38.5, 41.5] cm) from right armhole CO edge, ending after a WS row.

BEGIN STOCKINETTE ST

INC ROW: (RS) K3, remove m, p1, pm, knit and inc 8 (7, 7, 8, 7, 8, 8) sts evenly spaced across to last 4 sts, pm, p1, remove m, k3—95 (96, 98, 99, 100, 101, 103) sts.

NEXT ROW: (WS) K1, p2, k1, sl m, purl to last 4 sts, sl m, k1, p2, k1.

NEXT ROW: K3, p1, knit to m, p1, k3.

Rep the last 2 rows until piece meas 22¾ (25¼, 27¾, 30¼, 32¾, 35¼, 37¾)" (58 [64, 70.5, 77, 83, 89.5, 96] cm) from beg, and 12 (13, 14, 15, 16, 17, 18)" (30.5 [33, 35.5, 38, 40.5, 43, 45.5] cm) from right armhole CO edge, ending after a WS row.

SHAPE LEFT ARMHOLE

NEXT ROW: (RS) K3, p1, sl m, k19 for collar, BO 24 (25, 26, 28, 29, 30, 31) sts, knit to last 4 sts, sl m, p1, k3—23 collar sts rem and 48 (48, 49, 48, 48, 48, 49) body sts rem.

Place first 23 sts onto st holder or waste yarn for collar. Cont working body sts as foll:

left body

Cont in patt as est over last 48 (48, 49, 48, 48, 48, 49) sts until piece meas 26¾ (30¼, 33¾, 37¼, 40¾, 44¼, 47¾)" (68 [77, 85.5, 94.5, 103.5, 112.5, 121.5] cm) from beg, and 4 (5, 6, 7, 8, 9, 10)" (10 [12.5, 15, 18, 20.5, 23, 25.5] cm) from armhole BO edge, ending after a RS row. Place sts onto st holder or waste yarn and set aside, keeping yarn attached.

left collar

Return 23 held collar sts to needle and join yarn preparing to work a WS row. Work in patt as est until piece meas 3 (4, 4½, 5½, 6, 6½, 7)" (7.5 [10, 11.5, 14, 15, 16.5, 18] cm) from armhole BO edge, ending after a RS row. Break yarn.

Return 48 (48, 49, 48, 48, 48, 49) held left body sts to needle holding the left collar sts, and with WS facing cont as foll:

JOINING ROW: (WS) Work in patt over 48 (48, 49, 48, 48, 48, 49) body sts, turn to RS, use knitted method to CO 24 (25, 26, 28, 29, 30, 31) sts for armhole, turn to WS, work in patt over 23 collar sts to end—95 (96, 98, 99, 100, 101, 103) sts.

left front

Work in patt until piece meas 28½ (32, 35½, 39, 42½, 46, 49½)" (72.5 [81.5, 90, 99, 108, 117, 125.5] cm) from beg, and 1¾" (4.5 cm) from left armhole CO edge, ending after a RS row.

DEC ROW: (WS) K1, p2, k1, remove m, purl and dec 8 (7, 7, 8, 7, 8, 8) sts evenly across to last 4 sts, remove m, k1, p2, k1—87 (89, 91, 91, 93, 93, 95) sts.

BEGIN SLIP-STITCH PATT

ROW 1: (RS) K2, sl 1 wyb, pm, work Row 1 of slip-stitch patt to last 3 sts, pm, sl 1 wyb, k2.

ROW 2: K1, p1, sl 1 wyf, sl m, work Row 2 of slip-stitch patt to last 3 sts, sl m, sl 1 wyf, p1, k1.

ROW 3: K1, sl 1 wyb, k1, sl m, work Row 3 of slip-stitch patt to m, sl m, k1, sl 1 wyb, k1.

ROW 4: P1, sl 1 wyf, p1, sl m, work Row 4 of slip-stitch patt to m, sl m, p1, sl 1 wyf, p1.

ROW 5: K2, sl 1 wyb, pm, work Row 3 of slip-stitch patt to m, sl m, sl 1 wyb, k2.

ROW 6: K1, p1, sl 1 wyf, sl m, work Row 4 of slip-stitch patt to m, sl m, sl 1 wyf, p1, k1.

Rep the last 4 rows until piece meas 31 (34¾, 38½, 42¼, 46, 49¾, 53½)" (79 [88.5, 98, 107.5, 117, 126.5, 136] cm) from beg, and 4¼ (4½, 4¾, 5, 5¼, 5½, 5¾)" (11 [11.5, 12, 12.5,

13.5, 14, 14.5] cm) from left armhole, ending after a WS row.

BEGIN STOCKINETTE ST

INC ROW: (RS) K3, remove m, p1, pm, knit and inc 8 (7, 7, 8, 7, 8, 8) sts evenly spaced across to last 4 sts, pm, p1, remove m, k3—95 (96, 98, 99, 100, 101, 103) sts.

NEXT ROW: (WS) K1, p2, k1, sl m, purl to last 4 sts, sl m, k1, p2, k1.

NEXT ROW: K3, p1, knit to m, p1, k3.

Rep the last 2 rows until piece meas 32 (36, 40, 44, 48, 52, 56)" (81.5 [91.5, 101.5, 112, 122, 132, 142] cm) from beg, and 5¼ (5¾, 6¼, 6¾, 7¼, 7¾, 8¼)" (13.5 [14.5, 16, 17, 18.5, 19.5, 21] cm) from left armhole CO edge, ending after WS row.

INC ROW: (RS) Work 4 sts in patt, remove m, work in patt to last 4 sts and inc 23 (22, 20, 24, 23, 22, 20) sts evenly spaced across, remove m, work to end—118 (118, 118, 123, 123, 123, 123) sts.

BEGIN 3X2 RIB

Work 7 rows in 3×2 rib, ending after a WS row.

BO all sts in patt.

finishing

Weave in loose ends.

Block piece to measurements.

THIS STUNNING reversible cowl is made in a beautiful cross and zigzag stitch that produces fabric with two very distinct and unexpected sides. Using two similar shades of yarn gives another dimension to this fabric.

|| *designed by* **SIMONA MERCHANT-DEST**

zlatý dešť COWL

FINISHED SIZE
7½" (19 cm) wide and 54" (137 cm) circumference.

YARN
Worsted weight (#4 Medium).

Shown here: Anzula For Better Or Worsted (80% superwash merino, 10% cashmere, 10% nylon; 200 yd [182 m]/4.06 oz [115 g]): temperance (color A) and butter (color B), 1 skein each.

NEEDLES
Size U.S. 9 (5.5 mm) straight.

Adjust needle size if necessary to obtain correct gauge.

NOTIONS
Cable needle (cn); tapestry needle; 2 yd (2 m) of worsted yarn of contrasting color; spare size U.S. 9 (5.5 mm) needle for BO.

GAUGE
20 sts and 28 rows = 4" (10 cm) in cross and zigzag stitch.

NOTE
This cowl is worked as a scarf starting with provisional cast-on, then joined with three-needle BO to form a cowl.

STITCH GUIDE

SL 1 WYON (SLIP ONE WITH YARN OVER NEEDLE)

Slip 1 stitch purlwise carrying yarn float over the needle from front to back (see Glossary).

MOD 1/2 RC

Sl 2 sts onto cn, hold in back, k1 dropping the extra yarn over needle from previous row, (p1, k1) from cn.

MOD 1/2 LC

Sl 1 onto cn dropping the extra yarn over needle from previous row, hold in front, k1, p1, k1 from cn.

1/1 LC

Sl 1 sts onto cn, hold in front, p1, k1 from cn.

CROSS AND ZIGZAG STITCH

(multiple of 3 sts + 4)

ROW 1: (WS) K2, *sl 1 wyon, p1, k1; rep from * to last 2 sts, k2.

ROW 2: K2, *mod 1/2 RC; rep from * to last 2 sts, k2.

ROW 3: K2, *Sl 1 wyon, k1, p1; rep from * to last 2 sts, k2.

ROW 4: K2, 1/1 LC, * mod 1/2 LC, rep from * to last 3 sts, k1 dropping the extra yarn over needle from previous row, k2.

Rep Rows 1–4 for patt.

cowl

With provisional CO (see Glossary) and color A, CO 37 sts.

Knit 1 row.

Work in cross and zigzag stitch (see Stitch Guide) until piece meas 27" (68.5 cm) from beg. Break yarn.

Change to color B and cont working cross and zigzag stitch until piece meas 54" (137 cm) from beg.

finishing

Carefully remove waste yarn from provisional CO and place 37 sts onto empty needle. With RS facing each other, use three-needle bind-off (see Glossary) to join CO sts together with live sts.

Weave in loose ends. Block to measurements.

knit

THIS CLASSIC yoke sweater is knit in the round from the bottom up in two colors. A cast-on in a contrasting color along with a two-color slip-stitch pattern is used as a border on all the edges. Another slip-stitch pattern is placed as a few stripes to adorn the yoke. You will learn how to use slip-stitch patterns in yoke construction, how to place stitch patterns as a border, and how to shape without disturbing the pattern. || designed by **FAINA GOBERSTEIN**

koketka SWEATER

FINISHED SIZE

33½ (37½, 41¼, 45, 49, 51, 52¾, 54¾)" (85 [95, 105, 114.5, 124.5, 129.5, 134, 139] cm) bust/chest circumference. Top shown measures 33½" (85 cm).

YARN

DK weight (#3 Light).

Shown here: Blue Sky Alpaca Alpaca Silk (50% alpaca, 50% silk; 146 yd [133 m]/1¾ oz [50 g]): #131 kiwi (color A), 6 (7, 8, 8, 9, 10, 10, 11) skeins; #143 papaya (color B), 1 (1, 1, 2, 2, 2, 2, 2) skeins.

NEEDLES

Size U.S. 4 (3.5 mm): 29–32" (73.5–81.5 cm) circular (cir) and set of 5 double-pointed (dpn).

Adjust needle size if necessary to obtain the correct gauge.

NOTIONS

Markers (m); cable needle (cn); tapestry needle.

GAUGE

25 sts and 34 rnds = 4" (10 cm) in St st.

NOTES

Slip sts as if to purl with yarn in back unless stated otherwise.

STITCH GUIDE

Note: When working 1/1 LC or 1/1 RC, one of the sts is an elongated stitch that was slipped on 2 previous rnds. Treat it as a "normal" stitch.

1/1 LC

Slip 1 st onto cn, hold in front, k1, k1 from cn.

1/1 RC

Slip 1 st onto cn, hold in back, k1, k1 from cn.

TWISTED RIB

(multiple of 2 sts)

RND 1: *K1 tbl, p1; rep from * to end.

Rep Rnd 1 for patt.

BORDER STITCH

(multiple of 2 sts)

RND 1: With color B, * sl1 wyb, k1; rep from *.

RND 2: With color B, * sl1 wyb, p1; rep from *.

RND 3: With color A, * k1, sl1 wyb; rep from *.

RND 4: With color A, * p1, sl1 wyb; rep from *.

Rep Rnds 1–4 for patt.

COLOR GARLAND

(multiple of 5 sts)

RND 1: With color B, knit.

RND 2: With color A, knit.

RNDS 3 AND 4: With color B, knit.

RNDS 5 AND 6: With color A, *k2, sl2 wyb, k1; rep from *.

RND 7: With color A, *k1, 1/1 RC, 1/1 LC; rep from *.

TIP

To make decreases at the end and beg of rnd even, you can work one decrease before beg-of-rnd marker, follow the written instructions for decreases, and skip the last decrease.

sleeves

With color B and using long-tail method (see Glossary), CO 64 (70, 82, 88, 94, 96, 100, 106) sts. Divide sts evenly over 3 or 4 dpn. Pm for beg of rnd and join for working in rnds, being careful not to twist sts.

Change to color A and work in twisted rib (see Stitch Guide) for 5 rnds. Knit 2 rnds.

Work 8 rnds in border stitch. Break color B.

Change to color A and knit 4 rnds.

SHAPE SLEEVE

INC RND: K1, M1L (see Glossary), knit to last st, M1R (see Glossary), k1—2 sts inc'd.

Knit 3 (3, 3, 5, 5, 5, 5, 3) rnds.

Rep the last 4 (4, 4, 6, 6, 6, 6, 4) rnds 3 more times—72 (78, 90, 96, 102, 104, 108, 114) sts.

Cont to work even in St st (knit all sts, every rnd) until piece meas 4½ (4½, 4½, 5, 5, 5, 5, 5½)" (11.5 [11.5, 11.5, 12.5, 12.5, 12.5, 12.5, 14] cm) from beg.

DIVIDE FOR UNDERARM

NEXT RND: Knit to last 8 (9, 10, 11, 12, 13, 13, 14) sts, remove m, BO 16 (18, 20, 22, 24, 26, 26, 28) sts—56 (60, 70, 74, 78, 78, 82, 86) sts rem. Place sts onto holder or waste yarn.

Make second sleeve the same as the first.

body

With color B, cir and using long-tail method, CO 111 (123, 135, 147, 159, 165, 173, 177) sts, pm for "side seam," CO 111 (123, 135, 147, 159, 165, 173, 177) sts, pm for "side seam" and beg of rnd and join for working in rnds, being careful not to twist sts—222 (246, 270, 294, 318, 330, 346, 354) sts.

Change to color A and work 5 rnds of twisted rib. Knit 2 rnds.

Work 8 rnds in border stitch (see Stitch Guide or chart). Break color B.

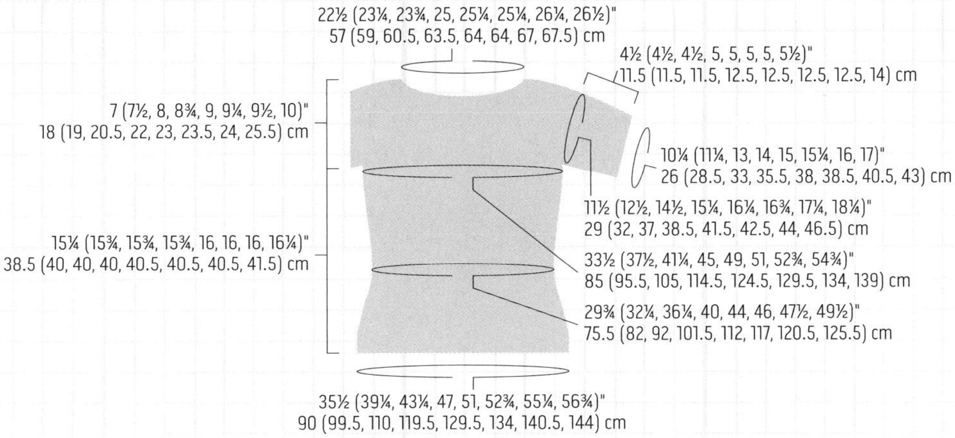

Change to color A and knit 4 rnds.

SHAPE WAIST

DEC RND: *K1, k2tog, knit to 3 sts before m, ssk, k1; rep from * once more—4 sts dec'd.

Knit 5 (3, 3, 3, 3, 3, 3, 3) rnds.

Rep the last 6 (4, 4, 4, 4, 4, 4, 4) rnds 2 (9, 9, 10, 10, 10, 9, 10) more times—210 (206, 230, 250, 274, 286, 306, 310) sts rem.

SIZES 33½ (37½, 41¼, 52¾)" ONLY:
[Rep dec rnd, then knit 3 (1, 1, 1) rnd(s)] 6 (1, 1, 2) time(s)—186 (202, 226, 298) sts rem.

ALL SIZES:
Work even until piece meas 8¼ (8¼, 8¼, 8½, 8½, 8½, 8½, 8½)" (21 [21, 21, 21.5, 21.5, 21.5, 21.5, 21.5] cm) from beg.

SHAPE HIP

INC RND: K1, M1L, knit to 2 sts before m, M1R, k1, sl m; rep from * once more—4 sts inc'd.

Knit 7 (5, 5, 5, 5, 5, 5, 5) rnds.

Rep the last 8 (6, 6, 6, 6, 6, 6) rnds 5 (7, 6, 6, 5, 5, 5, 4) more times—210 (234, 254, 278, 298, 310, 322, 330) sts.

SIZES 41¼ (45, 49, 51, 52¾, 54¾)" ONLY:
[Rep inc rnd, then knit 7 rnds] 1 (1, 2, 2, 2, 3) time(s)—258 (282, 306, 318, 330, 342) sts.

ALL SIZES:
Work even until piece meas 15¼ (15¾, 15¾, 15¾, 16, 16, 16, 16¼)"

(38.5 [40, 40, 40, 40.5, 40.5, 40.5, 41.5] cm) from beg.

DIVIDE BACK AND FRONT

NEXT RND: Knit to last 8 (9, 10, 11, 12, 13, 13, 14) sts, BO 16 (18, 20, 22, 24, 26, 26, 28) sts removing m.

NEXT RND: Knit to 8 (9, 10, 11, 12, 13, 13, 14) sts before the "side" m, BO 16 (18, 20, 22, 24, 26, 26, 28) sts removing m, knit to end—89 (99, 109, 119, 129, 133, 139, 143) sts rem for each front and back.

yoke

JOIN SLEEVES AND BODY

Notes: To make it more convenient to decrease for yoke and hide any color changing, we will place beg-of-rnd marker on the next rnd at the connection of back and left sleeve. We mark the center of back for point of reference as we do short-rows after all decreases are completed. It is hard to keep track of sts for back because we decrease sts evenly spaced.

NEXT ROW: (RS) Return 56 (60, 70, 74, 78, 78, 82, 86) held sts from 1 sleeve to

COLOR GARLAND

	with A, knit
·	with A, purl
	with B, knit
·	with B, purl
v	sl pwise wyb
⧄	with A, 1/1 RC
⧅	with A, 1/1 LC
☐	pattern repeat

BORDER

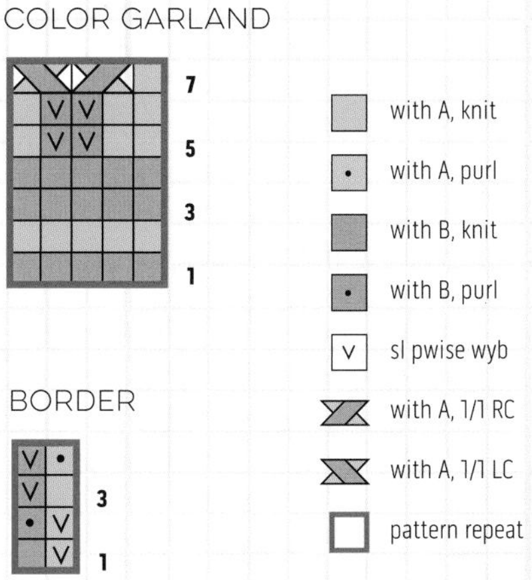

dpn, then knit across with cir for left sleeve, k89 (99, 109, 119, 129, 133, 139, 143) for front, return 56 (60, 70, 74, 78, 78, 82, 86) held sts from second sleeve to dpn, then knit across with cir for right sleeve, k44 (49, 54, 59, 64, 66, 69, 71), pm for center back, k1, pm, k44 (49, 54, 59, 64, 66, 69, 71), pm for beg of rnd—290 (318, 358, 386, 414, 422, 442, 458) sts.

Knit 9 (10, 11, 13, 13, 14, 14, 15) rnds.

SHAPE YOKE

DEC RND 1: Knit and dec 0 (3, 3, 1, 4, 2, 2, 3) st(s) evenly spaced—290 (315, 355, 385, 410, 420, 440, 455) sts rem.

Work Rnds 1–7 of color garland patt (see Stitch Guide or chart).

Change to color A only and knit 10 (11, 12, 14, 14, 15, 15, 16) rnds.

Work Rnds 1–7 of color garland patt.

Change to color A only and knit 2 rnds.

DEC RND 2: (K2, k2tog) 10 (5, 0, 5, 3, 5, 8, 10) times, *k1, k2tog, (k2, k2tog) 1 (2, 17, 5, 9, 4, 4, 3) times; rep from * to last 40 (20, 0, 20, 8, 20, 14, 40) sts, (k2, k2tog) 10 (5, 0, 5, 2, 5, 7, 10) times to end—210 (230, 265, 285, 305, 310, 325, 335) sts.

Knit 7 (8, 9, 11, 11, 12, 12, 13) rnds.

Work Rnds 1–7 of color garland patt.

Change to color A only and knit 2 rnds.

SIZES 33½ (45)" ONLY:
DEC RND 3: *K1, k2tog; rep from * —140 (190) sts rem.

SIZES 37½ (41¼, 49, 51, 52¾, 54¾)" ONLY:
DEC RND 3: (K1, k2tog) 0 (3, 0, 0, 3, 0) times, *k2, k2tog, (k1, k2tog) 14 (7, 19, 9, 9, 21) times; rep from * to last 0 (6, 0, 0, 6, 0) sts, (k1, k2tog) 0 (3, 0, 0, 3, 0) times to end—155 (180, 205, 210, 220, 225) sts.

ALL SIZES:
Knit 2 (4, 4, 4, 5, 5, 6, 6) rnds.

DEC RND 4: Knit and dec 0 (9, 32, 34, 47, 52, 56, 59) sts evenly spaced—140 (146, 148, 156, 158, 158, 164, 166) sts rem.

Knit 2 (2, 3, 3, 4, 4, 5, 5) rnds.

Work 6 rnds of border stitch, ending after Rnd 2.

Change to color A only and knit 1 rnd.

SHAPE BACK NECK

Work back and forth in short-rows (see Glossary) as foll:

Note: Short-rows are building symmetrically with respect to center back marker. Follow instructions and work wraps tog with wrapped sts when you come to them.

SHORT-ROW 1: Knit to center back m, remove m, k5 (5, 5, 6, 6, 7, 7, 8) sts, wrap next st, turn work.

SHORT-ROW 2: (WS) P10 (10, 10, 12, 12, 14, 14, 16), wrap next st, turn work.

SHORT-ROW 3: K20 (20, 20, 22, 22, 24, 24, 26), wrap next st, turn work.

SHORT-ROW 4: P30 (30, 30, 32, 32, 34, 34, 36), wrap next st, turn work.

SHORT-ROW 5: K40 (40, 40, 42, 42, 44, 44, 46), wrap next st, turn work.

SHORT-ROW 6: P50 (50, 50, 52, 52, 54, 54, 56), wrap next st, turn work.

SHORT-ROW 7: Knit to end-of-rnd m, working wraps tog with wrapped sts when you come to them.

Resume working all sts in the rnd as foll:

Work 5 rnds of twisted rib.

Change to color B only and BO all sts.

finishing

Sew underarm seams. Weave in loose ends. Block to measurements.

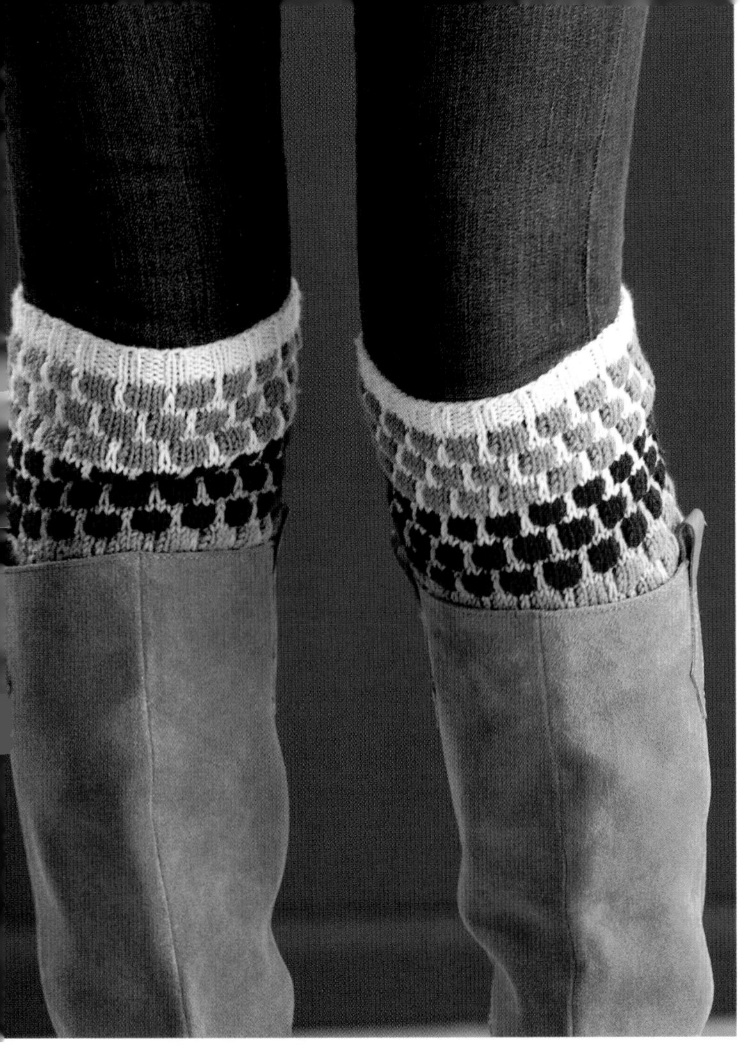

CHAPTER 5

reversible SLIP-STITCH PATTERNS

UNLIKE TRADITIONAL, woven, and fancy stitches, the classification of reversible patterns is very simple and cuts across all the other groupings of slip-stitch patterns. As you read through this book and look at the traditional, woven, or fancy stitch patterns, you'll see that many of them are also reversible.

Slip-stitch patterns are by far the most versatile stitch patterns; with simple manipulations or modifications of basic stitches, you can easily create reversible stitch patterns.

In this chapter, we introduce ten wildly different stitch patterns, which all have a distinctive look to them and are attractive on both sides. For these, we used a modern color scheme to accentuate the fashion-forward style slip stitch has to offer.

Reversible slip-stitch patterns have a wide use in the design of garments and accessories. They're a great way to get multiple uses out of one project. Both sides of the reversible pattern can also be featured in the same garment as design elements. This can produce an interesting look of the design while the gauge stays the same.

These stitch patterns were chosen because they have a very distinct stitch pattern on the right side and wrong side of the work.

We encourage you to explore the possibilities of producing more reversible stitches with just a little change in the given instructions.

reversible STITCHES DICTIONARY

STITCH GUIDE

1/1 LC
Sl 1 st onto cn, hold in front, k1; k1 from cn.

T2 (TUCK STITCH)
With LH needle, catch 2 floats on the back of next elongated st, so floats are on top of needle and in front of elongated st (3 loops on needle: 1 live st and 2 floats). Knit all loops tog.

T4 (TUCK STITCH)
With LH needle, catch 4 floats on the back of next elongated st, so floats are on top of needle and in front of elongated st (5 loops on needle: 1 live st and 4 floats). Knit all loops tog.

M3 (MAKE 3)
Sl next 3 elongated sts (dropping the extra wrap) to RH needle, bring all 3 sts to LH needle, then work into all 3 sts tog as foll: k1, yo, k1.

M5 (MAKE 5)
Sl next 5 elongated sts (dropping the extra wrap) to RH needle, bring all 5 sts to LH needle, then work into all 5 sts tog as foll: (k1, yo) twice, k1.

K1-DBLWRAP
Insert RH needle into the next stitch and wrap yarn twice around the needle, then knit the st withdrawing all the wraps along with the needle.

RIB WITH A TWIST

(MULTIPLE OF 3 STS + 1)

- Fabric is not elastic; cannot be used as a substitute for a regular rib.
- Creates soft and not very dense fabric.
- Begin with WS row, but chart shows RS of work.
- Can also be classified as a fancy stitch.

ROW 1: (WS) Sl 1 wyf, *k2, sl 1 wyf; rep from *.
ROW 2: *Sl 1 wyb, p2; rep from * to last st, sl 1 wyb.
ROW 3: Rep Row 1.
ROW 4: *K1, 1/1 LC; rep from * to last st, k1.
Rep Rows 1–4 for patt.

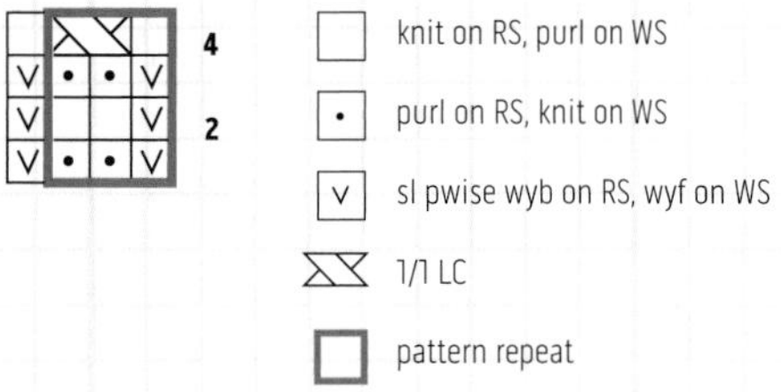

WIDE SLIPPED RIB

(MULTIPLE OF 4 STS + 2)

- Creates a textured and sturdy fabric.
- Great for accessories and skirts.
- Can also be classified as a traditional stitch.

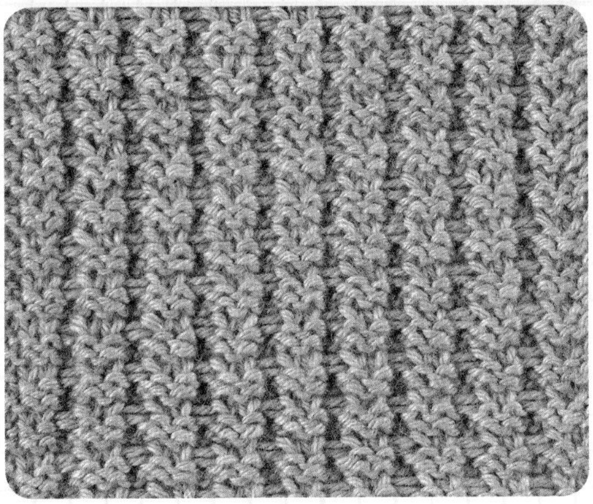

ROW 1: (RS) *P2, sl 2 wyb; rep from * to last 2 sts, p2.

ROW 2: K2, *sl 2 wyf, k2; rep from *.

ROW 3: Knit.

ROW 4: Purl.

Rep Rows 1–4 for patt.

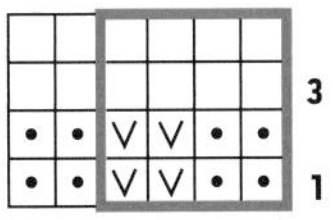

- ☐ knit on RS, purl on WS
- • purl on RS, knit on WS
- V sl pwise wyb on RS, wyf on WS
- ☐ pattern repeat

TEXTURED PILLARS

(MULTIPLE OF 3 STS + 1)

- Very different look on RS and WS.
- Uses both front and back floats for texture.
- Works well in different-weight yarns.
- Perfect for accessories.
- Can also be classified as a traditional stitch.

ROW 1: (RS) *K1, sl 1 wyb, sl 1 wyf; rep from * to last st, k1.

ROW 2: P1, *k1, p2; rep from *.

ROW 3: *K1, sl 1 wyf, sl 1 wyb; rep from * to last st, k1.

ROW 4: P1, *p1, k1, p1; rep from *.

Rep Rows 1–4 for patt.

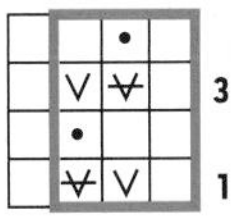

- ☐ knit on RS, purl on WS
- • purl on RS, knit on WS
- V sl pwise wyb on RS, wyf on WS
- V̶ sl pwise wyf on RS, wyb on WS
- ☐ pattern repeat

TUCK RIB

(MULTIPLE OF 6 STS + 3)

- Interesting patterns on each side.
- Suitable for many yarn weights.
- Can look like lace when worked with thin yarn and large needle.
- Can also be classified as a fancy stitch.

ROWS 1 AND 3: (RS) *K3, p1, sl 1 wyb, p1; rep from * to last 3 sts, k3.

ROWS 2 AND 4: P3, *k1, sl 1 wyf, k1, p3; rep from *.

ROW 5: *K3, p1, T4, p1; rep from * to last 3 sts, k3.

ROW 6: P3, *k1, p1, k1, p3; rep from *.

Rep Rows 1–6 for patt.

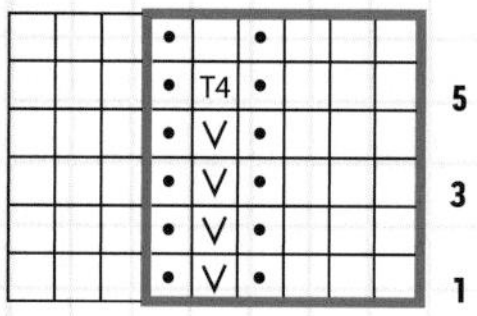

- knit on RS, purl on WS
- purl on RS, knit on WS
- sl pwise wyb on RS, wyf on WS
- T4-yon
- pattern repeat

SLIPPED GRANITE

(MULTIPLE OF 4 STS + 1)

- Shows best on solid-color yarn.
- Slightly dense fabric.
- Suitable for garments.
- Can also be classified as a traditional stitch.

ROW 1: (RS) *K2, sl 1 wyb, k1; rep from * to last st, k1.

ROW 2: P1, *p1, sl 1 wyf, p2; rep from *.

ROW 3: *K1, p1; rep from * to last st, k1.

ROW 4: P1, *k1, p1; rep from *.

ROW 5: *Sl 1 wyb, k3; rep from * to last st, sl 1 wyb.

ROW 6: Sl 1 wyf, *p3, sl 1 wyf; rep from *.

ROW 7: Rep Row 3.

ROW 8: Rep Row 4.

Rep Rows 1–8 for patt.

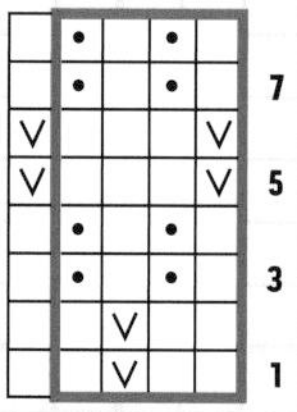

- knit on RS, purl on WS
- purl on RS, knit on WS
- sl pwise wyb on RS, wyf on WS
- pattern repeat

SLIPPED AND GARTER CHECKS

(MULTIPLE OF 12 STS + 1)

- RS and WS look very similar.
- Perfect for scarves and any project where full reversibility is required.
- Fabric is soft and elegant in its appearance.
- Can also be classified as a traditional stitch.

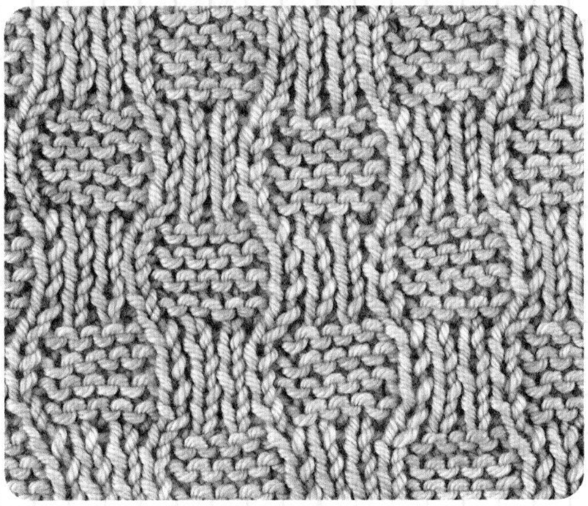

ROWS 1, 3, 5, AND 7: (RS) *P1, k5, (p1, sl 1 wyb) 3 times; rep from * to last st, p1.

ROWS 2, 4, AND 6: K1, *(p1, k1) 3 times, k6; rep from *.

ROW 8: Knit.

ROWS 9, 11, 13, AND 15: *(P1, sl 1 wyb) 3 times, p1, k5; rep from * to last st, p1.

ROWS 10, 12, AND 14: K1, * k6, (p1, k1) 3 times; rep from *.

ROW 16: Knit.

Rep Rows 1–16 for patt.

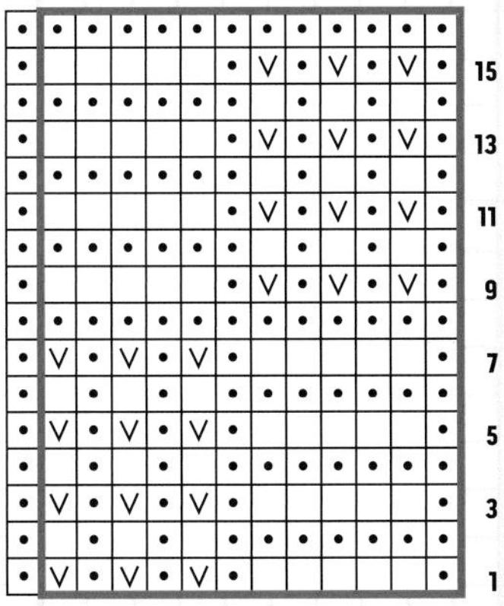

knit on RS, purl on WS

purl on RS, knit on WS

sl pwise wyb on RS, wyf on WS

pattern repeat

TWO-COLOR TRELLIS

(MULTIPLE OF 6 STS + 5)

— Two-color swatch. Purple is named A and gray is named B. Each color is worked for 2 or 4 rows.

— Features mix of stockinette and garter sts with slipped sts.

— Color must have enough contrast to show the pattern best.

— Can also be classified as a fancy stitch.

ROW 1: (RS) With A, k1, p3, *sl 3 wyf, p3; rep from * to last st, k1.

ROW 2: P1, *k3, sl 3 wyb; rep from * to last 4 sts, k3, p1.

ROW 3: With B, k1, p3, *k3, p3; rep from * to last st, k1.

ROW 4: P1, *k3, p3; rep from * to last 4 sts, k3, p1.

ROW 5: K4, *k1, T2, k4; rep from * to last st, k1.

ROW 6: Rep Row 4.

ROW 7: With A, p1, sl 3 wyf, *p3, sl 3 wyf; rep from * to last st, k1.

ROW 8: K1, *sl 3 wyb, k3; rep from * to last 4 sts, sl 3 wyb, k1.

ROW 9: With B, k4, *p3, k3; rep from * to last st, k1.

ROW 10: P1, *p3, k3; rep from * to last 4 sts, p4.

ROW 11: K2, T2, k1, *k4, T2, k1; rep from * to last st, k1.

ROW 12: P1, *k3, p3; rep from * to last 4 sts, k3, p1.

Rep Rows 1–12 for patt.

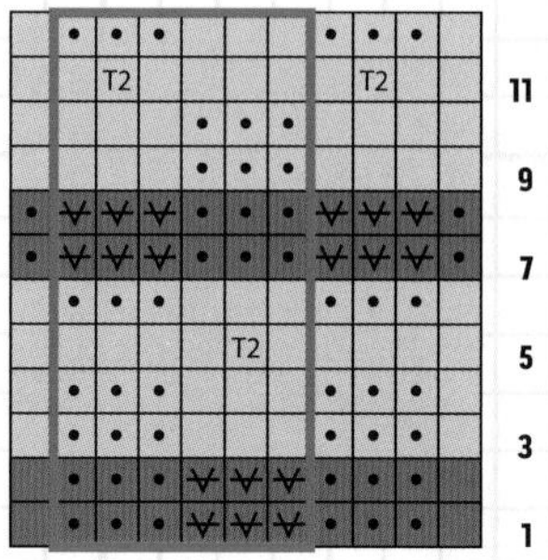

with A, knit on RS, purl on WS

with B, knit on RS, purl on WS

with A, purl on RS, knit on WS

with B, purl on RS, knit on WS

sl pwise wyf on RS, wyb on WS

T2 T2-yon

pattern repeat

THREE-COLOR GARTER GARLAND

(MULTIPLE OF 2 STS + 3)

- Three-color swatch. Colors are named A, B, and C. Each color is worked for 2 rows.
- Dense fabric with a subtle pattern on WS.
- Can also be classified as a traditional stitch.

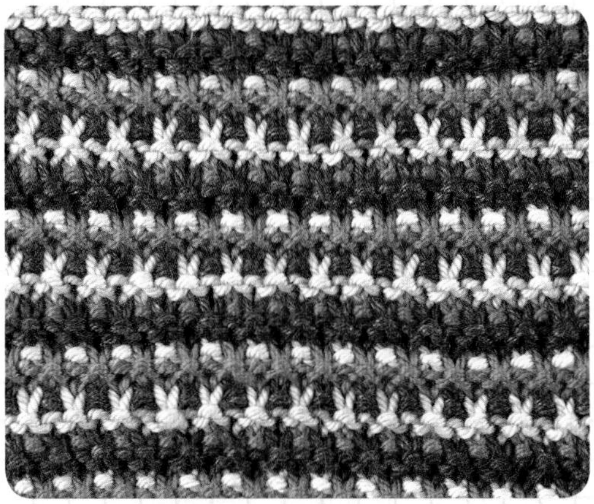

ROW 1: (RS) With A, knit.

ROW 2: Rep Row 1.

ROW 3: With B, K1, *sl 1 wyb, k1; rep from * to last 2 sts, sl 1 wyb, k1.

ROW 4: K1, sl 1 wyf, *k1, sl 1 wyf; rep from * to last 1 st, k1.

ROW 5: With C, knit.

ROW 6: Rep Row 5.

ROW 7: With A, k1, *k1, sl 1 wyb; rep from * to last 2 sts, k2.

ROW 8: K2, *sl 1 wyf, k1; rep from * to last 1 st, k1.

Rep Rows 1–8, changing colors in order of A, B, C every 2 rows for patt.

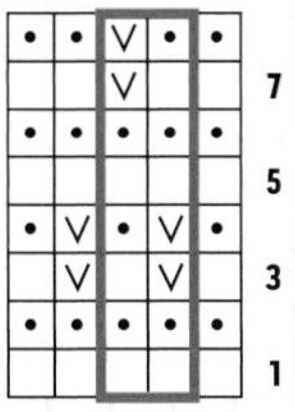

knit on RS, purl on WS

purl on RS, knit on WS

sl pwise wyb on RS, wyf on WS

pattern repeat

LITTLE STARS

(MULTIPLE OF 6 STS + 4)

- Two-color swatch. Pink is named A and gray is named B. Each color is worked for 2 rows.
- The RS pattern is more pronounced.
- Suitable for accessories.
- Make more yarnovers to create bigger stars.
- Can also be classified as a fancy stitch.

ROW 1: (RS) Knit.

ROW 2: Rep Row 1.

ROW 3: Sl 1 wyb, *k5-dblWrap, sl 1 wyb; rep from * to last 3 sts, k3-dblWrap.

ROW 4: M3, *sl 1 wyf, M5; rep from * to last st, sl 1 wyf.

ROW 5: Rep Row 1.

ROW 6: Rep Row 1.

ROW 7: K3-dblWrap, sl 1 wyb, *k5-dblWrap, sl 1 wyb; rep from *.

ROW 8: *Sl 1 wyf, M5; rep from * to last 4 sts, sl 1 wyf, M3; rep from *.

Rep Rows 1–8 for patt.

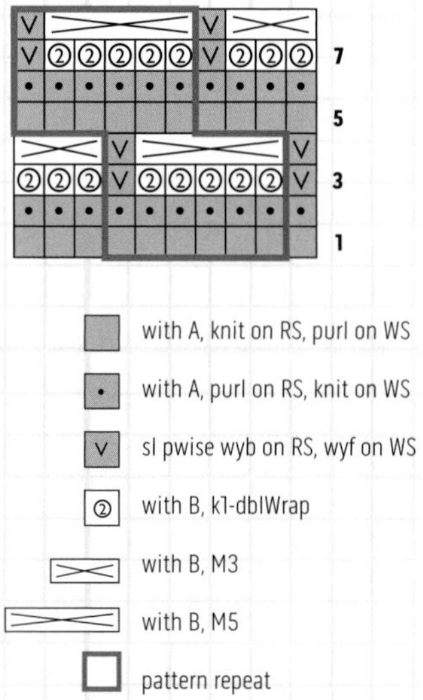

SPECKLED DIAGONALS
(MULTIPLE OF 5 STS)

- Beautiful textured pattern.
- Dense and sturdy fabric that is suitable for projects that need to hold shape.
- Can also be classified as a woven stitch.

ROW 1: (RS) *P2, sl 3 wyb; rep from *.

ROW 2: *Sl 3 wyf, k2; rep from *.

ROW 3: *P1, sl 3 wyb, p1; rep from *.

ROW 4: *K1, sl 3 wyf, k1; rep from *.

ROW 5: *Sl 3 wyb, p2; rep from *.

ROW 6: *K2, sl 3 wyf; rep from *.

ROW 7: *Sl 2 wyb, p2, sl 1 wyb; rep from *.

ROW 8: *Sl 1 wyf, k2, sl 2 wyf; rep from *.

ROW 9: *Sl 1 wyb, p2, sl 2 wyb; rep from *.

ROW 10: *Sl 2 wyf, k2, sl 1 wyf; rep from *.

Rep Rows 1–10 for patt.

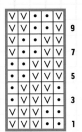

V	V	•	•	V	
V	V	•	•	V	9
V	•	•	V	V	
V	•	•	V	V	7
•	•	V	V	V	
•	•	V	V	V	5
•	V	V	V	•	
•	V	V	V	•	3
V	V	V	•	•	
V	V	V	•	•	1

- • purl on RS, knit on WS
- V sl pwise wyb on RS, wyf on WS
- ☐ pattern repeat

BOOT TOPPERS are a wonderful accessory. They look like handknit socks, but it takes only a fraction of the time to make them. Because they're so quick, they make great gifts for everyone on your list. These were designed to be worn in any direction for many styling possibilities. || *designed by* **SIMONA MERCHANT-DEST**

jetelinka BOOT TOPPERS

FINISHED SIZE
13¾" (35 cm) calf circumference and 6¼" (16 cm) long.

YARN
DK weight (#3 Light).

Shown here: LB Collection Superwash Merino (100% superwash merino wool; 306 yd [280 m]/3 1/2 oz [100 g]): #98 ivory (color A), #174 spring leaf (color B), #127 mahogany (color C), #107 sky (color D), 1 skein each.

NEEDLES
Ribbing: Size U.S. 3 (3.25 mm): set of 5 double-pointed (dpn).

Body: Size U.S. 4 (3.5 mm): set of 5 dpn.

Adjust needle sizes if necessary to obtain the correct gauge.

NOTIONS
Marker (m); tapestry needle.

GAUGE
21 sts and 38 rnds = 4" (10 cm) in bubble patt on larger needles.

NOTES
The boot toppers are worked in the round.
To make this design reversible without a "line" of yarns carried up at beg of round, with each color change, break off "old" yarn, join "new" yarn, and weave in ends as you go along.

STITCH GUIDE

T4 (TUCK STITCH)
With LH needle, catch 4 floats on the back of next elongated st, so floats are on top of needle and in front of elongated st (5 loops on needle: 1 live st and 4 floats). Knit all loops tog.

K2, P2 RIB
(multiple of 2 sts)

RND 1: *K2, p2; rep from *.

Rep Rnd 1 for patt.

boot topper

With color A and smaller dpn, CO 72 sts. Divide sts over 4 dpn as foll: 20 sts on Needle 1, 16 sts on Needle 2, 20 sts on Needle 3, and 16 sts on Needle 4. Place marker (pm) for beg of rnd and join to work in the rnd, being careful not to twist sts.

Work 5 rnds in k2, p2 rib.

Change to larger dpn and work Rnds 1–48 of bubble patt.

Change to smaller dpn and color D and work 5 rnds in k2, p2 rib.

BO all sts in patt.

finishing

Weave in loose ends. Block to measurements.

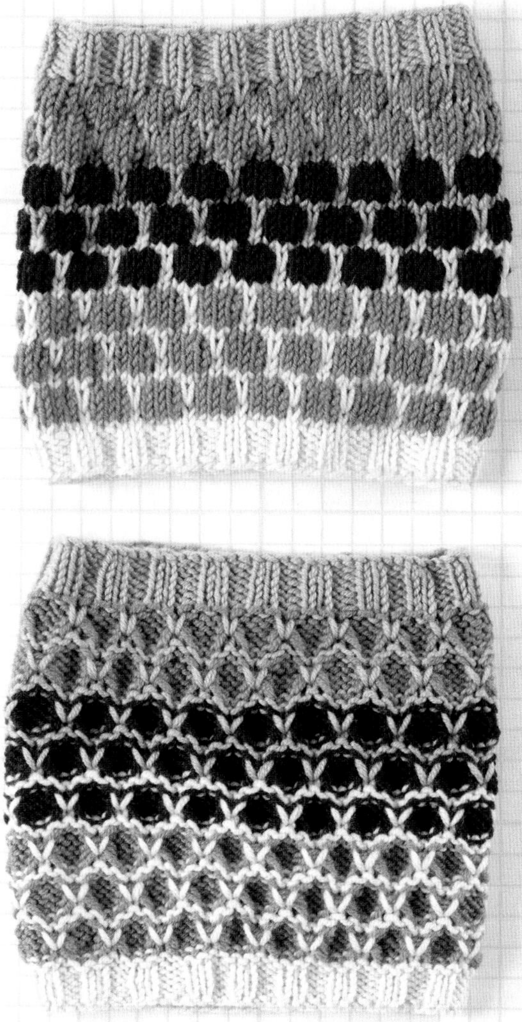

BUBBLE

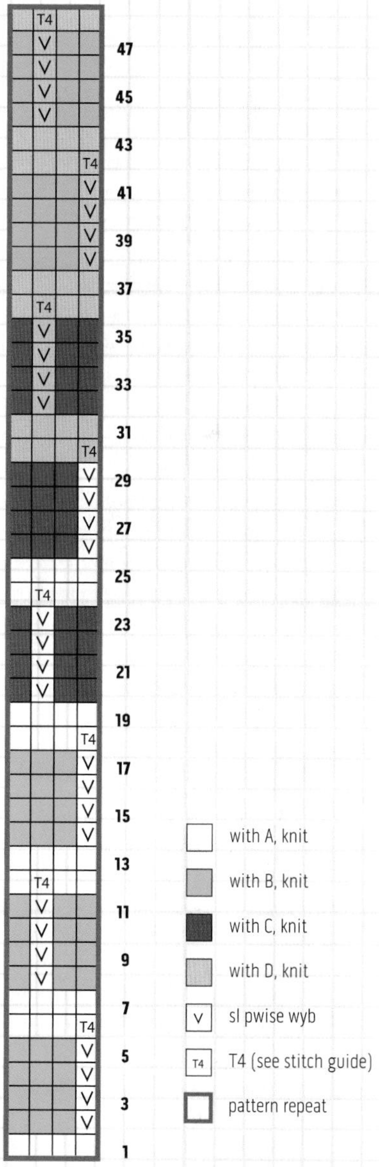

THESE BOOT TOPPERS are worked in a fairly simple slip-stitch pattern that plays with the placement of the slipped stitches, the way the floats are carried, the placement of knit and purl stitches, and color changes. You can make a wide variety of alternative designs by simply substituting different color choices. || *designed by* **SIMONA MERCHANT-DEST**

fialka BOOT TOPPERS

FINISHED SIZE
11¾" (30 cm) calf circumference and 8¼" (21 cm) long.

YARN
DK weight (#3 Light).

Shown here: LB Collection Superwash Merino (100% superwash merino wool; 306 yd [280 m]/3½ oz [100 g]): #141 wild berry (color A), #139 peony (color B), #98 ivory (color C), and #107 sky (color D), 1 skein each.

NEEDLES
Ribbing: Size U.S. 3 (3.25 mm): set of 5 double-pointed (dpn).

Body: Size U.S. 4 (3.5 mm): set of 5 dpn.

Adjust needle sizes if necessary to obtain the correct gauge.

NOTIONS
Marker (m); tapestry needle.

GAUGE
26 sts and 35 rnds = 4" (10 cm) in slip-stitch pattern on larger needles.

NOTES
The warmers are worked in the round. To make this design reversible without a "line" of yarns carried up at beg of round, with each color change, break off "old" yarn, join "new" yarn, and weave in ends as you go along.

STITCH GUIDE

K2, P2 RIB
(multiple of 2 sts)

RND 1: *K2, p2; rep from *.

Rep Rnd 1 for patt.

boot toppers

With color A and smaller dpn, CO 76 sts. Divide sts over 4 dpn as foll: 20 sts on Needle 1, 18 sts on Needle 2, 20 sts on Needle 3, and 18 sts on Needle 4. Place marker (pm) for beg of rnd and join to work in the rnd, being careful not to twist sts.

Work in k2, p2 rib until piece meas 1" (2.5 cm) from beg.

Change to larger dpn and work Rnds 1–54 of stripe patt.

Change to smaller dpn and color B only. Work in k2, p2 rib for 1" (2.5 cm).

Break yarn.

Make second boot topper the same as the first.

finishing

Weave in loose ends. Block to measurements.

STRIPE

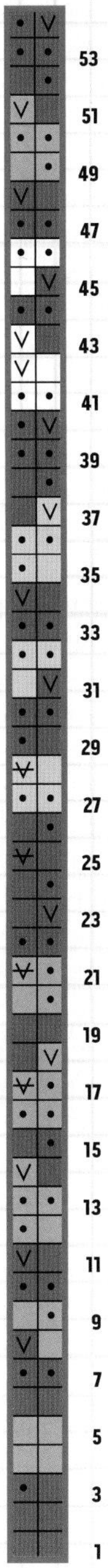

- with A, knit
- with A, purl
- with B, knit
- with B, purl
- with C, knit
- with C, purl
- with D, knit
- with D, purl
- sl pwise wyb on RS, wyf on WS
- sl pwise wyf on RS, wyb on WS
- pattern repeat

THE TWO-FOR-ONE hat begins with a dramatic 2×2 rib at the brim, followed by a reversible slip-stitch pattern. On one side, crossed slipped stitches form a geometric, polygon-like pattern; on the reverse side a basketweave pattern is showing. Modifying the slip stitch invisibly tapers the top of the hat and forms yet another geometric pattern on its own. // *designed by* **SIMONA MERCHANT-DEST**

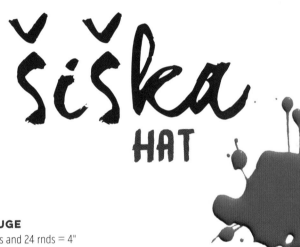

šiška HAT

FINISHED SIZE

18 (19½, 20¾)" (45.5 [49.5, 52.5] cm) head circumference at brim and 10¼" (26 cm) long from beg of brim. Shown in size 19½" (49.5 cm).

YARN

Worsted weight (#4 Medium).

Shown here: Malabrigo Worsted (100% kettle-dyed pure merino wool; 210 yd [192 m]/3½ oz [100 g]): #504 rattan, 2 skeins.

NEEDLES

Brim: Size U.S. 5 (3.75 mm): 16" (40.5 cm) circular (cir).

Body and Crown: Size U.S. 7 (4.5 mm): 16" (40.5 cm) cir and set of 5 double-pointed (dpn).

Adjust needle sizes if necessary to obtain the correct gauge.

NOTIONS

Markers (m); 2 cable needles (cn); tapestry needle.

GAUGE

18 sts and 24 rnds = 4" (10 cm) in body patt with larger needle.

23 sts and 24 rnds = 4" (10 cm) in k2, p2 rib, slightly stretched with smaller needle.

STITCH GUIDE

K1-DBLWRAP
Insert RH needle into the next stitch and wrap yarn twice around the needle, then knit the st withdrawing all the wraps along with the needle.

1/4 LC-DBLWRAP
Sl 1 st onto cn, hold in front, k1-dblWrap, k3; k1 from cn.

1/4 RC-DBLWRAP
Sl 4 sts onto cn, hold in back, k1; k3, k1-dblWrap from cn.

1/3 LC-DBLWRAP
Sl 1 st onto cn, hold in front, k1-dblWrap, k2; k1 from cn.

DEC-1/2 LC
Sl 1 st onto cn, hold in front, k2tog, k1; k1 from cn—1 st dec'd.

DEC-1/1 LC
Sl 1 st onto cn, hold in front, k2tog; k1 from cn—1 st dec'd.

MOD-DEC-1/1 LC
Sl 1 st onto cn, hold in back; sl next st to second cn, hold in front, return st from first cn to LH needle and k2tog; k1 from second cn—1 st dec'd.

K2, P2 RIB
(multiple of 2 sts)

RND 1: *P2, k2; rep from *.

Rep Rnd 1 for patt.

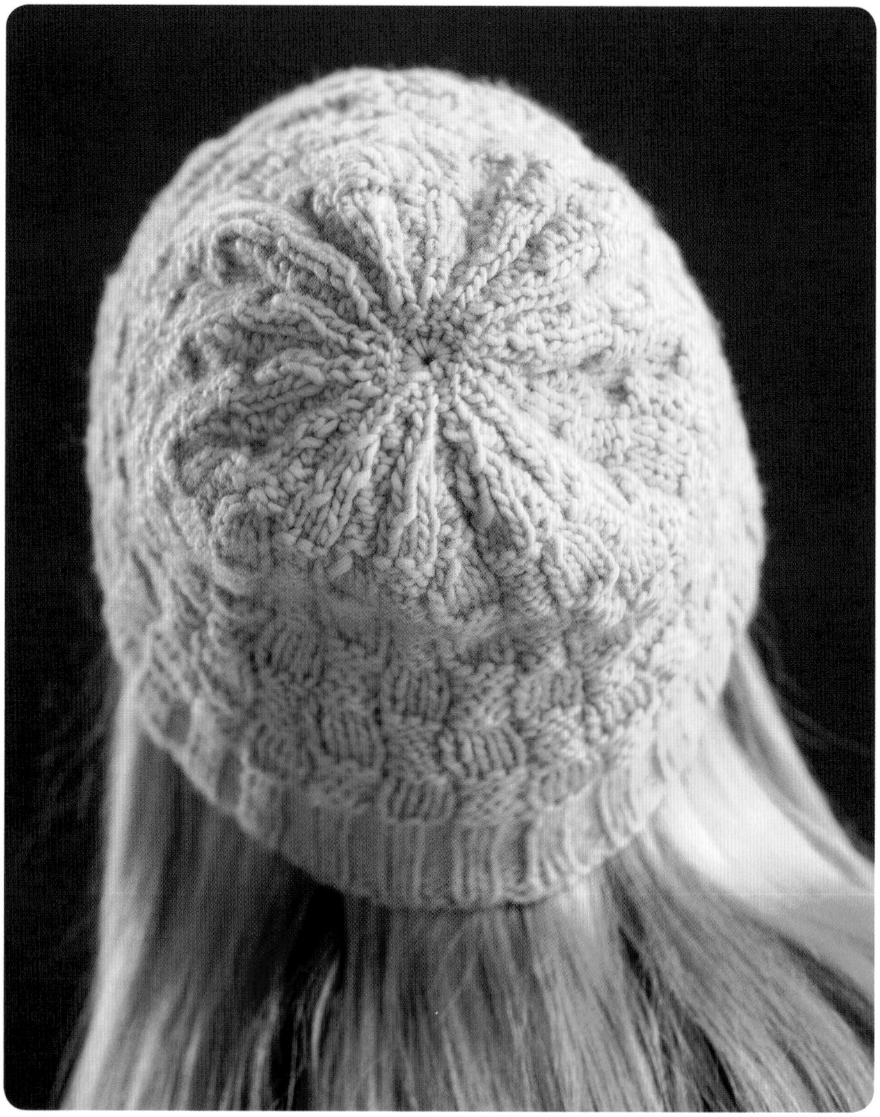

hat

BRIM

With smaller cir, CO 104 (112, 120) sts. Place marker (pm) for beg of rnd and join to work in the rnd, being careful not to twist sts.

Work in k2, p2 rib until piece meas 2" (5 cm) from beg.

BODY

Change to larger cir and knit 1 rnd.

Work Rnds 1–20 of body patt once, then work Rnds 9–20 once more.

[Piece meas about 7¼" (18.5 cm) from beg.]

SHAPE CROWN

Work Rnds 1–17 of crown shaping patt—26 (28, 30) sts rem. Change to dpn when sts no long fit on cir.

DEC RND: *K2tog; rep from *—13 (14, 15) sts rem.

Break yarn, leaving 8" (20.5 cm) tail. Thread tail through tapestry needle and draw through rem sts, pull tightly to close.

finishing

Weave in ends. Block if desired.

BODY

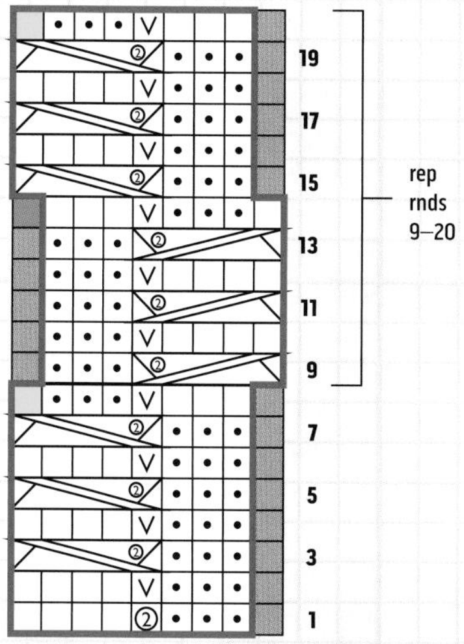

CROWN

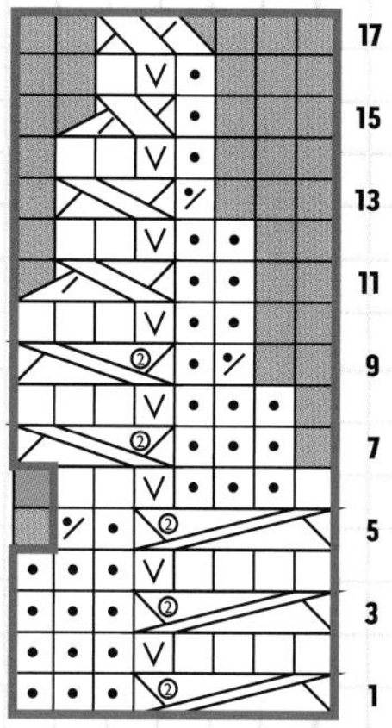

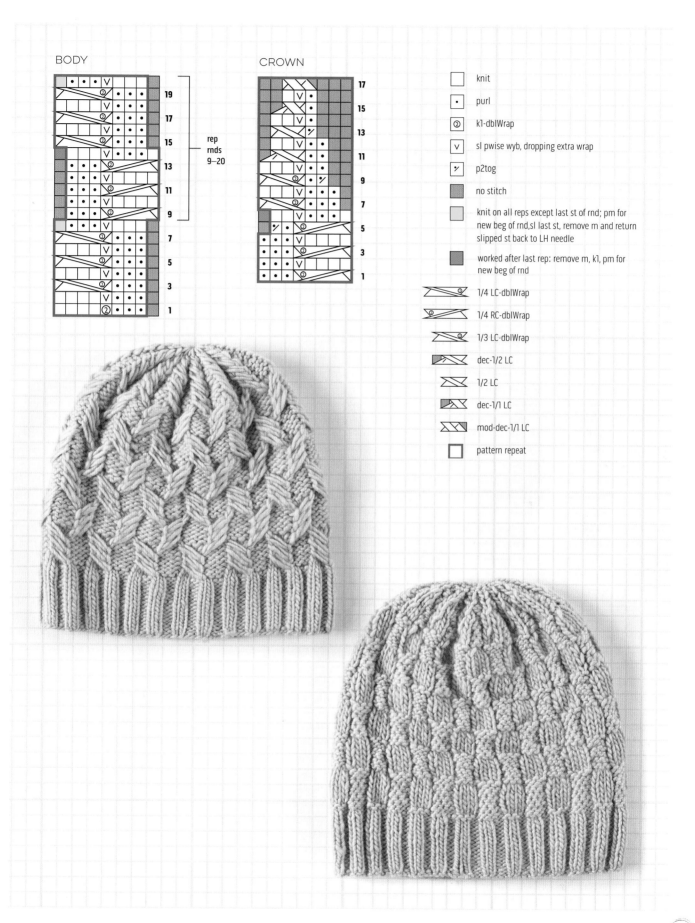

- knit
- purl
- k1-dblWrap
- sl pwise wyb, dropping extra wrap
- p2tog
- no stitch
- knit on all reps except last st of rnd; pm for new beg of rnd,sl last st, remove m and return slipped st back to LH needle
- worked after last rep: remove m, k1, pm for new beg of rnd
- 1/4 LC-dblWrap
- 1/4 RC-dblWrap
- 1/3 LC-dblWrap
- dec-1/2 LC
- 1/2 LC
- dec-1/1 LC
- mod-dec-1/1 LC
- pattern repeat

THIS VEST SHOWCASES the versatility of reversible slip-stitch patterns. The main stitch pattern, lace and slipped rib, is a reversible stitch that is visible on the wrong side as the garment moves. After the shoulders are joined, a multicolored scarf is worked in reversible tuck tile–stitch pattern and is attached to top of fronts and the back neck. // designed by FAINA GOBERSTEIN

seren VEST

FINISHED SIZE

About 28 (31, 34, 37, 40, 43)" (71 [79, 86.5, 94, 101.5, 109] cm) bust circumference.

Vest shown measures 28" (71 cm) with 7" (17.5 cm) negative ease.

YARN

DK weight (#3 Light).

Shown here: The Fibre Company Road to China Light (65% baby alpaca, 15% silk, 10% cashmere, 10% camel; 159 yd [145 m]/1 ¾ oz [50 g]): tamzanite (color A), 6 (7, 8, 9, 10, 11) skeins; amethyst-dark (color B) and grey pearl (color C), 2 (2, 2, 2, 3, 3) skeins each.

NEEDLES

Vest: Size U.S. 6 (4.0 mm): 32" (80 cm) circular (cir).

Scarf: Size U.S. 4 (3.5 mm) straight needles.

Adjust needle sizes if necessary to obtain the correct gauge.

NOTIONS

Markers (m); stitch holders or waste yarn; tapestry needle.

GAUGE

24 sts and 36 rows = 4" (10 cm) in lace and slipped rib stitch (see Stitch Guide or chart) with larger needles.

27 sts and 36 rows = 4" (10 cm) in tuck tile stitch (see Stitch Guide or chart) with smaller needles.

NOTES

For a nice selvedge, do the following: Every row: Sl 1 wyf, work to last st, k1.

Keep the yarn in front if next st after selvedge is a purl; bring the yarn to back if the next st is a knit.

When decreasing lace and slipped rib patt, if there are not enough sts to work both yo and p2tog (or ssk), work these sts in Rev St st (purl on RS, knit on WS) instead.

STITCH GUIDE

T2 (TUCK STITCH)

With LH needle, catch 2 floats on the back of next elongated st, so floats are on top of needle and in front of elongated st (3 loops on needle: 1 live st and 2 floats). Knit all loops tog.

LACE AND SLIPPED RIB

(multiple of 9 sts + 12)

With color A,

ROW 1: (WS) [K1, p1] twice, *ssk, yo, k2, p1, [k1, p1] twice; rep from * to 8 sts before m, ssk, yo, k2, [p1, k1] twice.

ROW 2: (RS) [P1, sl1 wyb] twice, p2tog, yo, p2, *sl1 wyb, [p1, sl1 wyb] twice, p2tog, yo, p2; rep from * to 4 sts before m, [sl1 wyb, p1] twice.

Rep Rows 1 and 2 for patt.

TUCK TILE

(multiple of 4 sts + 1)

With color C,

ROW 1: (RS) Sl1 wyb, *k3, sl1 wyb; rep from *.

ROW 2: Sl1 wyf, *p3, sl1 wyf; rep from *.

With color B,

ROW 3: T2 (see Stitch Guide), *p1, k1, p1, T2; rep from *.

ROW 4: K1, *p1, k1; rep from *.

With color C,

ROW 5: K1, *k1, sl1 wyb, k2; rep from *.

ROW 6: P1, *p1, sl1 wyf, p2; rep from *.

With color B,

ROW 7: K1, *p1, T2, p1, k1; rep from *.

ROW 8: P1, *k1, p1; rep from *.

Rep Rows 1–8 for patt.

TIPS

– Place markers between the pattern repeats. Slip the markers every row as you come to them.

– Use different color markers for side seams.

body

With color A, larger needle, and using long-tail method (see Glossary), CO 1 st, pm, CO 84 (93, 102, 111, 120, 129) sts for right front, pm for side "seam," CO 84 (93, 102, 111, 120, 129) sts for back, pm for left side "seam," CO 84 (93, 102, 111, 120, 129) sts for left front, pm, CO 1 st—254 (281, 308, 335, 362, 389) sts.

Knit 2 rows.

EST PATT: (WS) Sl 1 wyf, sl m, *work Row 1 of Lace and Slipped Rib stitch (see Stitch Guide or chart) to m, sl m; rep from * 2 more times, k1.

NEXT ROW: (RS) Sl 1 wyf, sl m, *work Row 2 of Lace and Slipped Rib Chart to m, sl m; rep from * 2 more times, k1.

Work 1 more row even as est.

SHAPE FRONT

Note: Read ahead; armhole shaping begins before front shaping is completed.

FRONT DEC ROW: (RS) Sl 1 wyf, sl m, (p1, sl 1 wyb) twice, k2og or p2tog keeping in patt, work in est patt to last 6 sts, ssk or ssp keeping in patt, (sl 1 wyb, p1) twice, sl m, k1—2 sts decreased.

Work 5 (3, 3, 3, 3, 3) rows even in patt.

Rep the last 6 (4, 4, 4, 4, 4) rows 2 (68, 63, 60, 56, 53) more times.

[Work front dec row, then work 3 (1, 1, 1, 1, 1) row(s) even in patt] 64 (3, 15, 24, 34, 42) times.

At the same time, when piece meas 20¼ (21, 21¼, 21½, 21¾, 22)" (51.5 [53.5, 54, 54.5, 55, 56] cm), end after a RS row. Cont working front shaping as est while shaping armholes as foll:

NEXT ROW: (WS) *Work in est patt to 8 sts before m, work next 16 sts as follows: k1, p1, k2, (p1, k1, p1, k2) twice, p1, k1; rep from * once more, work to end.

NEXT ROW: (RS) *Work in est patt to 8 sts before m, work next 16 sts as follows: p1, sl 1, (p2, sl 1, p1, sl 1) twice, p2, sl 1, p1] twice, work to end.

Cont in est patt and rep the last 2 rows until piece measures 21¾ (22½, 22¾, 23, 23¼, 23½)" (55 [57, 58, 58.5, 59, 59.5] cm), ending after a RS row.

Divide for back and front

Note: The count of front sts at this point varies with size. Make sure the count of both fronts is the same. Take note of the rem front shaping you'll need to work when you come back to fronts, after the back is finished.

NEXT ROW: (WS) *Work to 6 (6, 8, 8, 8, 10) sts before m, removing side m BO 12 (12, 16, 16, 16, 20) sts for underarm; rep from * once more, work to end for right front—72 (81, 86, 95, 104, 109) back sts rem, 6 (6, 8, 8, 8, 10) sts dec'd for each front.

Keep yarn attached to work right front later. Place right front and left front sts onto separate holders or waste yarn, leaving back sts on needle.

back

Join a new ball of yarn, preparing to work a RS row. Work even in patt, keeping selvedge sts as est, until armholes measure 8½ (8¾, 9, 9¼, 9½, 9¾)" (21.5 [22, 23, 23.5, 24, 25] cm), ending after a WS row.

NEXT ROW: (RS) Work next 12 (16, 16, 19, 22, 24) right shoulder sts in patt, BO 48 (49, 54, 57, 60, 61) sts for neck, work to end—12 (16, 16, 19, 22, 24) sts rem on each side.

SHAPE LEFT SHOULDER

Work 12 (16, 16, 19, 22, 24) left shoulder sts even as est for 8 more rows. Place left shoulder sts onto holder. Break yarn.

SHAPE RIGHT SHOULDER

Join yarn at neck edge, preparing to work a WS row. Work even as est for 8 more rows. Place right shoulder sts onto holder. Break yarn.

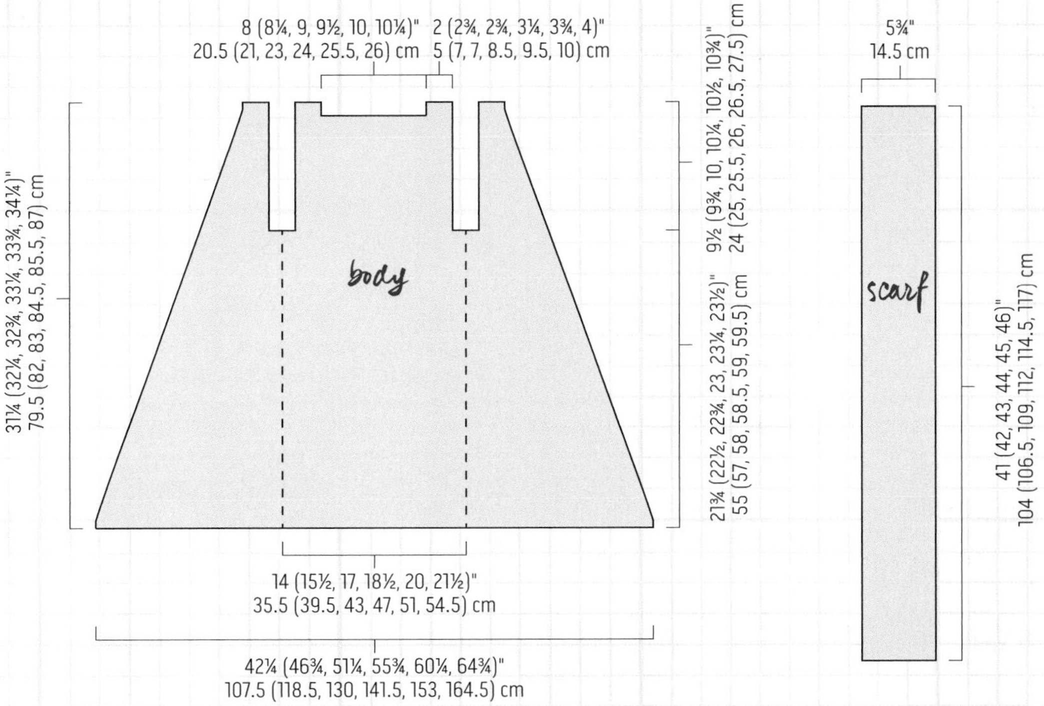
8 (8¼, 9, 9½, 10, 10¼)"
20.5 (21, 23, 24, 25.5, 26) cm
2 (2¾, 2¾, 3¼, 3¾, 4)"
5 (7, 7, 8.5, 9.5, 10) cm
31¼ (32¼, 32¾, 33¼, 33¾, 34¼)"
79.5 (82, 83, 84.5, 85.5, 87) cm
body
9½ (9¾, 10, 10¼, 10½, 10¾)"
24 (25, 25.5, 26, 26.5, 27.5) cm
21¾ (22½, 22¾, 23, 23¼, 23½)"
55 (57, 58, 58.5, 59, 59.5) cm
14 (15½, 17, 18½, 20, 21½)"
35.5 (39.5, 43, 47, 51, 54.5) cm
42¼ (46¾, 51¼, 55¾, 60¼, 64¾)"
107.5 (118.5, 130, 141.5, 153, 164.5) cm
5¾"
14.5 cm
scarf
41 (42, 43, 44, 45, 46)"
104 (106.5, 109, 112, 114.5, 117) cm

right front

Return right front sts to larger needle, preparing to work a RS row.

Cont working front shaping until completed, slipping the first st wyf and knitting the last st of every row—12 (16, 16, 19, 22, 24) sts rem. Work even in patt until armholes measure 8½ (8¾, 9, 9¼, 9¾, 9¾)" (21.5 [22, 23, 23.5, 24, 25] cm), ending after a WS row.

left front

Return left front sts to larger needle and rejoin yarn at armhole edge preparing to work a WS row. Work same as for right front.

color scarf/cowl

Notes: Use markers at each end to help isolate borders from main pattern. Although the tuck tile patt is a 4-st rep patt, 1 st is added for balance. Out of 39 sts, 29 sts between markers are worked in this patt.

With color B, smaller needle and long-tail method, CO 5 sts, pm, CO 29 sts, pm, CO 5 sts—39 sts.

BORDER

ROW 1: (WS) Sl 1 wyf, *p1, k1; rep from * to end.

ROW 2: (RS) Sl 1 wyf, (sl 1 wyb, p1) twice, sl m, *k1, p1; rep from * to 1 st before m, k1, sl m, (p1, sl 1 wyb) twice, k1.

ROW 3: Sl 1 wyf, (p1, k1) twice, sl m, *k1, p1; rep from * to 1 st before m, k1, sl m, (k1, p1) twice, k1.

ROW 4: Sl 1 wyf, (sl 1 wyb, p1) twice, sl m, *p1, k1; rep from * to 1 st before m, p1, sl m, (p1, sl 1 wyb) twice, k1.

Rep Rows 1–3 once more.

TUCK TILE

	•			•	
	•	T2	•		**7**
			V		
			V		**5**
T2	•		•	T2	**3**
V				V	
V				V	**1**

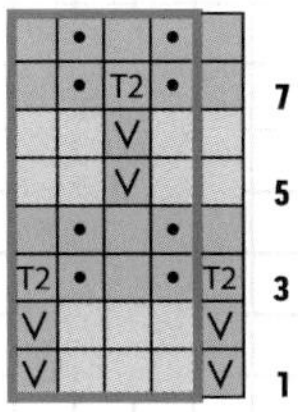

LACE AND SLIPPED RIB

•	V	•	V	•	•	O	⟋	V	•	V	•	V	•	•	O	⟋	V	•	V	•	**2**
•		•		•	⟋	O	•	•		•		•	⟋	O	•	•		•			

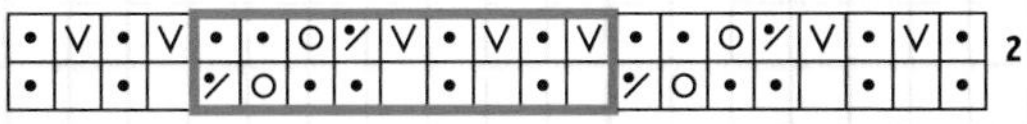

☐ with A, knit on RS, purl on WS	☑ V	sl pwise wyb on RS, sl pwise wyf on WS
▣ • with A, purl on RS, knit on WS	☑ ⟋	p2tog on RS, ssk on WS
▨ with B, knit on RS, purl on WS	☑ T2	T2 (see stitch guide)
▨ • with B, purl on RS, knit on WS	☑ o	yo
▨ with C, knit on RS, purl on WS	☐	pattern repeat

TUCK TILE PATT

On the next row, begin the tuck tile patt (see Stitch Guide or chart) between m, while cont borders in est patt, as foll:

NEXT ROW: (RS) Sl 1 wyf, (sl 1 wyb, p1) twice, sl m, work Row 1 of tuck tile patt to m, sl m, (p1, sl 1) twice, k1.

NEXT ROW: (WS) Sl 1 wyf, (p1, k1) twice, sl m, work Row 2 of tuck tile patt to m, sl m, (k1, p1) twice, k1.

Cont in est patt until piece meas 41 (42, 43, 44, 45, 46)" (104 [106.5, 109, 112, 114.5, 117] cm) or any desired length. Place sts onto st holder or waste yarn and set aside. Break yarn.

Make a second color scarf/cowl the same as the first. Break yarn, leaving a tail of color B about 1 yard (1 m) long.

finishing

Carefully block all pieces to measurements.

With RS tog, join shoulders using three-needle bind-off (see Glossary).

Return held scarf sts to smaller needles (1 piece on each needle). With WS tog, join scarf pieces using Kitchener stitch (see Glossary). Block seams only.

Using mattress stitch (see Glossary) and with RS of back and WS of scarf facing, pin the center of back to scarf seam.

Beg 5" (12.5 cm) down from shoulder seam, sew scarf along RS of right front, along back neck, and 5" (12.5 cm) down from shoulder seam along RS of left front.

Weave in loose ends.

abbreviations

beg(s)	begin(s); beginning
BO	bind off
cir	circular
cn	cable needle
CO	cast on
cont	continue(s); continuing
dec(s)('d)	decrease(s); decreasing; decreased
dpn	double-pointed needles
est	establish; established
foll(s)	follow(s); following
inc(s)('d)	increase(s); increasing; increase(d)
k	knit
k1f&b	knit into the front and back of same stitch
k2tog	knit 2 stitches together
k3tog	knit 3 stitches together
kwise	knitwise, as if to knit
LH	left hand
m	marker(s)
M1	make one (increase)
M1L	make one (left slant)
M1R	make one (right slant)
meas	measures
p	purl
p1f&b	purl into front and back of same stitch
p2tog	purl 2 stitches together
patt(s)	pattern(s)
pm	place marker
psso	pass slipped stitch over
pwise	purlwise; as if to purl
rem	remain(s); remaining
rep	repeat(s); repeating
RH	right hand
rnd(s)	round(s)
RS	right side
sc	single crochet
sl	slip
sl m	slip marker
ssk	slip, slip, knit (decrease)
ssp	slip, slip, purl (decrease)
St st	stockinette stitch
st(s)	stitch(es)
tbl	through back loop
tog	together
WS	wrong side
wyb	with yarn in back
wyf	with yarn in front
yd	yard(s)
yo	yarnover

glossary

BIND-OFFS

THREE-NEEDLE BIND-OFF

Place the stitches to be joined onto two separate needles and hold the needles parallel so that the right sides of knitting face together. Insert a third needle into the first stitch on each of two needles **(FIG. 1)** and knit them together as one stitch **(FIG. 2)**, *knit the next stitch on each needle the same way, then use the left needle tip to lift the first stitch over the second and off the needle **(FIG. 3)**. Repeat from * until no stitches remain on first two needles. Cut yarn and pull tail through last stitch to secure.

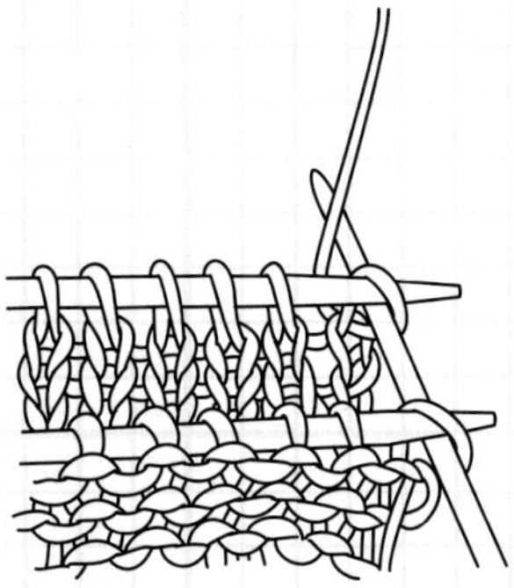

FIG. 1

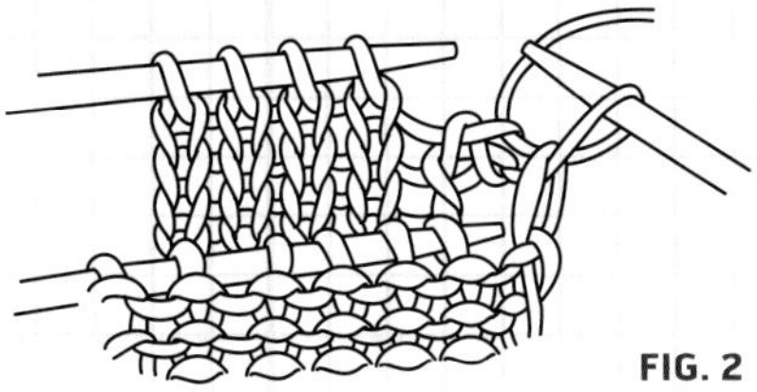

FIG. 2

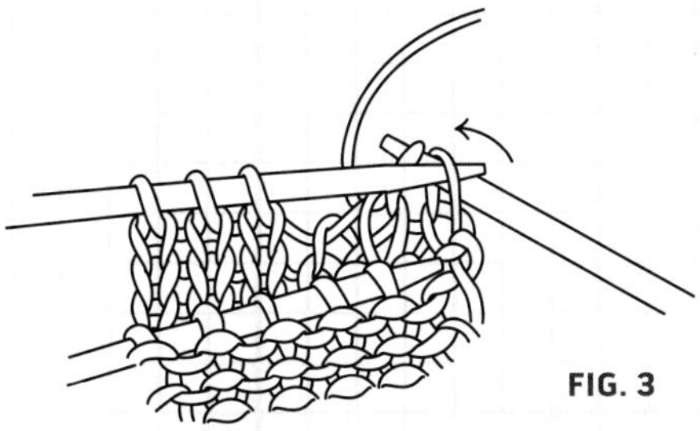

FIG. 3

BUTTONHOLES

ONE-ROW BUTTONHOLE

With RS facing, bring yarn to front, slip the next stitch purlwise, return yarn to the back, *slip the next stitch purlwise, pass the first slipped stitch over the second slipped stitch and off the needle; repeat from * two more times **(FIG. 1)**. Slip the last stitch on the right needle tip to the left needle tip and turn the work so that the wrong side is facing. **With yarn in back, insert right needle tip between the first two stitches on the left needle tip **(FIG. 2)**, draw through a loop and place it on the left needle]; rep from ** three more times, then turn the work so the right side is facing. With yarn in back, slip the first stitch and lift the extra cast-on stitch over the slipped stitch **(FIG. 3)** and off the needle to complete the buttonhole.

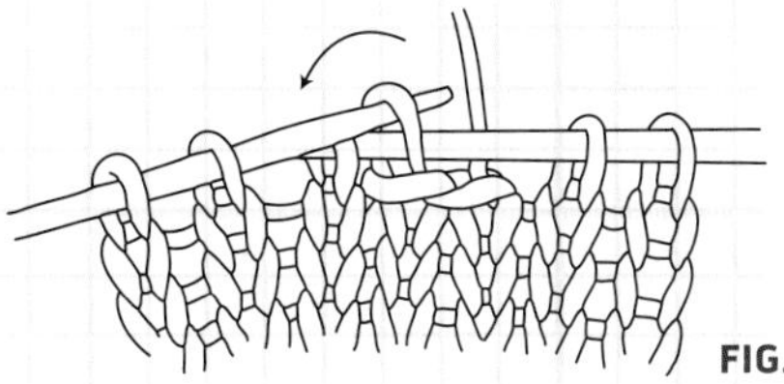

FIG. 1

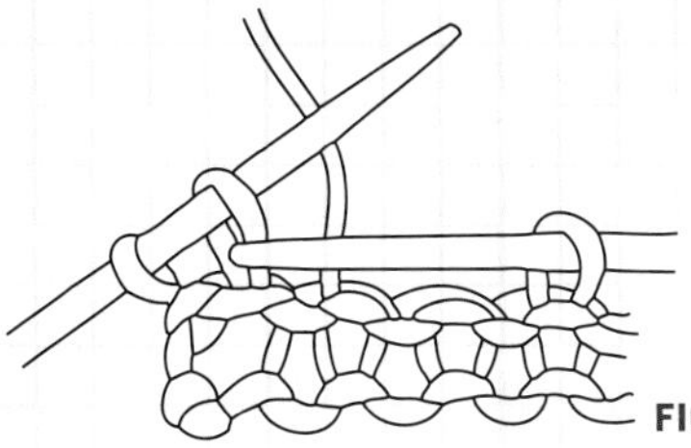

FIG. 2

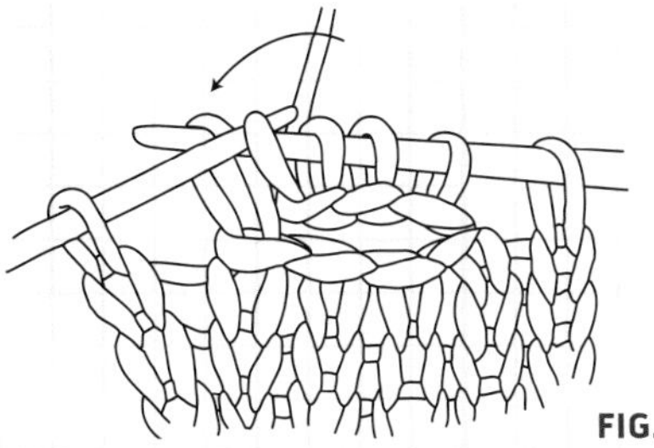

FIG. 3

CAST-ONS

BACKWARD-LOOP CAST-ON

*Loop working yarn and place it on needle backward so that it doesn't unwind. Repeat from *.

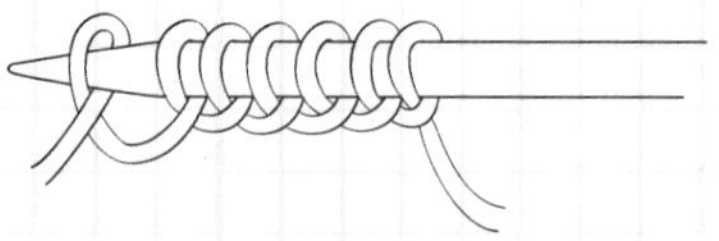

CROCHET CHAIN PROVISIONAL CAST-ON

With waste yarn and crochet hook, make a loose crochet chain (see page 167) about four stitches more than you need to cast on. With knitting needle, working yarn, and beginnning two stitches from end of chain, pick up and knit one stitch through the back loop of each crochet chain **(FIG. 1)** for desired number of stitches. When you're ready to work in the opposite direction, pull out the crochet chain to expose live stitches **(FIG. 2)**.

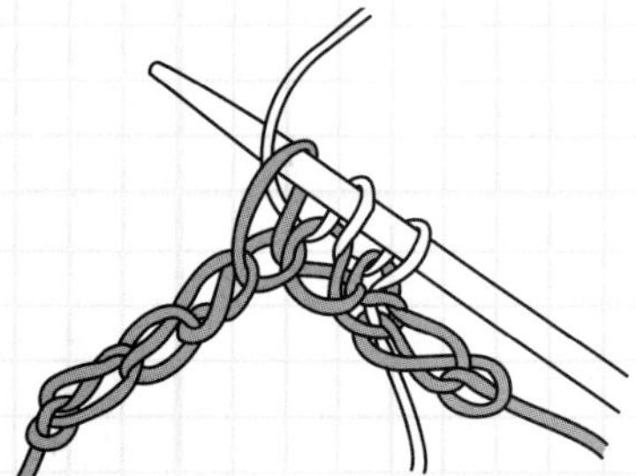

FIG. 1

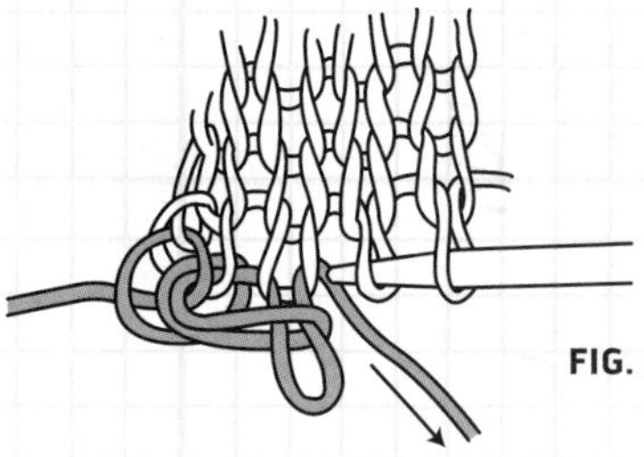

FIG. 2

KNITTED CAST-ON

If there are no stitches on the needles, make a slipknot of working yarn and place it on the left needle. When there is at least one stitch on the left needle, *use the right needle to knit the first stitch (or slipknot) on left needle **(FIG. 1)** and place new loop onto left needle to form a new stitch **(FIG. 2)**. Repeat from * for the desired number of stitches, always working into the last stitch made.

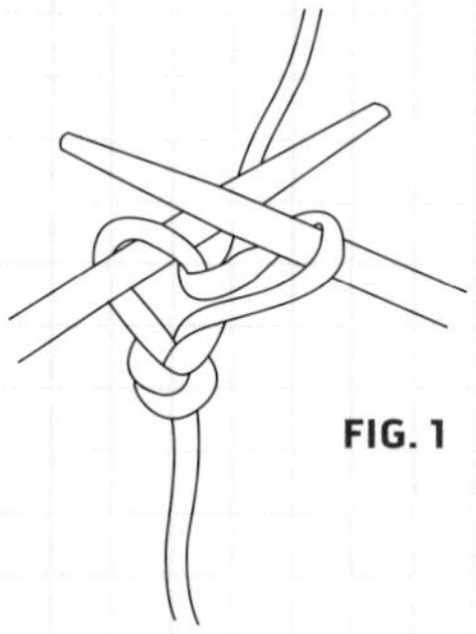

FIG. 1

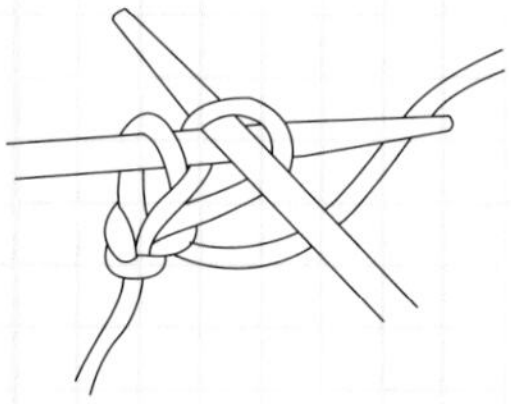

FIG. 2

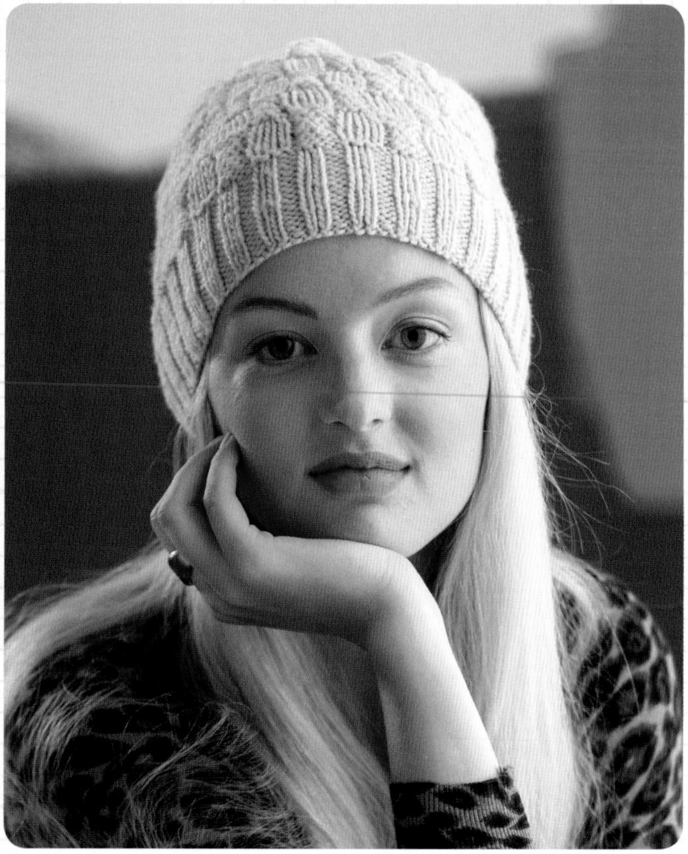

LONG-TAIL (CONTINENTAL) CAST-ON

Leaving a long tail (about ½" [1.3 cm] for each stitch to be cast on), make a slipknot and place on right needle. Place thumb and index finger of your left hand between the yarn ends so that working yarn is around your index finger and tail end is around your thumb and secure the yarn ends with your other fingers. Hold your palm upward, making a V of yarn **(FIG. 1)**. *Bring needle up through loop on thumb **(FIG. 2)**, catch first strand around index finger, and go back down through loop on thumb **(FIG. 3)**. Drop loop off thumb and, placing thumb back in V configuration, tighten resulting stitch on needle **(FIG. 4)**. Repeat from * for the desired number of stitches.

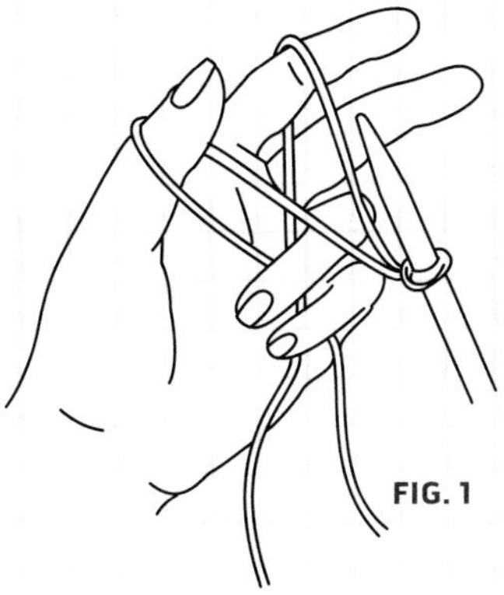

FIG. 1

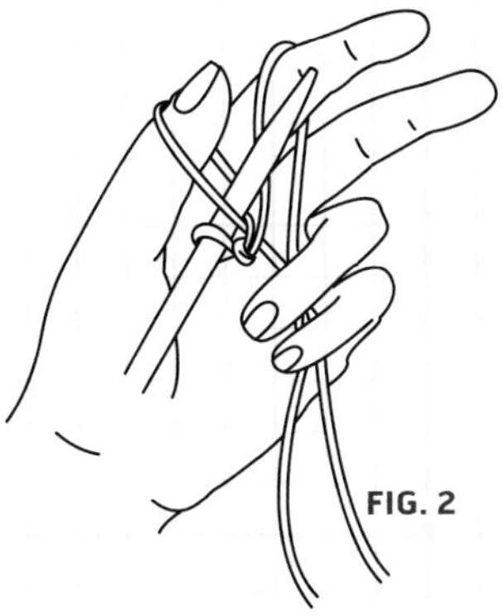

FIG. 2

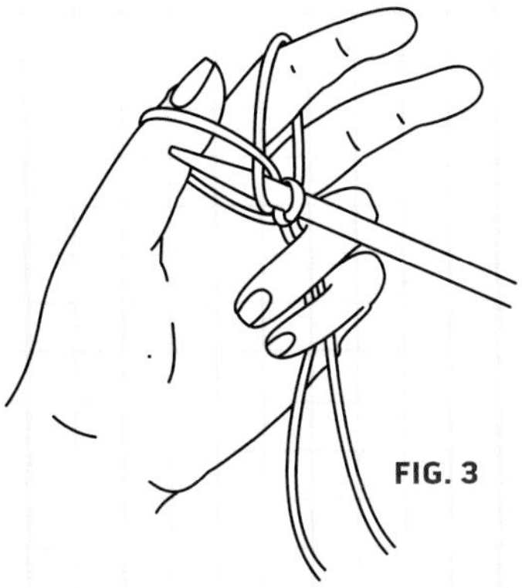

FIG. 3

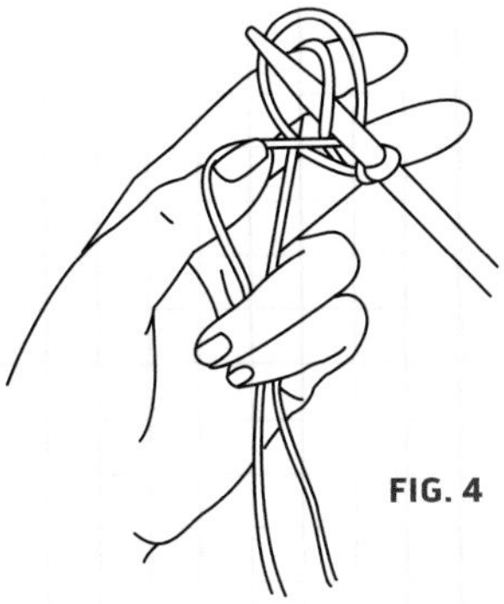

FIG. 4

CROCHET

CROCHET CHAIN

Make a slipknot and place it on crochet hook if there isn't a loop already on the hook. *Yarn over hook and draw through loop on hook. Repeat from * for the desired number of stitches. To fasten off, cut yarn and draw end through last loop formed.

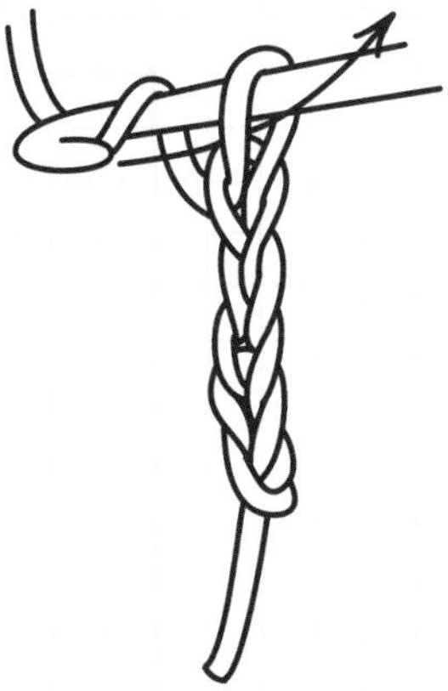

SINGLE CROCHET

*Insert hook into the second chain from the hook (or the next stitch), yarn over hook and draw through a loop, yarn over hook **(FIG. 1)**, and draw it through both loops on hook **(FIG. 2)**. Repeat from * for the desired number of stitches.

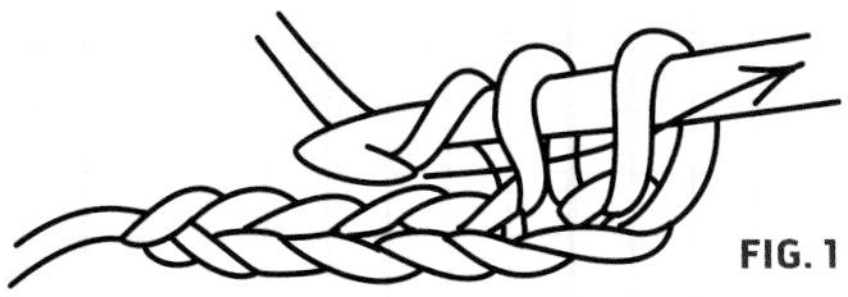

FIG. 1

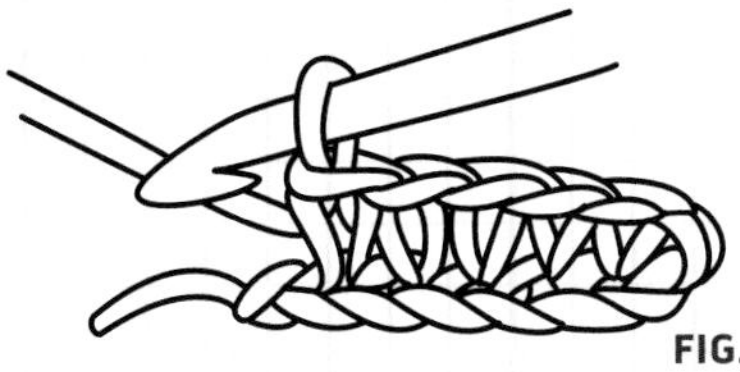

FIG. 2

SLIP STITCH

*Insert hook in stitch, yarn over and draw loop through stitch and loop on hook. Repeat from *.

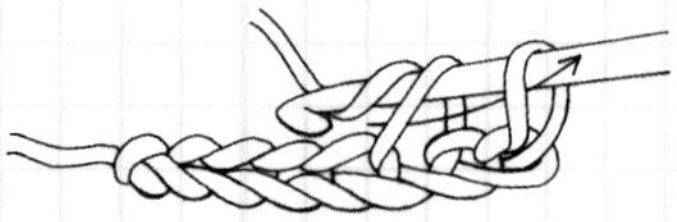

DECREASES

SSK

Slip two stitches individually knitwise **(FIG. 1)**, insert left needle tip into the front of these two slipped stitches, and use the right needle to knit them together through their back loops **(FIG. 2)**.

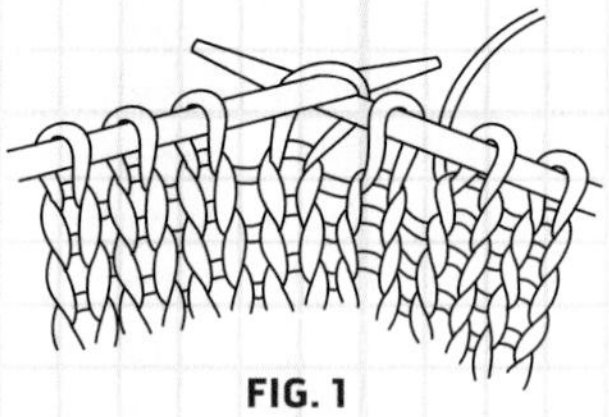

FIG. 1

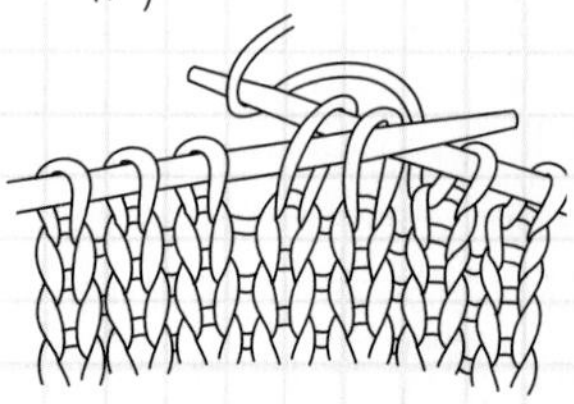

FIG. 2

SSP

Holding yarn in front, slip two stitches individually knitwise **(FIG. 1)**, then slip these two stitches back onto left needle (they will be twisted on the needle) and purl them together through their back loops **(FIG. 2)**.

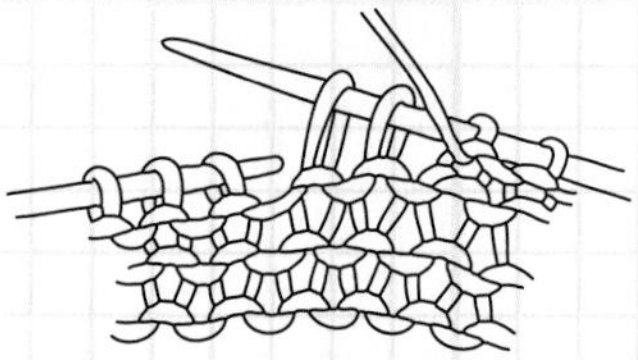

FIG. 1

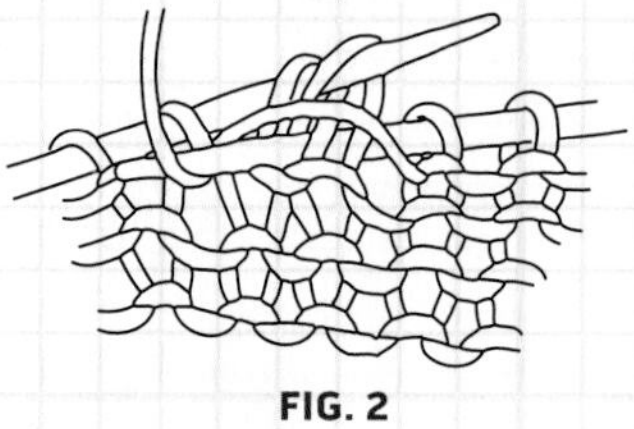

FIG. 2

INCREASES

MAKE ONE (M1) INCREASE

Note: Use the left slant if no direction of slant is specified.

RIGHT SLANT (M1R)

With left needle tip, lift the strand between the needles from back to front **(FIG. 1)**. Knit the lifted loop through the front **(FIG. 2)**.

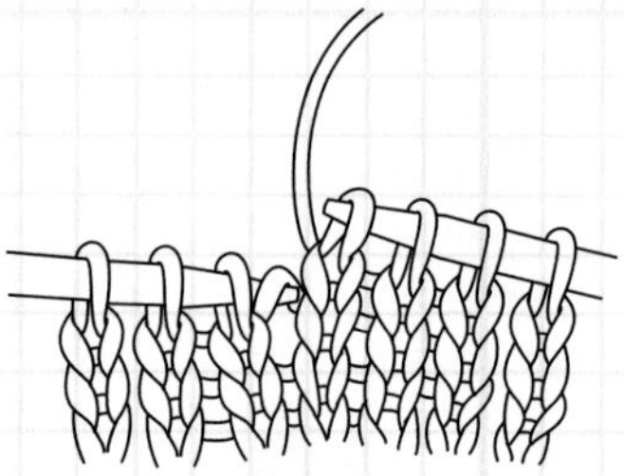

FIG. 1

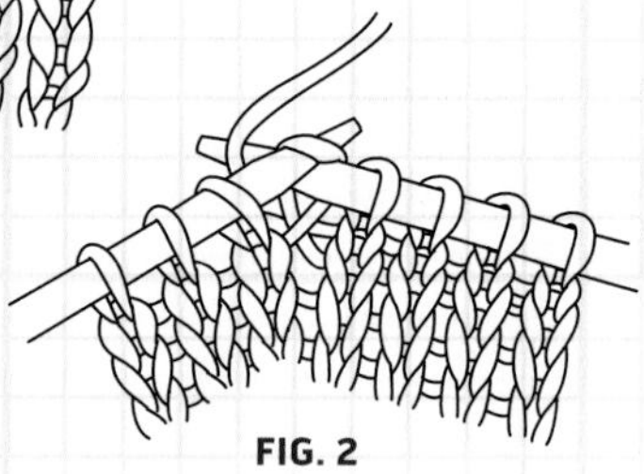

FIG. 2

LEFT SLANT (M1L)

With left needle tip, lift the strand between the last knitted stitch and the first stitch on the left needle from front to back **(FIG. 1)**, then knit the lifted loop through the back **(FIG. 2)**.

FIG. 1

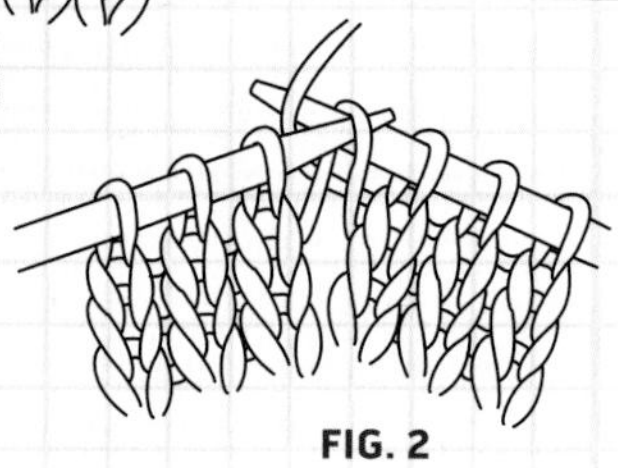

FIG. 2

RIGHT LIFTED INCREASE (RLI)

Knit into the back of stitch (in the "purl bump") in the row directly below the stitch on the left needle.

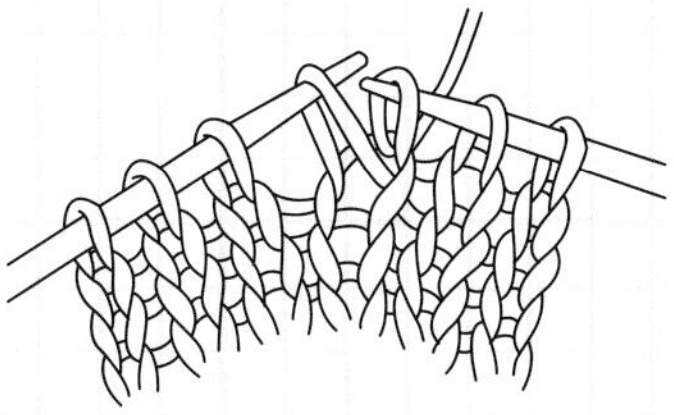

INTARSIA

ON RS:

When ready to switch from color A to color B, drop color A, join color B, and knit one stitch; *bring the strand of color B from under the strand of color A **(FIG. 1)** and work with B per pattern.* The B strand will wrap around the strand of color A and will prevent a hole from forming.

When the strand of the color you are switching to is already attached: Drop color A and work from * to *.

ON WS:

When ready to switch from color A to color B, drop color A, join color B, and purl one stitch; *bring the strand of color B from under the strand of color A **(FIG. 2)** and work with B per pattern. The B strand will wrap around the strand of color A and will prevent a hole from forming.

When the strand of the color you are switching to is already attached: Drop color A and work from * to *.

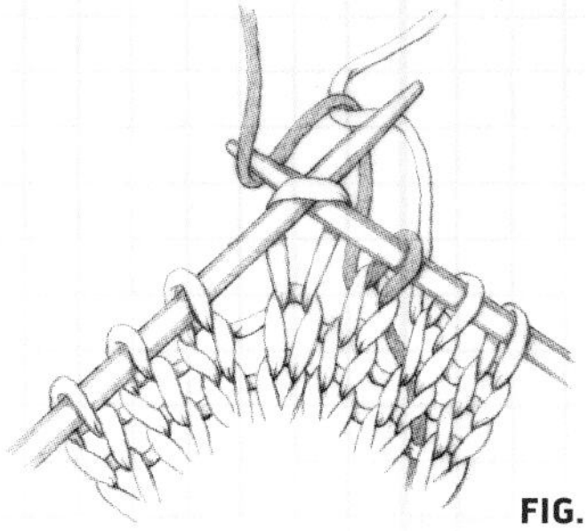

FIG. 1

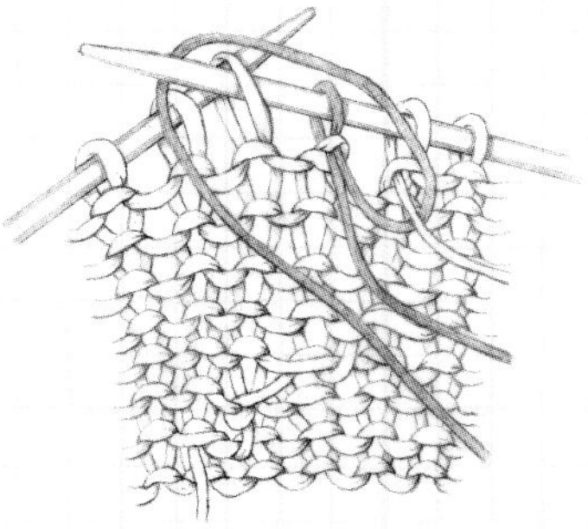

FIG. 2

GRAFTING

KITCHENER STITCH

Arrange stitches on two needles so that there is an equal number of stitches on each needle. Hold the needles parallel to each other with wrong sides of the knitting together. Allowing about ½" (1.3 cm) per stitch to be grafted, thread matching yarn on a tapestry needle. Work from right to left as follows:

Step 1. Bring tapestry needle through the first stitch on the front needle as if to purl and leave the stitch on the needle **(FIG. 1)**.

Step 2. Bring tapestry needle through the first stitch on the back needle as if to knit and leave that stitch on the needle **(FIG. 2)**.

Step 3. Bring tapestry needle through the first front stitch as if to knit and slip this stitch off the needle. Then bring tapestry needle through the next front stitch as if to purl and leave this stitch on the needle **(FIG. 3)**.

Step 4. Bring tapestry needle through the first back stitch as if to purl and slip this stitch off the needle. Then bring tapestry needle through the next back stitch as if to knit and leave this stitch on the needle **(FIG. 4)**.

Repeat Steps 3 and 4 until one stitch remains on each needle, adjusting the tension to match the rest of the knitting as you go. To finish, bring tapestry needle through the front stitch as if to knit and slip this stitch off the needle. Then bring tapestry needle through the back stitch as if to purl and slip this stitch off the needle.

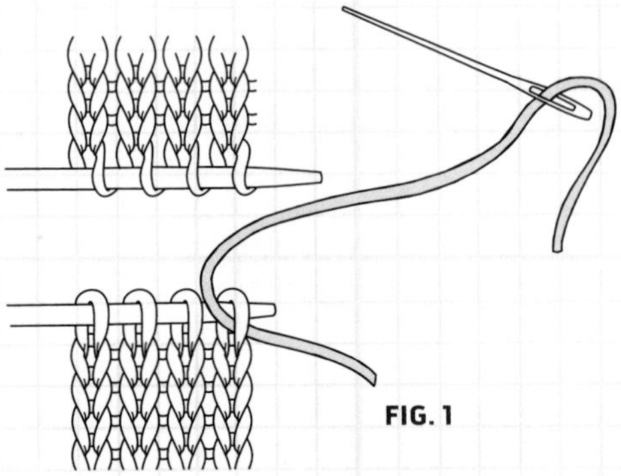
FIG. 1

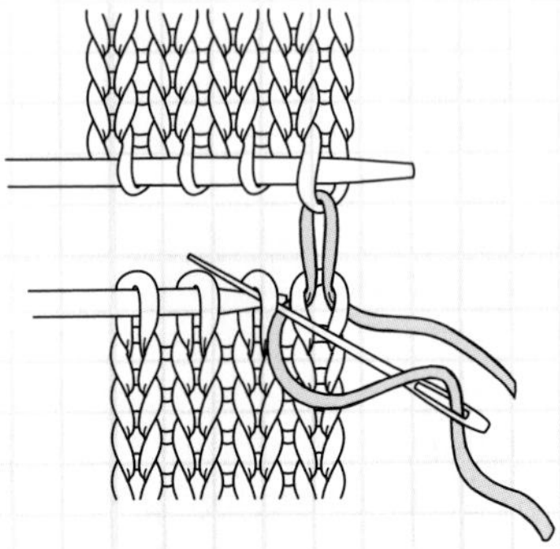
FIG. 3

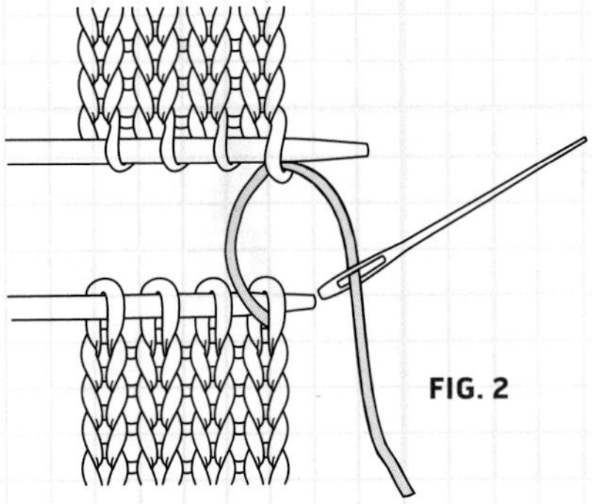
FIG. 2

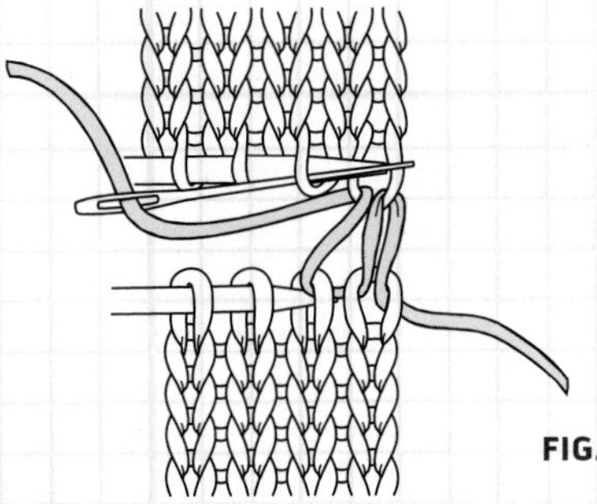
FIG. 4

PICK UP AND KNIT

ALONG CO OR BO EDGE

With right side facing and working from right to left, insert the tip of the needle into the center of the stitch below the bind-off or cast-on edge **(FIG. 1)**, wrap yarn around needle, and pull through a loop **(FIG. 2)**. Pick up one stitch for every existing stitch.

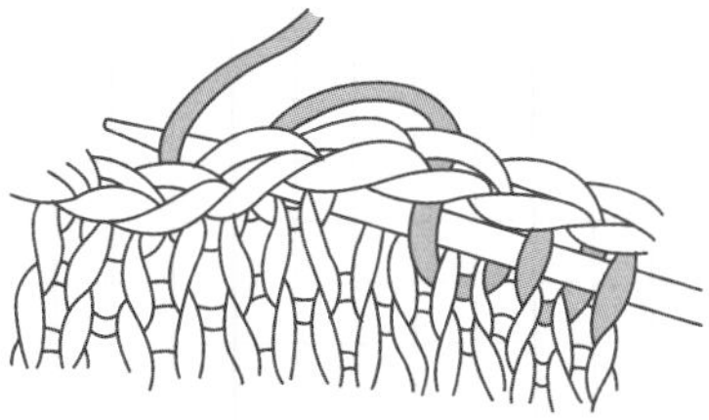

FIG. 1

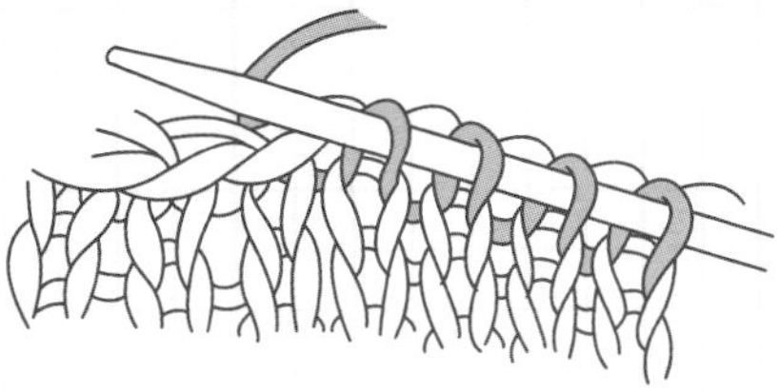

FIG. 2

ALONG SHAPED EDGE

With right side facing and working from right to left, insert tip of needle between last and second-to-last stitches, wrap yarn around needle, and pull through a loop. Pick up and knit about three stitches for every four rows, adjusting as necessary so that picked-up edge lies flat.

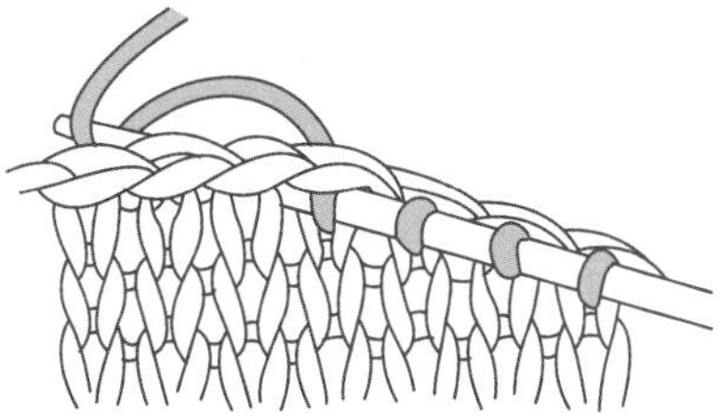

PICK UP AND PURL

With wrong side of work facing and working from right to left, *insert needle tip under purl stitch in the last row from the far side to the near side **(FIG. 1)**, wrap yarn around needle and pull a loop through **(FIG. 2)**. Repeat from * for desired number of stitches.

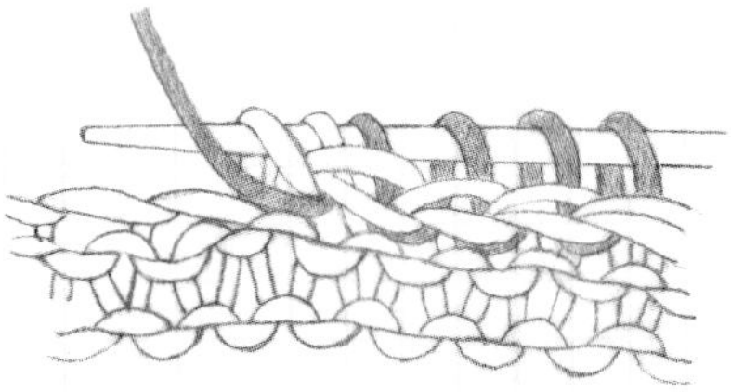

FIG. 1

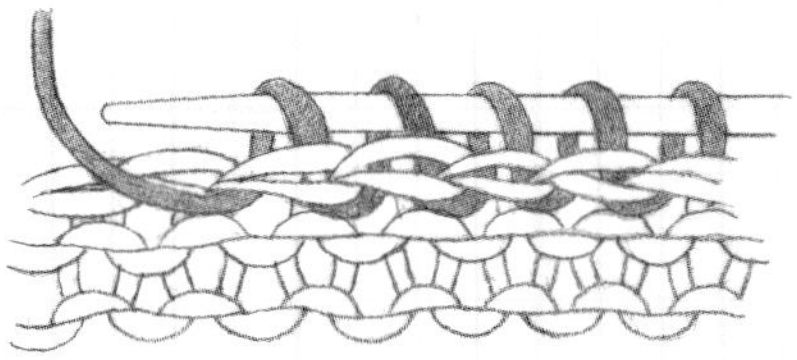

FIG. 2

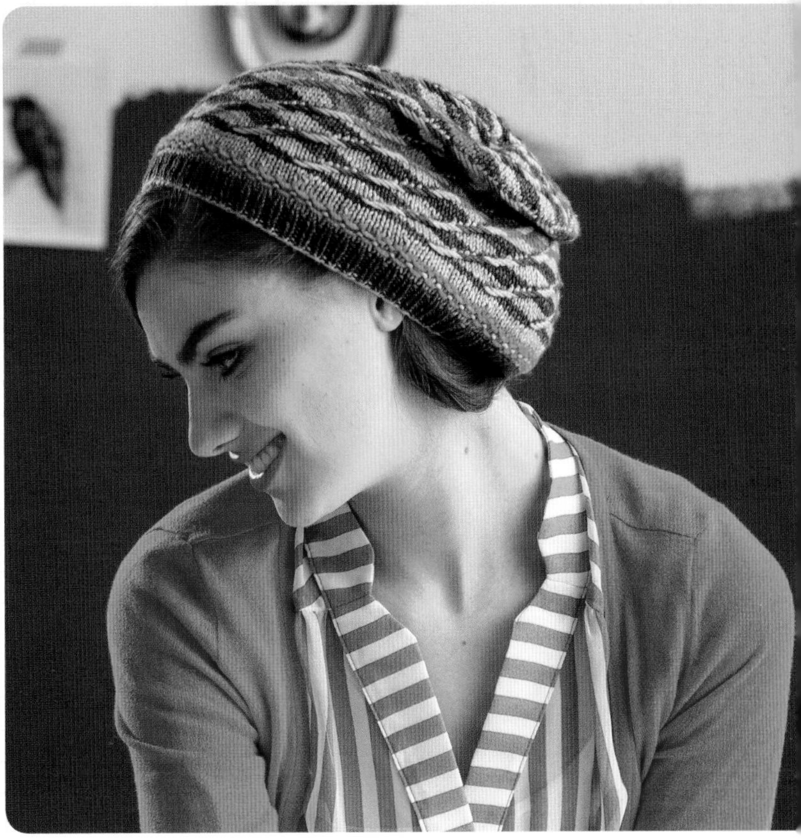

SEAMING

MATTRESS STITCH

With RS of knitting facing, use threaded needle to pick up one bar between first two stitches on one piece **(FIG. 1),** then corresponding bar plus the bar above it on other piece **(FIG. 2)**. *Pick up next two bars on first piece, then next two bars on other **(FIG. 3)**. Repeat from * to end of seam, finishing by picking up last bar (or pair of bars) at the top of first piece.

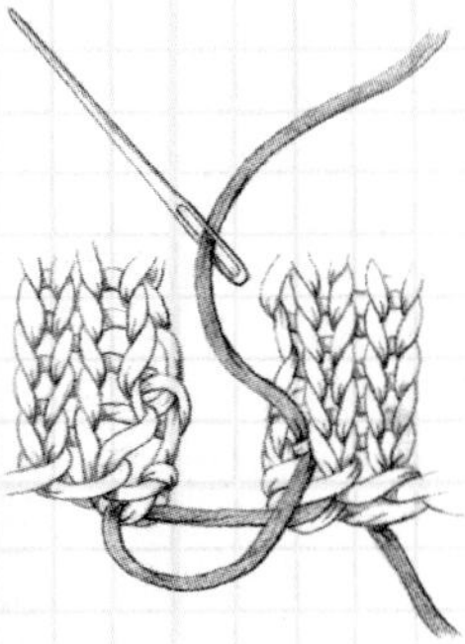

FIG. 1

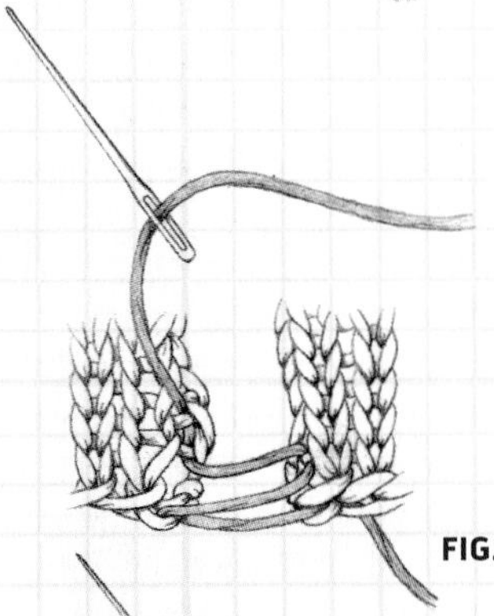

FIG. 2

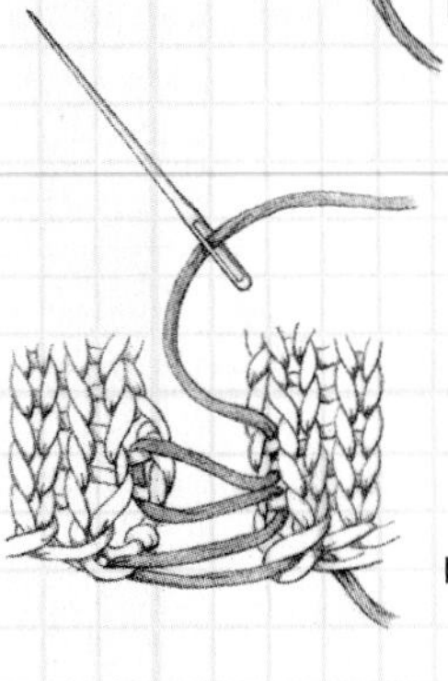

FIG. 3

WHIPSTITCH

Hold pieces to be sewn together so that the edges to be seamed are even with each other. With yarn threaded on a tapestry needle, *insert needle through both layers from back to front, then bring needle to back. Repeat from *, keeping even tension on the seaming yarn.

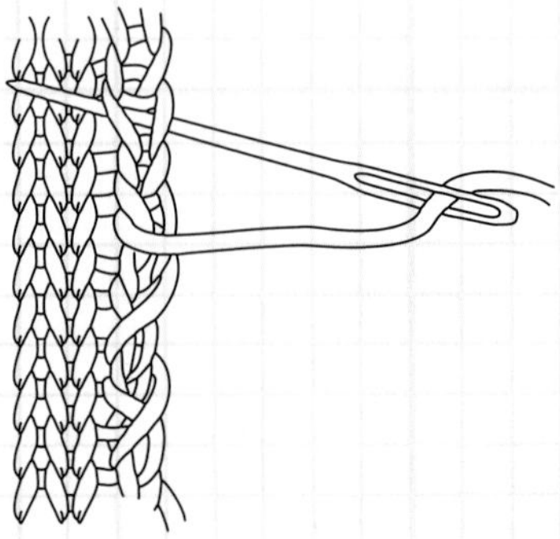

SEWING

BACKSTITCH

Working from right to left, bring the needle up at a and insert at b, ⅛" to ¼" (3 to 6 mm) from the starting point. Bring the needle back up at c and repeat.

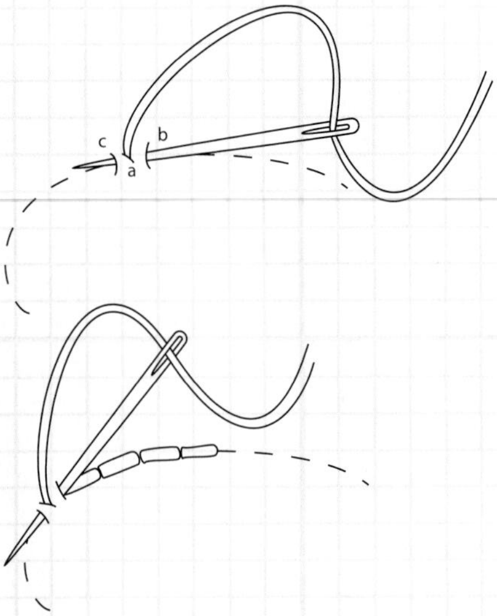

SHORT-ROWS

KNIT SIDE

Work to turning point, slip next stitch purlwise **(FIG. 1)**, bring the yarn to the front, then slip the same stitch back to the left needle **(FIG. 2)**, turn the work around and bring the yarn in position for the next stitch—one stitch has been wrapped, and the yarn is correctly positioned to work the next stitch. When you come to a wrapped stitch on a subsequent row, hide the wrap by working it together with the wrapped stitch as follows: Insert right needle tip under the wrap (from the front if wrapped stitch is a knit stitch; from the back if wrapped stitch is a purl stitch; **FIG. 3**), then into the stitch on the needle, and work the stitch and its wrap together as a single stitch.

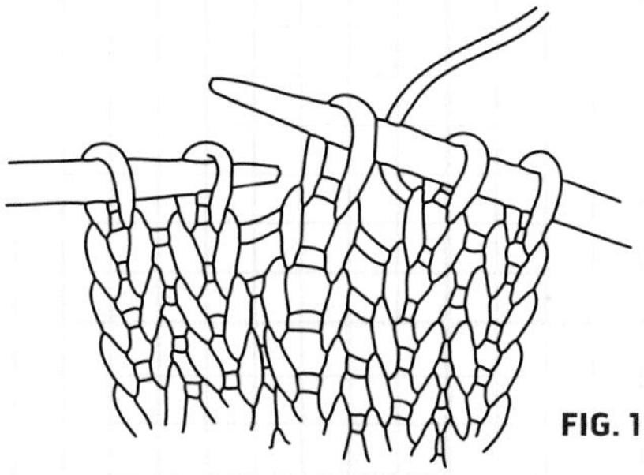

FIG. 1

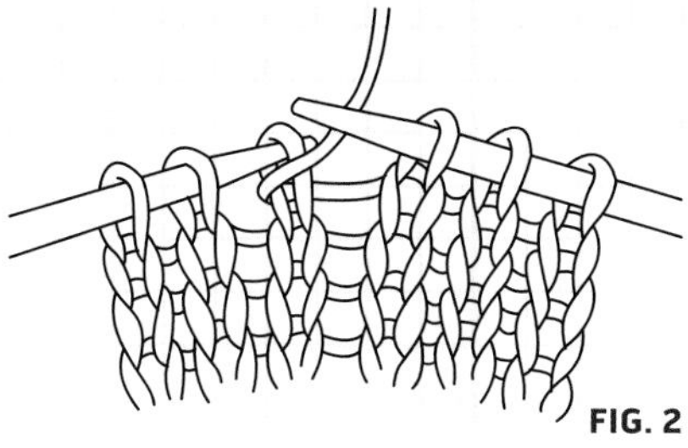

FIG. 2

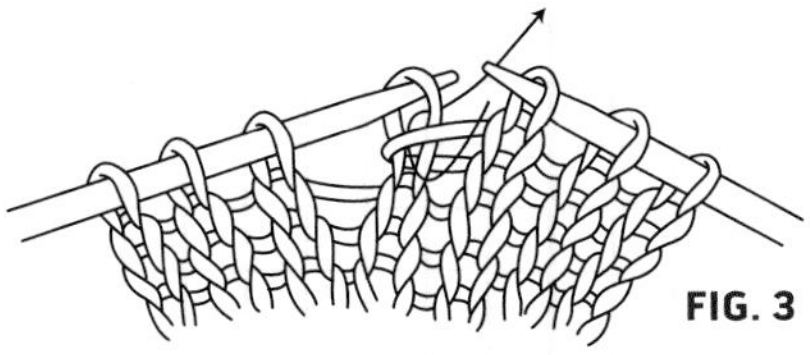

FIG. 3

PURL SIDE

Work to the turning point, slip the next stitch purlwise to the right needle, bring the yarn to the back of the work **(FIG. 1)**, return the slipped stitch to the left needle, bring the yarn to the front between the needles **(FIG. 2)**, and turn the work so that the knit side is facing—one stitch has been wrapped, and the yarn is correctly positioned to knit the next stitch. To hide the wrap on a subsequent purl row, work to the wrapped stitch, use the tip of the right needle to pick up the wrap from the back, place it on the left needle **(FIG. 3)**, then purl it together with the wrapped stitch.

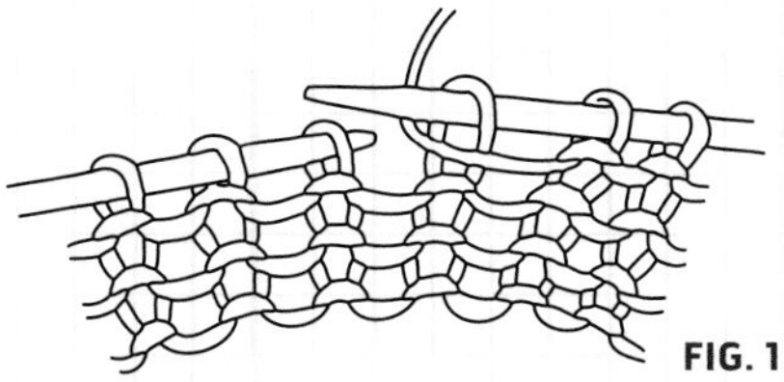

FIG. 1

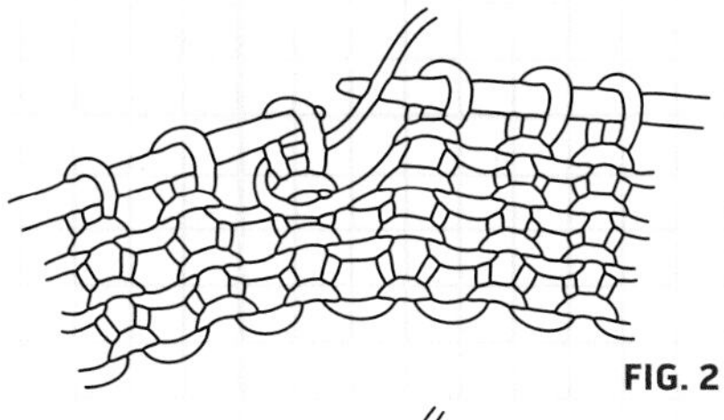

FIG. 2

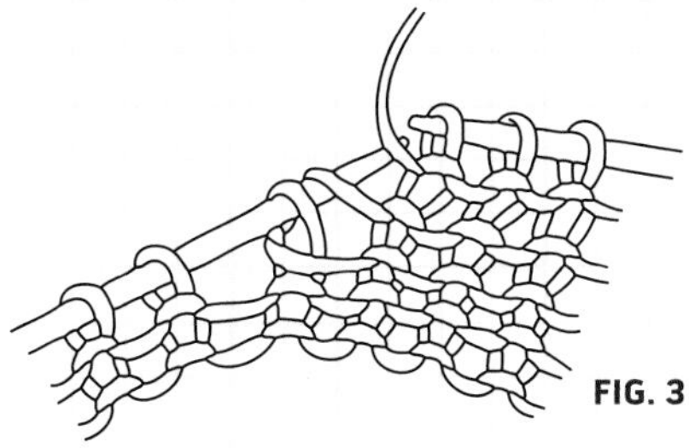

FIG. 3

SOURCES FOR YARN

Anzula
740 H St.
Fresno, CA 93721
anzula.com

Bijou Basin Ranch
PO Box 154
Elbert, CO 80106
bijoubasinranch.com

Blue Sky Alpacas
PO Box 88
Cedar, MN 55011
blueskyalpacas.com

Cascade Yarns
PO Box 58168
1224 Andover Park E.
Tukwila, WA 98188
cascadeyarns.com

Claudia Hand Painted Yarns
40 W. Washington St.
Harrisonburg, VA 22802
claudiaco.com

Fibre Company
Distributed by
Kelbourne Woolens
2000 Manor Rd.
Conshohocken, PA 19428
kelbournewoolens.com

Lion Brand Yarn Company
34 West 15th St., Floor 7
New York, NY 10011
lionbrand.com

Lisa Souza Dyeworks
4550 Newtown Rd.
Placerville, CA 95667
lisaknit.com

Malabrigo
malabrigoyarn.com

Manos del Uruguay
Distributed in the United States by Fairmount Fibers
PO Box 2082
Philadelphia, PA 19103
fairmountfibers.com

Skacel Collection, Inc
PO Box 88110
Seattle, WA 98138
skacelknitting.com

acknowledgments

Our warmest thanks to everyone who in one way or another helped to bring this book to fruition.

Special thanks to Michelle Bredeson, our exceptional editor, who was as excited about this project as we were. We are very grateful for her guidance, knowledge, enthusiasm, respect, and endless support.

Huge thanks to Kristen TenDyke for her expertise and precise technical editing and to editorial director Allison Korleski for believing in us once again.

Big thank-you to the talented staff at Interweave who made this book so stunning: associate art director Charlene Tiedemann, beauty photographer Joe Hancock, still photographer Ann Swanson, illustrator Kathie Kelleher, hair and makeup artist Kathy MacKay, designer Pamela Norman, photo stylist Tina Gill, and production designer Kerry Jackson.

We would also like to express a heartfelt thank-you to our sample knitters, Christopher Bahl, Lynn Bloch, Jill Bigellow Suttel, Karen Morin, Irina Semenets , and Kim Schneibolk, who helped us make some of the projects and swatches for this book.

We also would like to thank the yarn companies who donated their beautiful yarns for our projects: Anzula, Bijou Basin Ranch, Blue Sky Alpacas, Cascade Yarns, Claudia Hand Painted Yarns, Fibre Company, Lion Brand, Lisa Souza Dyeworks, Malabrigo, Manos del Uruguay, Skacel Collection, and JUL designs for gorgeous handles.

It was a pleasure to work with all of you.

PROJECT NAMES

Here are the translations and pronunciations of the Russian and Czech titles used for the designs in this book:

Traditional Slip-Stitch Patterns

Svítání Pullover
(Czech for sunrise; pronounced *svee-TAH-nyee*)

Kromka Hoodie
(Russian for border; pronounced *KROME-kah*)

Čekanka Jacket
(Czech for chicory flower; pronounced *chih-KAN-kah*)

Bordo Shawl (Russian for Bordeaux, pronounced *BORE-doh*)

Woven Slip-Stitch Patterns

Gobelen Bag
(Russian for tapestry; pronounced *go-BEE-lyen*)

Mák Cardigan
(Czech and Russian word for poppy flower; pronounced *mahk*)

Volna Scarf
(Russian for wave; pronounced *val-NAH*)

Spiral Hat
(Russian for spiral; pronounced *spee-RAL*)

Fancy Slip-Stitch Patterns

Nebo Pullover
(Russian for sky; pronounced *NYÉ-boh*)

Káva Vest
(Czech for coffee; pronounced *KAH-vah*)

Koketka Sweater
(Russian for yoke; pronounced *ko-KYET-kah*)

Zlatý déšť Cowl
(Czech for "Golden Rain," the name for the laburnum bush or tree; pronounced *zlah-TEE desht*)

Reversible Slip-Stitch Patterns

Jetelinka Boot Toppers
(Czech for clover; pronounced *YEH-teh-leen-kah*)

Fialka Boot Toppers
(Czech for violet flower; pronounced *FEE-al-kah*)

Šiška Hat
(Czech for pine cone; pronounced *SHEESH-kah*)

Seren' Vest
(Russian for lilac; pronounced *SEE-ren*)

BIBLIOGRAPHY

400 Knitting Stitches: A Complete Dictionary of Essential Stitch Patterns. New York: Potter Craft, 2007.

Big Book of Knitting Stitch Patterns. New York: Sterling Publishing Co., Inc., 2005.

Das Grosse Buch vom Stricken. Freiburg, Germany: Christophorus Verlag GmbH & Co. KG, 2010.

Hemmons Hiatt, June. *The Principles of Knitting.* New York: Touchstone, 2012.

The Harmony Guides: 450 Knitting Stitches, Volume 2. New York: Collins and Brown, 2004.

Miyashita, M. *2000 Patterns of Design and Figure Knitting.* Tokyo: Miyashita Shojl CO., Ltd.

Pudilova, Zdena. *Patterns for Hand Knitting, 5th Edition.* Prague, Czech Republic: SNTL Nakladatelstvi Technicke Literatury, 1989.

Walker, Barbara, G. *Mosaic Knitting.* Pittsville, Wisconsin: Schoolhouse Press, 1997.

Walker, Barbara G. *A Treasury of Knitting Patterns.* New York: Charles Scribner's Sons, 1968.

index